CORPORATE SOVEREIGNTY

Corporate Sovereignty

LAW AND GOVERNMENT UNDER CAPITALISM

Joshua Barkan

University of Minnesota Press
Minneapolis
London

A different version of chapter 3 previously appeared as "Liberal Government and the Corporate Person," *Journal of Cultural Economy* 3, no. 1 (2010): 53–68, reprinted by permission of Taylor & Francis. A portion of chapter 5 previously appeared in "Roberto Esposito's Political Biology and Corporate Forms of Life," *Law, Culture, and the Humanities* 8, no. 1 (2012): 84–101, reprinted with permission of SAGE Publications.

Published by the University of Minnesota Press
111 Third Avenue South, Suite 290
Minneapolis, MN 55401-2520
http://www.upress.umn.edu

Library of Congress Cataloging-in-Publication Data

Barkan, Joshua
  Corporate sovereignty : law and government under capitalism / Joshua Barkan.
  Includes bibliographical references and index.
  ISBN 978-0-8166-7426-8 (hc : alk. paper)
  ISBN 978-0-8166-7427-5 (pb : alk. paper)
  1. Corporation law. 2. Corporate power. 3. Corporate governance—Law and legislation. 4. Corporate state. 5. Sovereignty. 6. Capitalism. I. Title.
  K1315.B36 2013
  346'.066—dc23

                     2013010385

The University of Minnesota is an equal-opportunity educator and employer.

For Frieda Koren Barkan (1919–2007)
and for Susan and Sasha, with love

CONTENTS

Introduction   1

1 The Sovereign Gift   19

2 Property   41

3 Personhood   65

4 Territory   87

5 Responsibility   111

6 The Corporate University   139

   Conclusion   161

   Acknowledgments   167

   Notes   171

   Index   223

Even a cursory glance at recent headlines indicates the social, political, and economic importance of corporations, along with major problems concerning their regulation. In the United States, events such as the 2008 financial crisis and the 2001–2 accounting scandals highlighted, in spectacular fashion, the dramatic impacts of corporate decisions on local, national, and global economies. Likewise, the 2010 oil spill in the Gulf of Mexico or the controversies over the actions of corporate military contractors in the Iraq War are only the most recent in a growing list of corporate abuses of the environment and human life. That severe problems in corporate regulation are a fixture of the daily news cycle underscores the centrality of corporations in contemporary models of governance. From urban redevelopment projects coordinated through public–private partnerships to the subcontracting of military, prison, and security functions, corporations play a fundamental role in providing public goods and exercise powers customarily associated with formal state institutions.

Although each of these events—from large-scale corporate abuses to the more mundane aspects of privatized government—is geographically localizable and emerges out of specific historical trajectories, the problems of corporate power are global in scope. As the geographer Peter Dicken notes, "more than any other single institution the transnational corporation has come to be regarded as the primary shaper of the contemporary global economy and a major threat to the economic autonomy of the nation-state."[1] Corporations are intimately intertwined with projects of national economic development across the so-called third world. Structural adjustment programs associated with the Washington Consensus have equated corporate-led privatization, deregulation, foreign direct investment, and liberal corporate governance with national fiscal health. Consequently, we see corporations empowered in new ways in places ranging from the increasingly ubiquitous export processing zones to the proliferating enclaves associated with resource extraction. Meanwhile, protest movements against corporate-led globalization raise fundamental questions about the social and political impacts of global business corporations, particularly in the absence of democratic accountability for corporate actions.

Confronted with the breadth of problems involving corporations and their regulation, reflections on corporations move along well-traveled paths. Economists, who in many cases dominate policy discussions, have ceased to identify corporate power as a problem worthy of serious consideration in its own right. What others term *corporate power* simply reflects the efficiencies of firms in lowering transaction costs and coordinating production processes.[2] Largely abstracting the corporation from its political, social, and geographic contexts, dominant economic discourses present corporations as one option among others that entrepreneurs might choose for organizing capitalist enterprises. Owing to the methodological individualism of the discipline, contemporary economists treat corporations not as political institutions created by law but as private institutions produced through agreements (a "nexus of contracts," as law and economics scholars put it).[3] Although economists dating back to Adam Smith criticized state-backed corporations for introducing market imperfections,[4] inasmuch as contemporary economics treats today's corporations as private capitalist enterprises, they provide little insight into the roles of politics and power in shaping what corporations are or what they do.

In contrast, much of the rest of the social sciences have converged in recognizing that political institutions shape corporate behavior and economic outcomes. Economic historians now emphasize the role of law and political institutions in the formation and growth of corporate economies.[5] For instance, the contemporary U.S. corporate economy reflects the historical outcomes of earlier political struggles over the institutional form of corporations and corporate governance. Although other pathways of economic development were available in the past, much of the contemporary regulatory structure for corporations in Anglo-American law was consolidated in the early twentieth century.[6] Likewise, mainstream political scientists argue that national political and economic institutions shape corporate actions and governance.[7] Ongoing corporate abuses, then, derive from problems in the ways political institutions interact with the economic preferences of corporate stakeholders—including workers, managers, and shareholders—as they struggle to shape the rules of corporate law and governance. Grounded in rational choice methods, mainstream social science seeks institutional fixes to problems in corporate regulation. They attempt to identify institutions that can align the preferences of various stakeholders in ways that promote economic growth while simultaneously satisfying competing interests.

Critical scholars generally agree with the mainstream emphasis on the political constitution of the contemporary corporate economy while challenging the perceived neutrality of political institutions. Given societies rife with social antagonisms, they cast doubt on the possibility of institutional compromises that can satisfy competing groups in positions of radical inequality. Instead, a long tradition of critical writing on corporations suggests that political institutions are already structured toward corporate economic interests over those of communities or the public at large.[8] To understand the major corporate fiascos mentioned earlier, we should look at the processes of lax regulation and regulatory capture that allowed corporate banks to engage in unsustainable and predatory lending, accounting firms to fudge accounts, and oil companies to shirk basic maintenance and environmental oversight. Likewise, corporate-led globalization becomes a story about corporate economic interests hijacking programs of economic development in ways that benefit shareholders or managers over local populations. For those of us concerned with corporate power, this narrative powerfully shapes progressive strategies for challenging corporations. It suggests that more just and equitable economic relations require the reassertion of broad public interests against the narrow concerns of corporations, their managers, and the powerful institutional investors that continually pressure companies to increase profits.

While sympathetic to these criticisms and deeply interested in alternative forms of economic organization, this book argues that these approaches mischaracterize the nature of politics and power. In particular, two conceptual flaws limit our understanding of corporations. First, while much of the best work on corporations recognizes that modern corporate power emerges at the intersection of capitalist economic systems and liberal systems of law and politics, scholars continue to examine corporate power through a dualism between "the economy" and "politics." Scholars demarcate the corporation as an economic institution whose power threatens states. Although politically constituted and with political effects, corporations are considered to be separate from the fundamental structures of political order. Second, instances in which corporations play direct roles in politics and regulation are then presented as *errors* in which corporate economic interests overtake and wield undue influence within liberal law and public policy. This way of thinking about corporations has long characterized popular and academic writing on U.S. corporations.

It is mirrored in discussions of globalization that present the economic power of corporations as undermining state sovereignty.

This book argues that corporate power should be rethought as a mode of political sovereignty. Rather than beginning with distinctions between the economic power of corporations and the political sovereignty of states, this book argues that corporate power and sovereign power are *ontologically linked*. Situating analysis of U.S., British, and international corporate law alongside careful readings in political and social theory, *Corporate Sovereignty* shows that the Anglo-American corporation and modern political sovereignty are founded in and bound together through a principle of *legally sanctioned immunity from law*. The problems corporate-led globalization presents for democratic politics do not result from regulatory failures as much as from an Anglo-American conception of corporate immunity that has been increasingly exported across the globe.[9]

After all, corporations are legal creations—fictitious persons formed when states recognize the power of individuals to organize collectively. Seen in this light, the supposed opposition between the corporation and the state is itself revelatory. Corporations are fictions, created by states, but given such social power that they threaten to undermine the political sovereignty that created them. In other words, corporations are an "imaginary relationship of individuals to their real conditions of existence" produced by the state and the law and thus, strictly speaking, ideological.[10] They are also the means by which states attempt to marshal the collective power of individuals toward public ends by granting them a special legal status. This paradoxical relation, in which corporations emerge from law but continually threaten the validity and existence of the state, suggests something more complicated than the declining power of states in the face of a global corporate economy. Although the relationship appears as adversarial, it is in fact a kind of *doubling,* in which the fate of state sovereignty and corporate power are conjoined and also in conflict.

Double Bodies

On its face, the claim that corporations and states double one another is not particularly controversial. Corporate states and states-as-corporations have been a mainstay of Anglo-American literature and popular culture for more than a hundred years. From Edward Bellamy's utopian account of the corporate state in his best-selling *Looking Backward: 2000–1887* to the corporate conglomerates populating dystopian novels, corporations provide useful figures to plumb the promises and pitfalls of political power and social organization.[11] Certainly corporations and states share some family resemblances. Both corporations and states are collective entities composed of individuals united in a single body. They are both created, usually sharing some animating act of incorporation that establishes their legal existence, and these acts are codified, or, more accurately, constituted, through charters and constitutions. Once constituted, corporations and states share a range of techniques—from the consensual to the coercive— for establishing order within their institutional structures and across the places and territories in which they operate. Historically, corporations, like states, have been used to achieve ends of government. In addition to the most well known early modern corporations, such as the Roman Catholic Church or the infamous imperial trading companies that administered lands, politics, war, trade, and diplomacy, corporations have run schools, hospitals, and prisons, while also managing infrastructure for communication and transportation. Similarly, states are increasingly asked to function like corporations, deploying managerial techniques to make government efficient for citizen–consumers. Most important, corporations, particularly the large transnational sort, and states both command great political and economic power, a relation expressed in the oft-repeated lists of the world's "largest economies," which render the profits of multinationals comparable to the gross national products of nation-states.[12]

In addition, there is a tradition within Anglo-American legal and historical writing that considers the corporation in relation to political culture and governmental power. Frederic Maitland, reworking the political thought of Otto von Gierke, emphasized corporate associations as central to the emergence of liberal government in early modern England.[13] Early-twentieth-century legal realists, such as Morris Cohen and Robert Hale, writing in response to a previous period of corporate economic growth and consolidation, famously demonstrated the public roots of private power as well as the coercive aspects of private law in industrial relations.[14] Through the mid-twentieth-century, writers on corporations, including Adolf Berle, Sigmund Timberg, and Arthur S. Miller, considered the implications of the U.S. corporate economy for national politics and daily life, while also suggesting that corporations constituted a new form of social, political, and economic governance and administration.[15] And historians of U.S. state and economic relations, from the commonwealth studies of the 1940s and 1950s[16] to legal historians such as J. Willard Hurst, Morton Horwitz, Hendrik Hartog, Pauline Maier, and William Novak, have shown us how law promoted corporations as a means of economic development as well as a form of government and regulation.[17]

Although this book is indebted to these authors for making apparent aspects of corporate power that are normally obscured, it also departs from these discussions in decisive ways. First, the doubling that I identify with corporate sovereignty goes beyond resemblance to name a specific set of relationships. Corporations and states *model* each other's defining figures. Modern state sovereignty is *founded in* and *anchored to* a figure of the corporate political body. Likewise, modern corporate power *emerges from* and *mobilizes* apparatuses of sovereignty, discipline, and government. In this manner, corporate power and state sovereignty depend on one another, each establishing the other's condition of possibility. Nonetheless, the relation is full of tension, as these institutional ensembles mix and often threaten one another's existence. Doubling is not a simple antagonism leading to dialectical synthesis. The story of corporate sovereignty is not, as Hegel would have us believe, one in which corporations emerge as part of the development of the ethical life of the political community before being dialectically taken up and canceled in the movement from civil society to the rational state.[18] Doubling is much closer to the *supplement* that Derrida identified within the structures of signification and desire.[19] Yet, the proper formulation of this relationship is the *ban,* which Giorgio Agamben, among others, has located as the ontological structure of sovereign power.[20]

Readers of contemporary social and political theory might find the suggestion that corporations are somehow "banned" odd. For Agamben, the ban is inextricably connected with the exception and most often exemplified by figures "banned" through state-issued declarations of emergency.[21] Taking Carl Schmitt's definition of the sovereign as "he who decides on the exception,"[22] Agamben shows that the sphere of politics emerges through the suspension of law that founds and maintains legality as such. The ban names the "zone of indistinction" established by the exception, where the divisions that have structured the conception of politics in Western thought—between life and law, humans and animals, politically qualified life and bare biological existence, civilization and barbarism, the city and the forest, the state of law and right and the state of nature—are held in suspension and blur into one another.[23] By treating the ban as the ontological root of sovereign power, Agamben suggests that even in moments in which "normal" law is functioning, exception and abandonment exist virtually as a potential that is always already present in constituted legal orders.[24]

Before turning to the relation between the ban and corporate sovereignty, it is worth noting how the ban extends and reformulates Michel Foucault's trenchant account of modern power. As is well known, Foucault's studies of the 1970s focused on the ways in which life became an increasingly important object of political calculation, which he termed *biopolitics*. For Foucault, modernity entailed a transformation in the dominant organization of power, as juridical sovereignty—characterized by the "deductive power" of the sovereign to extract life in defense of the realm—gave way to new conceptions of power that connected state security to the optimal distribution of "men and things."[25] Foucault described the development of sciences of society (chief among them, political economy) that rationalized power in new ways. Instead of seeing them as emanating from a centralized legal authority, Foucault focused on the diverse ways modern power circulated through social formations, training bodies to be self-regulating, investing in the capacities of individuals, and ameliorating risks at the level of aggregate populations. The distinctiveness of modern power was its commitment to improve life: "It is no longer a matter of bringing death into play in the field of sovereignty, but of distributing the living in the domain of value and utility."[26] Beginning in the eighteenth century, these political rationalities were integrated into state projects associated with, first, cameralism, mercantilism, and police science and, much later, the social welfare state. Agamben, however, argues that juridical power and sovereignty continue to be foundational for modern biopolitical regimes. This is not because contemporary biopolitics necessarily involves a sovereign directly deciding who lives and dies but rather because contemporary society is structured by the paradox of the sovereign ban, in which legal exceptions and the abandonment of populations are justified as vital to the security of political communities.

Interest in the exception and the ban has coincided with the U.S. Global War on Terror and the ongoing suspensions and abrogation of laws that have accompanied that conflict.[27] Scholars have focused on the ban to explain how suspensions, withdrawals, and transgressions of law consolidate state sovereignty. Still, the ban's importance is not only for conceptualizing sovereign power in terms of nation-states;[28] more precisely, the ban suggests that sovereignty is a topological relation that goes beyond state territoriality or simple spatial processes of centralization and diffusion.[29] Sovereignty is the paradoxical structure of power that emerges out of a complex of concrete practices that attempt to govern life by establishing and transgressing the boundaries of law. In other words, sovereignty is not a property of a scale of government (national or local sovereignty, the new world order, etc.) but the outcome of a biopolitical process. Agamben emphasizes the point when arguing that the paradigmatic space of sovereignty is not the state but the camp: a figure or schema (rather than an empirical location) that comes into being through emergency measures and is included in the law only by suspending normal legal protocols for those trapped within its structure.

Corporations are not camps. Nevertheless, corporate sovereignty emerges from and is exercised over the border between the inside and outside of constituted political spheres. This border-structure situates corporations in the ambiguous position of being closely intertwined with law while simultaneously formally separate from (and even opposed to) state power. The ability of corporations to regulate life in fundamental ways certainly derives from specific laws. Just the same, the corporation, as a politicolegal concept, plays an important role in establishing the legally defined borders and limits of law as well as spaces and cases where laws apply only to the extent of not being applicable.

Such a formulation allows us to consider the doubling between state and corporation as an instance of the ban. Corporations govern life through the extension of law as well as through legally authorized suspensions, privileges, and immunities from law. Moreover, like sovereign power generally, these transgressions are justified in the name of our common welfare, even our salvation. Thus doubling is in part due to the ways that definitions of corporations in Anglo-American and international law have hinged on their immunities—from the chartered privileges of imperial trading companies to the constitutionally protected rights of contemporary multinationals. As this book demonstrates, these privileges and immunities enable corporations to function as a mode of sovereignty that emerged in conjunction with modern nation-states and has been particularly effective in governing populations under liberal forms of rule. Focusing on the role of immunity and the ban in contemporary corporate power forces us to confront the uncomfortable notion that a political theology underlies modern biopolitical regimes, including those associated with corporations and the corporate capitalist economy. Corporations gain legal recognition by arguing that their status benefits the common good. The ability of corporations to provide for the health, welfare, and security of the population (in other words, for the *salus publica*) is central to their constitution. As the famous legal maxim *salus publica suprema lex esto* signifies, if the pursuit of public welfare is the highest law, it can include dramatic powers up to and including transgression of the legal order. The exceptions and immunities granted to achieve public welfare have the potential to threaten not only the political existence of the very populations they are designed to save but their biological existence as well. Corporate sovereignty highlights the way the law's ability to suspend itself enabled corporations to exercise prerogatives of sovereign power in the name of governing life, while also explaining the politics of abandonment that results from such a formulation.

Finally, the ban clarifies that problems with corporate power are not just empirical issues concerning this or that set of corporate regulations. They are ontological problems concerning the modes of being of political power. Because corporate power is so intimately bound up with the figures orienting basic conceptions of politics in Western law, critiques of corporate power cannot simply deploy law, sovereignty, property, and right as innocent concepts. As the final chapters of this book demonstrate, the error made by contemporary political mobilizations that attempt to limit corporate power through assertions of law, regulation, human rights, or social responsibility is that each of these is already constitutive of and internal to the complex of corporate sovereignty. By charting the logic of the ban at the core of corporate sovereignty, this book provides a genealogy of corporate power able to parse the curious doubleness of corporations and states. The aim of such a project cannot be to confine the corporation to the dustbin of history, as these entities are at the very foundation of important ideas of collective power; rather, the task becomes one of understanding how this doubling works to deactivate its most pernicious elements while holding on to those that enable us to articulate new forms of sociality.

This approach has important implications for reframing the engagement with corporations today. Advocates for more stringent corporate governance suggest reforms ranging from additional government oversight to empowering shareholders as a check on managers. Others seek to redirect corporate actions by treating them as "citizens," with corresponding duties and responsibilities, or by making corporations, like states, accountable to public international law. Yet the panoply of reforms is united in conceptualizing law as something *above* the corporate economy that acts as a *limit* on corporate power. Focusing on the ways that law mutually constitutes sovereignty and the corporation, and explaining how corporate capitalism emerges as a mode of liberal government, this book clarifies how reforms unwittingly reinvest the sovereign powers they seek to subvert. It poses the question of a democratic response to corporate power that could serve life in common outside of any relation to legal immunity and its logics of abandonment. In addition, it raises two conceptual issues that are internal to the chapters that follow and thus require additional elaboration.

Capitalism and Life

The first concerns the ways corporate capitalism comes to function as a mode of biopolitical control as much as an economic system. As already suggested, one of the most pressing concerns about corporate power today is the ways that the economic strengths of corporations enable them to govern fundamental aspects of life without the checks associated with democratic government. Such concerns are heightened under neoliberal globalization, which elevates market competition to a universal logic of social organization. Peck and Tickell have usefully termed neoliberalism a "new religion," suggesting that its ideologies of market-based governance, privatization, and deregulation have taken, among their adherents, "the status of the Latinate church in Medieval Europe."[30] Corporations, as one of the primary institutional forms of globalizing capital, are central to this new assemblage of power. Considering the long-standing linkages between corporations, sovereign power, and political theology, Peck and Tickell's comparison between the Roman Catholic Church and neoliberal economics identifies a *genealogical,* and not simply a metaphorical, relation. Indeed, we can think of the ways corporations became articulated to particular circuits of capitalist accumulation as part of formulating capitalism itself as a mode of government, in which everyday life became governed by the production and circulation of abstract and socially necessary value.

Paolo Virno provides a way to break open this claim with his suggestion that biopolitics should be conceptualized in terms of *labor-power.* Like Agamben's analysis of sovereignty, for Virno, labor-power is an ontological category that indexes a material form of "potentiality."[31] His argument relies on a compelling reading of Marx from both the first volume of *Capital* and *Grundrisse.* Marx, who was a close reader of Aristotle, treated labor as a means by which the potential of the world was rendered actual and usable:

> Labour is, first of all, a process between man and nature, a process by which man, through his own actions, mediates, regulates and controls the metabolism between himself and nature. He confronts the materials of nature as a force of nature. He sets in motion the natural forces which belong to his own body, his arms, legs, head and hands, in order to appropriate the materials of nature in a form adapted to his own needs. Through this movement he acts upon external nature and changes it, and in this way he simultaneously changes his own nature. He develops the potentialities slumbering within nature, and subjects the play of its forces to his own sovereign power.[32]

Labor, then, prior to its determination as the commodity labor-power, appears as "living labor," a force that transforms the potentiality of nature and humanity into a world of useful objects. For Marx, this power is distinct to human life—distinguishing it from the weaving of the spider and the construction of the bee—as only humans apply purposeful thought to this metabolic exchange with nature.[33] Capitalism requires this autonomous potential within labor to produce the world. "Living labour must seize on these things, awaken them from the dead, change them from merely possible into real and effective use-values."[34]

Under capitalist social relations, where workers are forced to sell the capacity to work for wages, labor-power becomes the commoditized form of human potentiality. Capitalists, in buying labor-power, barter in potentiality. As such, Virno suggests that biological life becomes regulated "because it acts as the substratum of a mere faculty, labor-power, which has taken on the consistency of a commodity. . . . By the mere fact that it can be bought and sold, this potential calls into question the repository from which it is indistinguishable, that is, the living body."[35] In other words, the commodity form of living labor—labor-power—demands "the *entirety* of human faculties in as much as they are involved in productive praxis," and it is precisely for this reason that attention by the capitalist state and other ancillary institutions must be given to regulating life itself.[36]

For Virno, the body of the worker constitutes a force with the permanent potential to transgress constituted political and economic orders. But under capitalist social relations, capitalists constantly attempt to disconnect labor-power from the living body of the worker and treat it as a moment in the life of capital. Marx made this point clear, highlighting the way that labor-power appears only as an inversion of human potentiality once laboring is determined by capitalist social relations: "By incorporating living labour into their lifeless objectivity, the capitalist simultaneously transforms value, i.e. past labour in its objectified and lifeless form, into capital, value which can perform its own valorization process, an animated monster which begins to 'work,' 'as if its body were by love possessed.'"[37] While labor-power is the substratum of biopolitics, the productive capacity of humanity becomes hidden within the self-animating "monster" of capital. And the state increasingly confronts this monstrous body—the monstrous body of self-valorizing value set off from the body of the worker.

Virno's basic premise, that biopolitics emerges to manage human potentiality, requires that we recognize the relationship between biopolitical regulation and the sovereign ban. Though the living body might be a "tangible sign" of potentiality, the conditions of possibility for its regulation under liberal capitalist regimes are established through a series of legal fictions. As Marx put it, "the sphere of circulation or commodity exchange, within whose boundaries the sale and purchase of labour-power goes on, is in fact a very Eden of the innate rights of man. It is the exclusive realm of Freedom, Equality, Property and Bentham."[38] To understand the relation between biopolitics and capitalism within a liberal political order, we must not only understand the way that the potentiality of life becomes regulated as a commodity; we should also grasp the way that the law incorporates capital as necessary to the security of society through fictions that both expand and limit state sovereignty.

What is this monstrous form of capital today, if not the corporation? This seemingly autonomous form of capital is structured by the ban in at least two senses. First, corporations, as legal embodiments of capital, are one of the primary institutions by which states, social groups, and individuals regulate, channel, and direct *life toward value*. Because of their pivotal role in coordinating the production and distribution of goods and services, corporations, as much as states, have repeatedly claimed "exceptional" prerogatives that allow them to make decisions concerning the social value of people's lives. Capitalism provided a historically and geographically specific set of practices for establishing the border between lives that were valuable and those that could be abandoned. Second, within the ambit of the law, the corporation is itself considered a "life" worthy of political existence. As I demonstrate, this is the reason why lawyers and jurists refigured corporations as juridical persons with corresponding legal rights and privileges. It is also a crucial assumption that undergirds the claims that corporations bear political responsibilities or can exercise forms of citizenship. These two modes of regulating, directing, and channeling life toward capitalist value provide a way of conceptualizing the corporation as a hinge between capitalism and sovereignty, although one articulated through a radically different spatial politics than that associated with the sovereignty of the nation-state.

Spatial History

The second issue concerns the importance of space and territory in the development of political order. Territory, of course, has been central to definitions of sovereignty in the West as the taken-for-granted background over which power is exercised. Similarly, the argument that corporate economic power undermines state sovereignty depends on a notion of state territoriality in which states exercise sovereignty over the economic activities that occur within their borders. In both cases, space is presented as a static property of states. Even in some of the most sophisticated analyses of constituting power, spatial dynamics take a backseat to questions about temporality.[39] Political historians emphasize time as the medium through which diffuse forms of constituting power coalesce into revolutionary forces or new state institutions, and Marxists have explained the temporal movement by which living labor is transformed into capital.[40] Put in ontological terms, it is through time that the potentiality of the world is actualized in new political forms. Space might be implicitly useful for understanding the completion of these processes (in the sense that we often talk about groups conquering territory in the process of taking state power), but it is time that is usually presented as the domain in which multiple possibilities are realized as events in the movement of history.

How do we conceptualize an active role of space, place, and territory in the constitution of political order and in the history of the present?[41] One way of approaching this question is by focusing on the spatial and territorial assemblages by which corporate power is organized and consolidated. Just as states claim territories through spatial demarcations—violently bounding space and limiting flows of people and things across territorial borders, while also enabling and fostering other movements and linkages—so, too, does corporate sovereignty entail a series of spatial arrangements. Examples include the imperial trading companies' policing of trade routes, the juridical standing of legal personhood that enables corporations to be legally recognized in and out of multiple jurisdictions, or the free trade zones carved out of national territories and situated within an imagined global economic space. In each case, it is not just the territorialization itself (the trade route, the free trade zone) but larger assemblages of power that enable these territorializations to come into being. The present global order emerged out of the potentiality created within these diverse spatial assemblages. The present, with its problems and possibilities, is a particular realization or *actualization of potentiality* immanent to these spatial arrangements and configurations.

This suggests that history is an outcome of power relations that always work in and through space. We can press the importance of space even further by suggesting that it is not only the physical territorial arrangements that are important but also the implicit spatiality that structures thinking about the corporation itself.[42] This implies that space is not just the medium by which power is actualized; space also inhabits the frames of reference that orient our acting in the world. In this sense, the discourses shaping how the power of imperial trading companies, the corporate person, or free trade zones is thought about and understood are already structured by the spatial and institutional arrangements in which thinking emerges and by which it is conditioned. The concrete imperial geographies of the East India Company or today's fleet-footed multinationals were preceded by a colonial imagination that structured the basic understandings of what these corporations are, what they do, and on whose authority. The task of criticism is thus not only to outline the territorial configurations by which power was actualized, a project to which geographers have contributed useful and important discussions,[43] but also to engage the implicit spatiality conditioning our understanding of corporations in the first place.

It is in this sense that this study addresses the global. The global order in question is contemporary economic globalization. Although the term *global* retains its commonsense connotations as referring to phenomena that are all encompassing or concerning the entirety of human affairs, critical scholars have explained globalization as an uneven historical and geographical development in the capitalist world-system and as an ideology, most often linked to the term *neoliberalism,* promoting the universal applicability and benefits of free market capitalism.[44] Corporate power has been understood as central in both senses, as corporations are virtually synonymous with transnational capitalism and the globalization of production networks, while also playing an important role in fostering an ideology of global markets.[45] As my reading of the texts, cases, and arguments composing the specific archive of this book suggests, however, the outsized role of corporations in fostering a certain global order emerged within distinct assemblages of power, space, and knowledge. This book attempts to bring the singularity of these origins to light. As such, this genealogy does not view "global order" as an empirical location to be described (say, one made up of the totality of corporate actions or corporate laws across the planet); rather, "global" names an essential element in the way the potentiality of the past has been materialized in the present, along with the implicit spatiality structuring that process.

Genealogy

As should now be clear, this book is different from an empirical account of individual corporate laws, a case study of particular corporate actions, or even a history of the rise of global corporations. Instead, it is a genealogical inquiry into the shifting *problematic* governing corporate power. I borrow this term from Althusser, for whom the study of the problematic was inextricably linked with ideology. Resisting the notion of ideology as false consciousness, Althusser argued that all thinking emerges within the ideological constraints of social formations. For this reason, thought necessarily misrecognizes the objects it seeks to explain. The role of theory, then, is to expose the framework (i.e., the problematic) structuring this misrecognition. In this sense, the problematic refers to "the objective internal reference system" of a mode of thinking that structures the "questions commanding the answers given by the ideology."[46] To study the problematic is not simply to study the way a form of knowledge answers the questions it poses to itself; rather, it is an inquiry into the ways that certain problems become available for thinking, while others remain obscure.

Consequently, the modern disciplines of economics, political science, history, and legal analysis successfully answer the questions they pose to themselves about corporate power. Yet they are far less adept at explaining why those disciplinary questions are important, how those questions might be linked with the material and institutional structures shaping the disciplines, how corporate power might be embroiled in processes beyond the fields of vision of these disciplinary formations, or, most important, how corporations might be implicated in the institutional production of knowledge itself. For this reason, this study finds none of the disciplines individually or even under the combinatory logic of interdisciplinarity sufficient for understanding corporate sovereignty. Establishing the question to which contemporary corporate power constitutes the misunderstood answer requires something far different from empiricist social science. Althusser termed this type of investigation a *symptomatic reading*. We might also call it, following Nietzsche and Foucault, *genealogy*.[47]

Genealogies are similar to intellectual histories in that both focus on concepts inhabiting the past. Whereas intellectual history examines the causal forces shaping thought over time, genealogies are interested in concepts to the extent that they give meaning to practices. Capturing the inverted logic that Althusser attempted to identify in the problematic (or that Spinoza identified long before him),[48] genealogies treat objects and institutions as the effects of the discursive practices that attempt to define them. Understanding corporate power requires investigating the multiple modes of thought and practice that have attempted to define these institutions. Moreover, genealogy recognizes that these forces are multiple and heterogeneous rather than linear and unified. In this sense, it was not a simple logic of either "capitalism" or "politics" that established contemporary corporate power. What makes the corporation so interesting for genealogical research are the diverse lines of development that have constituted it as an object of knowledge and reflection as well as a legal and economic institution that acts in the world. As we will see, corporations have long and varied connections to industrialized capitalism and manufacturing, to be sure, but also to sovereignty, law, government, religion, police power, property, personhood, knowledge, territory, and so on.

This book explains how these different conceptual frameworks shaped the problematic of corporate power. To do so, each chapter reads specific texts and discourses that attempted to define, expand, engage, or limit corporate power in particular geographic and historical contexts. What emerges are accounts of assemblages of power that work through texts, institutions, laws, and events to reintroduce us to the submerged logics that govern our understanding of and relations to corporate power in the present. Chapter 1 examines early modern corporate sovereignty as it emerged from medieval religious thought. Historians have written of the ways medieval corporate law provided a framework for conceptualizing secular state sovereignty. Secular state sovereignty also transformed medieval corporations, which, up until that time, were institutions, such as universities, towns, or religious orders, whose incorporation provided a means of autonomy and self-government. Reading texts such as corporate charters, Hobbes's political theory, and Blackstone's writings on the common law, this chapter describes a new configuration of corporate power that emerged during the eighteenth century. The key to the new assemblage was the charter, which granted corporations legal standing, established corporate immunities and privileges, and provided a framework for governing towns, hospitals, poorhouses, learning societies, and churches as well as for commerce, banking, trade, and the administration of empire. These chartered grants were considered "gifts" from the sovereign and were, in the words of Thomas Hobbes, not law but "exemptions from law."[49] I argue that the chartered grant transformed corporations into *police institutions,* in the sense of eighteenth-century police science, whereby corporations were granted legal exemptions to benefit public welfare. This relation reached its apogee in the British imperial project, suggesting that corporate sovereignty and its political logic were governed by a colonial conception of space from the outset.

Chapter 2, examining corporate property, and chapter 3, on corporate personhood, explain the reworking of corporate sovereignty in the context of modern U.S. corporate law. To do so, these chapters read the vast nineteenth- and early-twentieth-century literature of lawyers, political economists, and public figures to understand how corporations changed from fundamental institutions of government into private, capitalist firms. Before the American Revolution, corporations had been the institutions of government, established through royal grants and charters. Many of the original colonies, including Virginia, Massachusetts, Connecticut, Rhode Island, Georgia, and the Carolinas, were corporations chartered by the Crown. Corporations also continued to provide the legal form for cities and towns, hospitals, churches, centers of learning, and institutions for managing the poor, infirm, underaged, unmarried, and abandoned.[50] Through the course of the nineteenth century, however, corporations were transformed from institutions of imperial government into privately held companies within a liberal capitalist economy. Corporate law became synonymous with business law, as new distinctions emerged between business corporations and other corporate entities. Although the general contours of this story are well known, these chapters approach the question of corporate power somewhat counterintuitively, showing the ways the concept of police that undergirded early modern corporate sovereignty, described in chapter 1, was translated into state police power, while discourses of political economy provided new logics for the exceptions granted by charters. In short, corporate privileges became private rights held *against the state.* Moreover, these changes articulated corporate rights to the production and circulation of capitalist value.

Chapter 4 and chapter 5 each address global ramifications flowing from these transformations. Although modern multinational corporations and transnational corporations are literal embodiments of global capitalism, historically, corporations have had close relations to the legal jurisdictions in which they were created. Chapter 4 examines how the articulation of corporate sovereignty to capitalist value enabled corporations to transact business and enter into legal proceedings in multiple jurisdictions. By considering the ways legal frameworks of comity (the deference one sovereign shows another sovereign within his territory) or personhood were applied and not applied to corporations extraterritorially, chapter 4 explains the coalescence of the pockmarked international regulatory structure for transnational corporations that emerged during the mid-twentieth century. Chapter 5, in turn, deals with one contemporary response to that uneven landscape: the use of discourses of corporate social responsibility and citizenship as relatively *deterritorialized* and *nonlegal* responses to problems of corporate regulation that nonetheless reiterate important elements in the problematic of corporate sovereignty.

The final chapter provides a response to corporate sovereignty by attempting to rearticulate the potential of the corporate university. Whereas today the corporate university stands for the subjugation of reason to the dictates of neoliberal ideology and global markets, chapter 6 attempts to expose the "corporateness" that resides within the university as an institution and within intellectual inquiry, or even within reason itself. As such, my genealogical approach to the corporatization of the university is a more modest response to contemporary problems than either the proposals for responsibility and citizenship that attempt to legislate corporate behavior, discussed in chapter 5, or the more radical direct confrontations with the corporate university that are erupting on campuses across the world as I write. Such a conclusion, however, is fitting for a project of this sort. Although the question of what is to be done is as urgent now as ever, it is also possible that criticism has different responsibilities from political praxis that are more narrow but, I argue, equally important; namely, it can expose us to the invisible, unrecognized, and repressed logics that govern our understanding of corporate power in the present, not to point out their inevitability but rather to punctuate the possibility for the world to be otherwise.

On Law and Corporate Power

Of course, the narrative charted here is *a* genealogy, not *the* genealogy, of law and government under capitalism. To admit as much is simply to say that this is one cut—partial and incomplete but also politically invested—at understanding the frames of intelligibility structuring politics and power today. What unites these disparate interventions into the genealogy of the corporation, however, is a close attention to law in the shaping of corporate power. A number of valid criticisms can be raised at such an approach. In particular, it pays short shrift to the other forms of reason that constitute corporations, including the cultural discourses of the workers, managers, shareholders, and community activists who engage corporations and corporate power in myriad ways, and it constantly risks treating the law as an autonomous discourse cordoned off from social politics, thereby reiterating, rather than destabilizing, one of liberal law's most pernicious ideological effects.

Despite these risks, focusing on law in the constitution of corporate power has its advantages. Critical social theorists ranging from Pierre Bourdieu to Gilles Deleuze have identified law and jurisprudence as active discourses that in many respects create the social world.[51] Moreover, although much critical work on globalization has considered the political forces constituting global structures of power, and although international relations theorists have studied the increased use of legal forms in structuring international politics, we are still far from understanding the complex spatiality of law and its historical and political production. I would argue that this lacuna is directly linked to the assumption that law operates over a sovereign territory. What becomes clear when focusing on the corporation and corporate law is that law empowers through both its *application* and its *nonapplication* as well as through overlapping jurisdictions, extraterritorial extensions, and intersecting regimes of customary and formal legal orders. By focusing on times and places in which legal force is used and those in which it is suspended, the book begins to map out the uneven terrain of today's global order.

CHAPTER ONE

The Sovereign Gift

To make a gift of something to someone is to make a present of some part of oneself.

— MARCEL MAUSS, *The Gift: Form and Reason for Exchange in Archaic Societies*

It is not uncommon to read comments on multinational corporations and economic globalization that begin with reference to the massive trading companies of the early modern era. The English and Dutch East India companies, the Royal African Company, and the Hudson Bay Company, among others, are often presented as the first multinationals, posing political and economic problems that are useful for understanding issues in contemporary international business. For some, these corporations, backed by European military power, provide a useful model for examining relations of exploitation between the global North and South. Others emphasize the differences between these older corporations, with their political ties and patronage, and the multinationals inhabiting today's global economy. In both cases, scholars treat the relations between past and present not in terms of causation—the bread and butter of historical inquiry—but in terms of metaphor and analogy, as these corporations allow us to consider the similarities and differences between contemporary globalization and the imperial past.[1]

There are, however, other ways to grasp the relevance of early modern corporations, of which the imperial trading companies were only one particularly important example. This chapter argues that early modern writing on corporations continues to be meaningful because it shaped the problematic for subsequent thinking about corporate power. My argument is twofold. First, I demonstrate that the corporation offered an image of sovereignty in a specifically liberal and decentralized mode. As we will see, historians have shown that medieval religious discourses on

the corporation were important in establishing the sovereignty of secular states in Europe. In this sense, the corporation provided an immanent
foundation for the conventional model of sovereign power, linking state,
nation, and territory into a unified body politic. Less attention has been
paid to how the articulation between the corporation and state sovereignty
influenced corporate bodies that were not states such as towns or religious
orders. I suggest that in seventeenth-century England, the corporate charter
became a technique by which the Crown both recognized the autonomy
of these groups and attempted to redirect their power toward the fiscal
and physical health of the state. As such, I argue that the corporation was
connected with the *police* of society—a term that, in its early modern us-
age, did not reference the police forces we think of today but rather was
connected with police science and denoted the wise superintendence and
distribution of things in society. Though these two figures of corporate
sovereignty intertwined with one another, it was this corporation-as-police,
as opposed to the state's corporate body, that shaped the problematic of
modern corporate sovereignty in its liberal and decentralized modes.

Second, building on the discussion of the exception and the ban in
the introduction, I suggest that the corporation-as-police was, both in
thought and practice, an exemption from law that enabled the disciplining of various individuals and populations. Corporate charters were liberties held against the state that gave legal standing to corporations. From
the state's perspective, the charters were grants or gifts of immunity from
the sovereign, designed to strengthen the state. By granting privileges and
immunities, the state encouraged groups of individuals to organize institutions such as poorhouses, religious orders, universities, cities, factories,
and colonies. Yet, because the grant could also specify certain portions of
land that were placed under the corporation's control, charters became a
way of providing for the health of the sovereign by exempting corporations from the state's monopolies on territory and force.

These two modes of sovereign power—the state's corporate body and
the corporation-as-police—constitute our first iteration of the doubling
to which I referred in the introduction as *corporate sovereignty*. As we
will see, the specifically *corporate* nature of sovereignty was integral in
both cases, establishing the common frame of intelligibility between these
modes of political organization.[2] Although scholars have examined the
importance of the exception and the ban for state sovereignty, we have yet
to consider this other mode of sovereign power, the corporation-as-police.
Here, too, the paradoxes of abandonment are apparent. For example, the
corporation-as-police was conceptualized as a threshold establishing the
limits of direct state power. Moreover, this limit was productive in the sense

that it enabled the regulation of individuals and populations in new ways. For many of the same reasons, however, corporations were also viewed as potential threats to state sovereignty and therefore as institutions that had to be reined in and controlled by the state. The tension between the alleged benefits of corporations for the public and the fears that they undermined the undivided sovereignty of the state would become a defining feature of political discourses on corporations, even after the meaning of the corporation went through a number of changes. We can understand what was at stake in this debate by explaining the emergence of its problematic.

Mystical Bodies

Hobbes's *Leviathan,* a pivotal text on sovereignty in the history of Western political thought, demonstrates the profound tension between the corporation-as-police and the state's corporate body. Responding to the turmoil enveloping mid-seventeenth-century English political society, Hobbes argued for a unitary and indivisible sovereign who could compel subjects to obey the law and put an end to internecine wars.[3] Hobbes's theoretical innovation was to ground sovereign power in human nature rather than divine providence. Instead of a sovereign power derived from God's command, fundamental aspects of human psychology, according to Hobbes, were the reason that humans formed the commonwealth. Hobbes defined this commonwealth as a "reall Unitie" of a multitude of individuals "united in one Person," which he referred to as "that great Leviathan, or rather (to speake more reverently) of that *Mortall God.*"[4]

By personifying the Leviathan, Hobbes drew on familiar imagery. Famously represented on the frontispiece of *Leviathan* (Figure 1), the commonwealth is a corporate body composed of innumerable individuals, with the sovereign as the head. The image of the body unifies individuals and territory, as the corporate sovereign gazes on the dominion of the realm. It also conjoins religion and politics, presenting the Leviathan as grasping both the sword of secular rule and the staff of religious order.

Commentators have noted, however, how the image of the Leviathan constitutes a conjuring trick.[5] Personification suggests that the social contract transforms the multitude of individuals from many into one. In this way, the corporation appears as a unified body representing the totality of individuals authorizing its creation.[6] Contract renders the corporate body of the state distinct from the individuals that composed it and the sovereign at its head. The metaphor erases potential conflicts between the range of individual interests and the sovereign's power and prerogative. Once

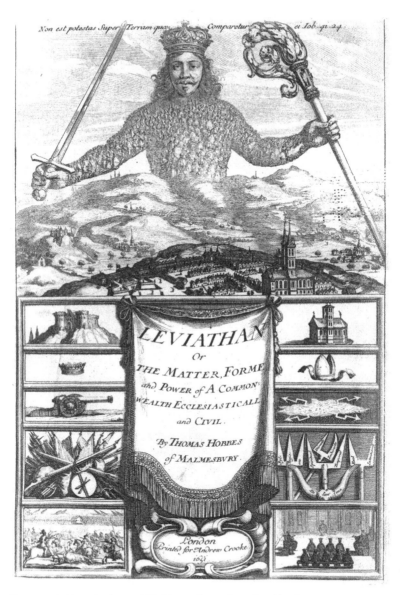

FIGURE 1. Frontispiece of Hobbes's *Leviathan*, by Abraham Bosse (1651). This image of the Leviathan, foundational to Western political thought, demonstrates the corporate nature of early modern theories of state sovereignty. The sovereign's body is a corporation, composed of a multitude of individuals.

constituted as a body, the commonwealth seems self-animating, a representation taking on a life of its own.[7] Although the corporate nature of the commonwealth suggests unity, the trick is that grounding sovereignty on individual desires for peace and security never eliminates the tension between the many and the one. If the sovereignty of the state emerges through agreements and contracts, what prevents the proliferation of sovereigns or the diffusion of sovereignty to smaller groups? What distinguishes the corporate body of the state from other corporate bodies in society?

In an era of religious civil wars, these were anxious questions Hobbes hoped to resolve. This anxiety was not just symptomatic of Hobbes's historical moment, however, as his vision borrowed and reframed a theological concept of the corporate body for secular ends.[8] Before the corporation had a relation with state power, and long before it had any relation to commerce or capitalism, it was a religious image that defined the relation between particular entities in subordination to a universal totality. Harkening back to the *universitates* and *collegium* of ancient Greece and Rome, theories of corporate existence were revived in late medieval European political and legal theory at the intersection of Christian theology and Aristotelian humanism.[9]

Ernst Kantorowicz has described the role of corporate imagery in the establishment of medieval political sovereignty. On one hand, the corporation became the basis for conceptualizing secular political power by transforming the religious notion of the *corpus mysticum*.[10] The *corpus mysticum* traditionally referenced the mystical body of Christ, embodied in the Eucharist. Twelfth-century canonists redefined it as the sociological structure of the Roman Catholic Church. The corporate body established the relation between the individual body of God and the collective body of believers who maintained their corporate status by partaking of the sacrament.[11] The corporal designation also imparted a new legal status on the ecclesiastical community as a *persona repraesentata* or *ficta*. In this manner, the community became a fictional person that represented the collective will of believers. As far back as the thirteenth century, corporateness was intimately intertwined with sacredness. Kantorowicz explained that shrouding politics in corporate imagery worked "to hallow the secular polities as well as their administrative institutions."[12]

The corporate form not only gave states a theological foundation but also provided a means for conceptualizing sovereignty as a superior power over both individuals and rulers that was unified *through time* and *across space*. Prefiguring the Hobbesian corporate sovereign, corporate legal doctrines were central to what Kantorowicz termed "the king's two bodies." Whereas the physical body of a particular sovereign lived and died, the essence of sovereignty resided in a second, corporate body that linked the larger political community and the sovereign. This corporate body was critical to the temporal continuity of sovereignty beyond the life and death of any individual ruler. Kantorowicz argued that the thirteenth-century English canonist Bracton made the difference between the physical and the sempiternal body central to the dual nature of sovereignty, although he also made clear that the duality was neither between the king's public and private functions nor even between the king's natural and political bodies. Rather, duality was internal to the concept of sovereignty as an "extra-territorial or extra-feudal realm within the realm, an 'eminent domain' the continuity of which, beyond the life of an individual king, had become a matter of common and public interest because the continuity and integrity of that domain were matters 'that touched all.'"[13]

In addition to maintaining sovereignty over time, the corporate body also established spatial relations between the state, territory, and public wealth. By the thirteenth century, the extraterritorial realm had taken on real territorial dimensions as the *fiscus* or fisc. The fisc named the public treasury, along with the physical lands and territory that reverted back to the Crown, in its corporate capacity, when tenants died without a will. These lands were public in the sense that they were controlled by the state but separated from the imperial patrimony; they were therefore land considered of common concern.[14] For this reason, the fisc was one of the central locations for the development of a discourse on the *salus publica* or public good. As common lands administered for public welfare, the fisc was designed to strengthen sovereignty in its corporate capacity instead of increasing the wealth of individuals. We can get a better idea of the particularly sacrificial relationship of secular sovereignty by noting that, etymologically, the corporate lands of the fisc are the root of both the adjective *fiscal* and the verb *to confiscate*.[15]

Thus, long before Hobbes posed the problem of sovereign power and individual desire, the corporate form was used to designate a complex assemblage of perpetual sovereignty, sacredness, land, and common welfare. In this way, the corporate body became central to the establishment of secular state sovereignty. Michel Foucault has used the term *deductive power* to describe the ways states drew on Christian ethics of sacrifice and linked the Roman concept of patriarchal power to secular sovereignty (see Figure 2).[16] Christian ethics redirected private and personal relations of fealty to an emergent concept of the common public good. It was not, therefore, metaphorical to see the extraction of taxes or the sacrifice of one's life for the sovereign in terms of the physical maintenance of the corporate body or the fisc. In addition to the reversion of lands to the fisc,

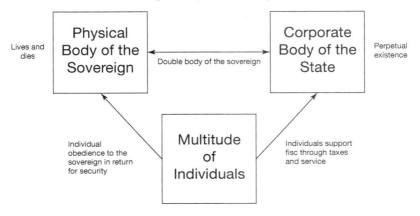

FIGURE 2. Deductive sovereignty. This schematic represents the logic of state sovereignty in its deductive mode. Here, too, we see the corporate nature of sovereignty in the double body of the sovereign that persists beyond the life of any individual ruler. See also Ernst Kantorowicz's *The King's Two Bodies: A Study in Medieval Political Theology* (Princeton, N.J.: Princeton University Press, 1957).

Kantorowicz provided other examples where sovereignty was equated with sacrifice for the corporate body of the state during periods of emergency that threatened the common welfare.[17] Kantorowicz located a new ethic of public sacrifice with the crusades in the twelfth and thirteenth centuries, which transformed a personal relationship between knights and their lords into a public sacrifice for the body of believers. Sacrifice included military service and the imposition of emergency taxes in defense of the realm and was conceptualized as an ethic of giving that sanctified death as part of membership in the collective body. Kantorowicz unequivocally stated, "At a certain moment in history the 'state' in the abstract or the state as a corporation appeared as a *corpus mysticum* and that death for this new mystical body appeared equal in value to the death of a crusader for the cause of God."[18] The sovereign's ability to demand service for the *salus publica* was captured by the twelfth-century legal maxim *necessitas legem non habet* (necessity knows no law).[19]

Police Science and Economic Government

Corporate imagery established the sacredness of state sovereignty and legitimated the power to abandon populations or compel death for the security of the state. This is the line of reasoning that eventually led to the corporate body of the Leviathan and that continues to undergird arguments about the exceptional nature of state sovereignty into the present. Unrecognized, however, is the function of the corporation in that other mode of modern power Foucault discussed in terms of the problematic of government. As Foucault demonstrated, governmental rationality was quite different from the deductive model of sovereign power and arguably more important for structuring liberal forms of rule.

First developed in the sixteenth-century revival of republicanism and civic humanism, discourses on government articulated strategies for shielding the political community against the unpredictability of fortune.[20] Foucault argued that government isolated the state as an institution that could be strengthened through "the right way of arranging *(disposer)* things in order to lead *(conduire)* them, not to the form of the 'common good,' as the texts of the jurists said, but to a 'suitable end,' an end suitable for each of the things to be governed."[21] Instead of emphasizing the personal status of the monarch, new discourses of government situated the prince in a relationship of externality and transcendence to his principality. Without this fundamental connection to God or Nature, the prince could only maintain control of territory and subjects through the manipulation of forces. Governmental reason problematized the best ways to harness those forces and thus became a flexible discourse that linked the government of a state to the governing of "a household, souls, children, a province, a convent, a religious order, a family."[22] In each sense, government relied on specific forms of knowledge: "the art of self-government, connected with morality; the art of properly governing a family, which belongs to economy; and finally the science of ruling the state, which concerns politics."[23]

Government aimed to increase the public welfare by organizing individuals and objects, along with their interrelations, in optimal ways. Unlike the deductive theory of sovereignty, whose ways of knowing were drawn from law and theology, the government of populations and things was first systematized in the *science of police*. In this sense, police science marked a passage between direct power over life associated with deductive theories of sovereignty and liberal modes of governmentality. As with later forms of liberal reason, police science was devoted to the optimal arrangement of things, yet police science still relied heavily on law and regulation, legislating "just distribution" primarily through legal codes known as police ordinances.

To be clear, police science and the early modern concept of police differ markedly from the modern municipal police forces that developed during the nineteenth century. First outlined in mid-sixteenth-century Central European legal codes,[24] the concept of police was more closely related to policy and signified both "a condition of order in the community" and "statute aimed at the institution and/or maintenance of order in the community."²⁵ Police was a massive program of regulation that attempted to foster the wealth, stability, and happiness of the state by producing knowledge that was at once totalizing, regulating whole populations toward the welfare, security, and happiness of the state, and individualizing, shaping the conduct of individuals in their particular relations. Police science received its most extensive elaboration in the German empire, while also being developed in Russia and France.²⁶ In England, police was not centralized in a state administrative structure, but the concept remained central to political debates.²⁷ As late as the eighteenth century, paradigmatically liberal thinkers, including the jurist William Blackstone and Adam Smith, continued to engage police and police science. Blackstone wrote of "wrongs" against "the Public Health, and the Public Police or Oeconomy" in his *Commentaries,* and Smith discussed police in both the 1762–63 *Lectures on Jurisprudence* and, more critically, in *The Wealth of Nations.*²⁸

Though concerned with the *salus publica,* police was not reducible to a republican discourse on civic virtue.²⁹ Whereas many articulations of republicanism held trade and finance in disdain as a corrupting influence, police, like cameralism, mercantilism, and political arithmetic, with which it is associated, addressed the physical and fiscal strength of the state as a problem not of virtue but of conduct.³⁰ As such, it was the first system that treated the government of the state as a question of economy, in its classical sense as relating to the government of the *oikos* or "household." Blackstone made the link clear when he referred to police as "the due regulation of domestic order of the kingdom: whereby the individuals of the state, like members of a well-governed family, are bound to conform their general behavior to the rules of propriety, good neighborhood, and good manners; and to be decent, industrious, and inoffensive in their respective stations."³¹ The power of the patriarch to govern in the service of public order grounded an expansive agenda of regulation. Blackstone included the following in his account of police: the quarantining of ships; the regulation of goods and marriage; limits on the movement of soldiers, mariners, and "Egyptians or gypsies"; nuisance ordinances concerning public highways, bridges, and rivers; regulations against "all disorderly inns or ale-houses, gaming-houses, bawdy-houses, stage-plays, unlicensed booths, and stages for rope-dancers, mountebanks and the like"; limits on lotteries, fireworks, and gunpowder; prohibitions against eavesdroppers, rogues, vagabonds, and "idle and disorderly persons"; sumptuary laws against luxurious dress and diet; and regulations concerning hunting, animals, slaves, and the poor.³²

Unlike later arguments for laissez-faire liberalism, the relationship between police and *oeconomy* did not imply that police was a tactic used by the state to limit the economy; likewise, the neighboring discourse of cameralism was not a science of administration in the modern sense, nor was mercantilism an economic or even protoeconomic theory. As Keith Tribe reminds us, "this neat separation [between politics and economics] is however only effective on the basis of modern conceptions of economy and polity that are not present in the eighteenth century."[33] The model of governing a state on the basis of *oeconomy* meant "a constant preoccupation with the ordering of productive activity."[34] Instead of constituting a separate sphere in social life, government, in this sense, was a technique of directing the actions of whole populations toward both individual and collective health. *Oeconomy* and conduct linked sumptuary laws, poor relief, slavery, labor management, the control of populations, and the regulation of trade and markets to public health, order, and happiness. Mitchell Dean has usefully provided the image of the traffic cop, who "shapes, structures and guides flows and forces," as opposed to the idea of an absolute sovereign who forces his will directly on his subjects as a way of illustrating the shift from theories of sovereignty to theories of government.[35] We can understand the role of police in this assemblage of power through the schematic in Figure 3.

Corporation-as-Police and the Chartered Grant

My central claim is that here, in the connections between corporation and police, our current mode of corporate sovereignty first developed. The police of society required corporate institutions to direct the conduct of individuals and things to optimal ends. Marc Raeff notes that corporate bodies were responsible for the enforcement of police ordinances in Western and Central Europe. He argues, "What was new is the greater degree of control and supervision exercised over the activities of these officials and institutions by the prince's councils and central offices."[36] His comment gets at the heart of a new set of relations emerging around the corporation in conjunction with theories of police. These new discourses positioned the corporation, like the family, as simultaneously an autonomous disciplinary apparatus and an object of regulation by the state.[37] Corporations were given exceptional powers to manage, direct, and channel the conduct of the corporate body, its individual members, and the lives of whole populations. Corporations also became situated as external to the official state apparatus and regulated with new forms of accountability and oversight.

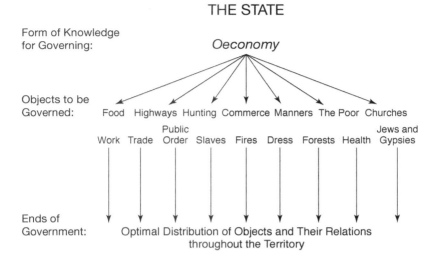

FIGURE 3. Police. A midpoint between the older deductive theories of sovereignty and liberal modes of government, the science of police was a massive regulatory project first articulated in mid-sixteenth-century European legal codes. Police science viewed the state as a household and used the logic of household management, or economy, to direct objects to an optimal distribution across a sovereign territory.

This amounted to nothing less than a fundamental reorganization of power between the sovereign and the corporation.

In seventeenth-century England, the Crown removed itself from the direct management of much of daily life, using corporations to manage hospitals, schools, philanthropy, and imperial trade in a specifically de-centralized and liberal mode of government. John P. Davis, in his early-twentieth-century study of corporations, explained that the decline of religious authority led to the reorganization of charities, like hospitals and almshouses, under new grants that were heavily supervised by the state. The 1601 Charitable Uses Act became the first legislative act to regulate these corporate bodies in England, with a preamble listing the variety of activities that the state had supported through grants of "land, tenements, rents, annuities, profits, hereditaments, goods, chattels, money and stocks of money," which included

> relief of the aged, impotent and poor people, some for
> maintenance of sick and maimed soldiers and mariners, schools of

learning, free schools, and scholars in universities, some for repair
of bridges, ports, havens, causeways, churches, sea-banks and
highways, some for education and preferment of orphans, some for
or towards relief, stock or maintenance for houses of correction,
some for marriages of poor maids, some for supportation, aid
and help of young tradesmen, handicraftsmen and persons
decayed, and others for relief or redemption of prisoners or
captives, and for aid or ease of any poor inhabitants concerning
payments of fifteens, setting out of soldiers and other taxes.[38]

In other words, *corporations became the very basis for regulating conduct.*
As late as 1793, the connection between police and corporation remained
close enough that Stewart Kyd began his treatise on the laws of corporation by noting the natural division of political communities into local
corporate structures for "a more convenient system of police."[39] We can
thus revise our earlier schematic of police to include the corporation as
the technique used to ensure public welfare (Figure 4).

The police function was embodied in charters, which situated lesser
bodies in hierarchical sets of relations that formed the sinews of power
in territorial states. In England, charters became necessary after the Statute of Mortmain, passed under Edward I in 1279, limited the ability of
ecclesiastical bodies to hold land.[40] The Crown raised revenues by selling charters to various groups. The charters established the legal standing of corporations as unified bodies that could exercise a variety of legal
privileges. This regulation was in turn contingent on a series of extralegal
practices of self-government and regulation that the corporation enforced
against its members as well as against nonmembers who interacted with
the corporate body. Legally, corporations were designated by a name and
a legally binding seal, and charters granted them the ability to hold property collectively, the right to sue or be sued, and exemption from physical
punishments. These privileges were codified in a recognizable and repeat-
able form that stabilized in the mid-sixteenth century.[41] Sir Edward Coke
famously outlined the "essence" of the grant of incorporation in *Case of
Sutton's Hospital* (1612). Coke distinguished between things necessary
for the corporation's independent existence and things necessary for the
corporation to carry out its appointed task. The essential elements—name,
location, and ability to sue and be sued—were those that linked the grant
back to the "Lawful authority" that established the corporation. This was
contrasted with things like revenue and the power to make ordinances,
which were "requisite for the good order and government of the poor, &c.
but not to the essence of the incorporation."[42] The enumerated list was

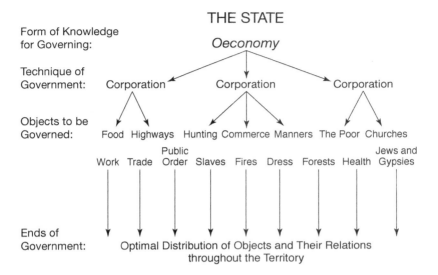

FIGURE 4. Corporation-as-police. Corporations played a central role in orchestrating the police of society and thus the distribution of things to optimal ends. This is the original formulation of modern corporate sovereignty.

reproduced in the anonymous *The Law of Corporations* in 1702. Blackstone followed Coke's reasoning, arguing that the essence of the corporation resided in its relation to the power that created it.[43]

The concern with the relationship between political authority and the corporation carried over into the language of the charters. In addition to the name and seal, the basic clauses of most charters established "the right of perpetual succession, of suing and being sued, of having a common seal, of dealing with lands and of making by-laws"—essentially the same list found in Coke and Blackstone and a mainstay of U.S. charters well into the nineteenth century.[44] Charters also provided protocols for "visitation" by the authorizing power and gave precise accounts of the form, frequency, and location of meetings. These meetings were to be directed by governors, whose election, succession, and terms were stipulated in the grants. While grants were construed to have benefits for the incorporators, the logic behind them was to benefit the King and good government. Almost all charters were incorporated by "special grace, certain knowledge, and mere motion" of the King. Blackstone glossed this phrase as designating that grants were made "not at the suit of the grantee" but at the will of the King.[45] These clauses were followed by recitations of the grant: of tax exemptions, of monopoly rights, of rights to land and sempiternal existence.

The logic was more pronounced with regulated companies, whose grants contained monopoly privileges intended to regulate industry and commerce in the national interest. Charters were pleaded for on the basis of the moral standing of the applicants and granted "in generous recognition of merit."[46] For example, the Mines Royal received "Letters Patents for divers good considerations."[47]

Privileges implied moral responsibilities. Good government and regulation were not strictly political or economic terms, and many of the phrases that would connect companies to "economic" processes still carried their older ethical meanings in the seventeenth century.[48] When the grant to the Merchants of London Trading to France was given to "merchants of good credit," it applied the interlinked concepts of credulity and the ability to secure loans.[49] Likewise, the Mines Royal grant "to their most profit and commodity" referenced good order and utility more than the useful object (i.e., the commodity) itself.[50] Such moral regulation was not left to happenstance; charters granted the corporation disciplinary power over the conduct of members of the corporation. Corporations drew on mechanisms for structuring behavior associated with older monastic and educational corporations. Merchant companies, universities, and fraternal organizations installed oaths for membership and required religious observance. Guilds and corporate towns could enforce their internal regulation even on individuals who were not members of the corporation yet participated in a trade or had business in a corporate town.[51]

Corporate bylaws established stringent controls. A regulation for the merchants and apprentices of the Eastland Company, a chartered company trading in the Baltics and Scandinavia, ordered

> that if any brother That is an apprentice or any other unruly
> person or persons of our Bretheren or any the kings Majesties
> subjects shall misbehave themselves or use whore houses, keepe
> dishoneste and unlawfull Company or Ryotinge or wastfully
> mispendinge his or their Masters or friends goods, or is missinge
> out of his hoasts house all nighte, Or after Eleven of the Clocke
> in the Sommer and tenne in the Winter (without he can prove he
> hath bin in honeste Company and urged to keepe their Company
> soe late). Or use Cards dyce or any other unlawfull games or
> gameinge for money hee or they soe offendinge shalbe punished at
> the discrecon of the deputie and assistants.[52]

Other regulations prohibited fighting, disclosing secrets, and using "unseemely words to the Governour." Yet the majority of acts and bylaws concerned the regulation of trade, working conditions, and accounts. In addition to acts regulating the conduct of apprentices and the "disordered sonnes servants," work regulations focused on who could and could not fill various positions within the company, their specific duties, and their recourses for offenses. Regulations for trade and accounting included the hiring of auditors, the standards for taking bills of exchange, and regulations for collecting duties.[53] The charter also gave bylaws legally binding force. Many grants for towns and trading companies included provisions for the establishment of courts. The Mines Royal charter gives a sense of the legal power of the corporation:

> to limit set ordain and put reasonable pains and penalties by fines forfeitures and imprisonments or any of them upon any, being a member or members of the body politic Society and Commonalty aforesaid or a minister officer or servant labourer or workman of the same, for any offence touching the said [Corporation] or their works affairs or other things contrary to the statutes acts ordinances and rules so to be devised and made as is aforesaid or any of them.[54]

The corporation-as-police also established territorial control. Most grants contained lists specifying the geographic parameters in which the corporation had jurisdiction. With the trading companies, the geographic designation usually included trade routes. In relation to state sovereignty, the clauses were by definition extraterritorial in scope. The Levant Company received a monopoly to bring Mediterranean goods into England and Wales, which included rights to travel protected routes in the Mediterranean Sea. Likewise, mining companies were granted rights to explore specific territories, and fishing companies had rights over certain waters. Grants of territorial control focused on taking possession of natural resources. The charters established relations that were extractive, returning wealth and power back to the Crown. The Newfoundland Company charter granted

> all the lands soil grounds havens ports rivers mines, as well royal mines of gold and silver as other mines, minerals pearls and precious stones woods quarries marshes waters fishings huntings hawkings fowlings commodities and hereditaments whatsoever, together with all prerogatives jurisdictions royalties privileges franchises and preeminences within any the said territories.[55]

Similar to guild regulations, traders could enforce their monopoly on other Englishmen conducting business in the region, even if they were not members of the corporation.

By granting special powers to corporations in territories beyond the boundaries of the nation, the state was able to direct the conduct of subjects abroad in ways that reinforced the *salus publica*. For instance, John Wheeler's 1601 *Treatise of Commerce* defended the monopoly privileges of the Merchant Adventurers by suggesting that the company strengthened the position of England in relation to its neighbors and trading rivals, that it ensured good prices for English textiles, and that "the Queenes Customes and Incomes, are augmented by maintaining the Companie."[56] The chartered grant also encouraged self-government, protecting merchants from "that naughtiness & corruption which is naturallie in him: for there is nothing in the world so ordinarie, and naturall unto men, as to contract, truck, merchandise, and traffike one with another."[57] The police functions of the corporation, especially its monopoly privileges and coercive powers, were thus central to the creation of the disciplined, liberal, male subject. When Wheeler was confronted with the strongest arguments that the monopoly on textiles hurt the cloth market in England and thereby restricted "the libertie of the subject," he replied that the monopoly controlled the "greedy appetite" that is a natural extension of the propensity to trade. Only "by their good gouerment & by their politike & merchantlike orders" was the corporation able to restrain avaricious human nature and render it productive for the Crown.[58] Trade required the self-organization of merchants into governable bodies that the state could observe and manage externally. If the pursuit of interest was in fact natural, then the creation of corporations and the enforcement of their bylaws and monopoly privileges represented a way for the state to benefit from the inherent greed of the population over whom it held authority.

While corporate privileges might have had salutary effects for the traders, in the colonies, the charter empowered corporations to deploy a wide array of disciplinary and military tactics. Colonization, in this respect, was the *logical outgrowth* of the charter's exemptions, as it established direct forms of sovereign power aimed at the policing of conduct.[59] Within the context of European colonization, charters set the legal framework for the control of territories and populations (Figure 5). They also demarcated legal jurisdictions and set the structures of colonial courts, provisions for maintaining standing armies, and protocols for conducting relations with colonial subjects or indigenous populations. The charter of the Royal African Company contained the following clause, which reappeared in the East India Company charter of 1683:

The Governor, Sub-Governor, Deputy Governor and Assistants of
the said Company for the time being or any seven of them duly
appointed in manner aforesaid shall and may have the ordering
rule and government of all such forts, factories, and plantations
as now are or shall be at any time hereafter settled by or under
the said Company . . . and also full power to make and declare
peace and war with any of the heathen nations that are or shall
be natives of any countries within the said territories . . . and also
to appoint governors there with powers of raising troops and
executing martial law; provision as to profits of gold mines.[60]

Charters characterized the colonies as vacant lands requiring settlement
or as an infinitely expandable list of territory, goods, and resources over
which the corporation could take control. Charters served the purposes
of the Crown, and in the case of the East India Company or Royal African Company, it codified the corporation's ability to suspend the law and
engage in warfare to achieve those ends.

The Double Body and the Parasite

Tracing these developments allows us to understand the anxiety besetting
advocates of state sovereignty. When presented as the figure of the commonwealth, the corporate body of the state suggested a unity between
the sovereign and the multitude, one that grounded a deductive theory of
sovereignty. Theorists of state power were also aware that the same ideas
could establish independent political bodies. Both Hobbes and Jean Bodin
argued that there was a tension between the state-as-corporation and nonstate corporations that held privileges against the state. Moreover, they
fretted that the minimal regulation provided by the charters was insufficient to control corporate power and direct it toward the public welfare.
Corporations could lead to divided sovereignty or, worse, a state within
a state, *imperium in imperio*.

Bodin, for instance, began his discussion of corporations in the *Six Books
of the Commonwealth* by presenting them as autonomous institutions directed toward religion and police. In their police function, corporations
"concerne but worldly things," including "the bringing vp of youth, or for
fellowship of physitians, or of other schollers, or of marchants, or of handie
craft and trades men, or of companies of husbandmen."[61] Bodin suggested
that the corporation's ability to regulate individual conduct relied on its autonomy, making corporations similar to households. Just as families were
natural associations built on love, Bodin argued that corporations develop

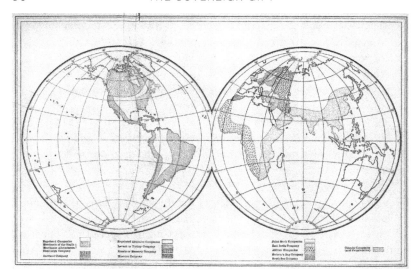

FIGURE 5. "Map Showing Areas of National External Corporations" from John P. Davis, *Corporations: A Study of the Origins and Development of Great Business Combinations and of the Relation to the Authority of the State* (New York: Knickerbocker Press, 1905). The map, a cartographic expression of corporate territoriality, presents the Hudson Bay Company across much of present-day Canada; the South Sea Company with territorial claims from the west coast of North America to the entire coastal region of Central and South America and the Caribbean; various colonial companies occupying the eastern North American seaboard; the domination of Africa on the east coast by the African Companies and on the west coast by other colonial companies; and the East India Company with dominion across South Asia. The map does not specify what historical era is represented. Davis also included an appendix discussing the difficulties of cartographically depicting the expansive legal grants of territory and property along with the areas practically controlled by companies in their day-to-day operations.

from the love and friendship of "men joined in alliance."[62] Without the sovereign, however, these "communitie ciuill" would have no legal standing. Corporations required the sovereign to establish their membership in the political community. "Where the word Lawfull importeth the authoritie of the soueraigne, without whose permission there can be no colledge."[63]

Hobbes took an even stronger stance against corporate autonomy. As we have already discussed, Hobbes used the image of the corporation to ground the power of the commonwealth. Still, if the corporate body of the state had the sole authority to represent the interests of the multitude, Hobbes faced the problem of existing corporations such as guilds, towns, or religious groups. He considered all associations as "Systemes, which resemble the similar parts, or Muscles of a Body naturall" and described the activities of "men joined in one Interest, or one Businesse"[64] by setting out a typology of the different classes of associations. These included groups that were political or private, lawful or unlawful, regular or irregular, and absolute or dependent, and they ranged from families, "Corporations of Beggars, Theeves and Gipsies,"[65] and conspirators to cities, colonies, political assemblies, religious groups, and the commonwealth itself. The critical aspect for Hobbes was that none of these groups could represent individuals in terms of political authority, which was the sole prerogative of the sovereign.[66] Both the charter and the laws of the commonwealth circumscribed the actions that a corporate body could undertake. Hobbes viewed corporations as threats to the welfare of the state and worried openly about the existence of groups whose interests were not clearly connected with state power, describing them in conjunction with things that weaken a commonwealth, as "the great number of Corporations; which are as it were many lesser Common-wealths in the bowels of a greater, like wormes in the entrayles of a naturall man."[67]

For this reason, Hobbes placed special emphasis on the chartered grant, which established the state's supremacy over corporations. Hobbes used the figure of *the gift* as opposed to universally binding law to accentuate the link between charter and sovereign power. Whereas laws are by nature universal, *the gift composed an extralegal relationship that founded corporate power*:

> Likewise *Lawes* and *Charters* are taken promiscuously for the same thing. Yet Charters are Donations of the Soveraign; and not Lawes, but exemptions from Law. The phrase of a Law is *Jubeo, Injungo, I Command,* and *Enjoyn*: the phrase of a Charter is *Dedi, Concessi, I have Given, I have Granted*: but what is given or granted, to a man, is not forced upon him, by a Law. A Law may be made to bind All the Subjects of a Common-Wealth: A Liberty, or Charter is only to One man, or some One part of the people. For to say all the people of a Common-Wealth, have Liberty in any case whatsoever; is to say, that in such case, there hath been no Law made; or else having been made, is now abrogated.[68]

In Hobbes's construction, the charter was a gift—an exemption from law—that *both suspended and established* the legal order. As a legally authorized exemption, the charter provided the basis for liberties held against the state while simultaneously asserting the power of the sovereign over corporations.

Hobbes's anxiety, and his peculiar resolution of it in the form of the sovereign gift, continues to trouble the world. The power granted to corporations enabled them to discipline both members and nonmembers, promoting a host of activities that benefited the sovereign. By disciplining individuals in poorhouses, orphanages, towns, religious orders, and hospitals, corporations used their legally granted privileges to produce forms of life that were proper or valuable for the state. In the case of the trading companies, corporations were empowered to optimally organize the relations between individuals, resources, and things, even beyond the political borders of the state. Through the granting of charters, the Crown created conditions for governing indirectly in a liberal and decentralized way not confined to the state's territory. Liberal government still entailed relations of force, but they were dislocated from the state and placed in the corporation. These powers also reinforced the autonomy of the corporation with respect to the state. Though the corporation relied on the state's legal privileges, it was also viewed by the state as a potential threat—a worm in its own entrails—that endangered the health and welfare of the public.

This early configuration of corporate sovereignty is relevant for understanding corporate power today, but not because modern multinationals are the same as their colonial forbearers. Although the tensions around corporations persisted into the eighteenth century and beyond in British and, later, U.S. legal thought, important transitions in both corporate and state power transformed the terms of the debate. For the state, the changes concerned the development of political theories of liberalism and popular sovereignty, which, unlike the discourses of state sovereignty we have been considering in this chapter, were rooted in civil society and its social relations. The changes with respect to the corporation concerned its increasing use for capitalist accumulation. As the next two chapters will attempt to explain, the ambiguous status of the corporation, as both a creation of the state and a liberty against the state, shifted when the corporation became thought of as a form of property, in terms of the market, and as a legal embodiment of capital.

Contemporary globalization nonetheless repeats certain components of the assemblage of power discussed here. Two repetitions seem particularly important. First, contemporary globalization radically expands the argument that corporate privileges and the concomitant abandonment of populations are necessary for public welfare. Though we will examine shifts in the terms by which necessity is calculated, this past formulation of corporate sovereignty resides within all of those projects that grant privileges and immunities to corporations for the salvation of populations. Second, globalization reiterates the strange spatial configurations of corporate sovereignty. The account of corporate sovereignty offered here suggests that states, sovereignty, and law were critical to the creation of a relatively decentralized form of government and order within corporations, relations that are manifest in the current uneven spatial assemblages of corporate power. In both cases, we can see a global order that is not the result of the imperial past but rather a particular realization of its latent potential.

CHAPTER TWO

Property

Today, we seldom think about corporate authority deriving from the sovereign grant of a corporate charter. In an age in which incorporation has become standardized and a normal legal device for business, we focus on more proximate and visible sources of corporate authority, namely, the managers running corporations and the shareholders and boards of directors that employ them and, at least nominally, direct their actions. This contemporary vision treats corporations as private institutions, governed by relations of property and contract, owned by shareholders, and managed by directors. Furthermore, it suggests that while laws are important in establishing a broad framework of property rights, the law (and by extension the state) are not directly involved in the organization of corporations or the corporate economy. Yet, as chapter 1 argued, the development of a legal framework in which corporations were equated with private property was in no way foreordained, as early modern corporations took their bearings from legal discourses concerning religious authority and the administration of public welfare. The treatment of corporations as a form of private property occurred within the context of wider debates over sovereignty, government, and political economy during the late eighteenth and early nineteenth centuries. This chapter explains that transition and its subsequent effects by focusing on the reorganization of the corporation as a private institution in U.S. law during this period.

I focus on nineteenth-century U.S. legal constructions of the corporation for two reasons. First, as historians have noted, this legal framework was important for establishing a regime of corporate or managerial capitalism that became dominant within the United States by the late nineteenth century and anchored U.S. economic growth through the course of the twentieth century.[1] The rise of the large industrial corporation was not only intertwined with the production of a national economy but also transformed political culture, including concepts of government, sovereignty, and rights. Second, U.S. corporate law, which coalesced during this period, has been aggressively exported through contemporary rounds of economic globalization and thus constitutes an important source for conceptualizing current aspects of the transnational or global political and economic order.[2] Although scholars have explained the general contours of these legal shifts, they have not situated these changes within the problematic governing corporate law and thus have failed to consider how the privatization of the corporation not only supported incipient forms of corporate capitalism but did so in ways that depended on and fostered new conceptions of sovereignty and government. Too often we simply reiterate a fable about the division between the economy and the state, attributing corporate capitalism to the former without recognizing the ways it is bound up with the latter. But state power, law, sovereignty, and government were the very terms in which corporate power was understood as corporations shifted from the institutions of imperial government during European colonization to privately held companies that, by the end of the nineteenth century, functioned within a nationally administered liberal capitalist economy.

Whereas the corporation-as-police constituted an important part of government in seventeenth-century England, by the late eighteenth century, liberal political economists were attacking both corporations and the police power. Liberals argued that sovereigns could never acquire adequate knowledge to effectively govern the complex interactions of people and things to optimal ends and viewed the division of labor and market exchanges as means of increasing the general wealth and welfare of society. In the early American republic, however, legal scholars reformulated the concept of police into a more formal police power that state legislatures *used to promote capitalism as a project of national development.* State police powers established the priority of the state over private interests but did so, in many ways, *to promote private property.*

Within this context, statesmen, lawyers, and other political actors vigorously debated the uses, meaning, and status of corporations. State legislatures continued to create corporations through special acts as a means of developing infrastructure and encouraging individuals to undertake quasi-public projects, ranging from the building and management of bridges, turnpikes, and canals to the creation of literary societies or the administration of poorhouses and orphanages. But such uses of public power were controversial. Discourses of popular sovereignty and republican government transformed these legislative acts into contracts establishing vested rights. As the division between private property and public power became more entrenched through the nineteenth century, the corporation straddled the line between public and private. Corporations could appear as expressions of public power undertaking risky ventures in the name of the common welfare, but they also could be seen as private property existing in a tense relation with the police power of the state.

Through much of the nineteenth century, these competing definitions of the corporation sat uneasily alongside one another. By the late nineteenth century, an expansion of federal administration led to a decisive shift in corporate regulation, as liberal legal thinkers argued that the maintenance of legal norms, rather than direct state intervention, was the best way to serve public welfare. At the state level, permissive general incorporation laws simplified and opened the process of incorporation for individuals seeking to undertake collective projects of various sorts, including those relating to business. At the federal level, an expanded administrative state sought to regulate business corporations based on their effects on prices and not in terms of their legal standing or through the act of incorporation. Agencies like the Interstate Commerce Commission, the Industrial Commission, the Bureau of Corporations, and the Federal Trade Commission argued that some corporate consolidation served the public welfare by promoting enterprises that were only profitable with limited competition. They advocated increased publicity and government oversight as a way of regulating anticompetitive behavior. Within the law, these changes drew a sharper division between the state and the corporation than had previously existed, ending the practice of dealing with corporations as extensions of public power.

Such changes have been understood as part of the way that the state promoted a form of corporate capital. Less commented on, but equally decisive, these changes depended on new concepts of government in which "economy," as "a level of reality, a field of intervention" (i.e., "the economy"), bore increasing responsibility for maintaining public welfare (Figure 6).[3] Economy, as a form and method of government, extended liberal critiques of the police. To govern on the basis of economy and through the economy meant recognizing the limits of the state in directing the productive relations of society and used law to establish "general forms of intervention."[4] The reformulation of the corporation as an economic entity was part of the state's attempt to create procedural norms that allowed individuals to address problems of economic organization.[5] By refiguring the corporation with powers to limit liability and hold subsidiary companies, which became generally available by the 1890s, the state found powerful tools to promote investment, while protecting capital from the full force of competition.

Thus the focus here on the "privatization" of the corporation is quite different from historical accounts of the rise of the large industrial business

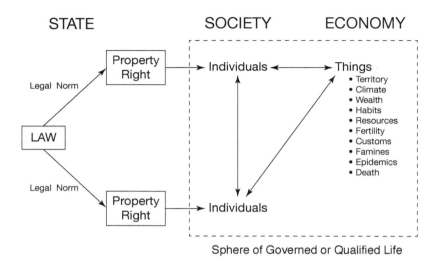

FIGURE 6. Liberalism, or government by economy. In the genealogy of governmental reason, liberalism can be usefully considered a form of "economic government" that extended the critique of police science. To govern on the basis of economy (as a form of reason) and through the economy (as a social field, i.e., "the economy") meant recognizing the limits of the state in directing the productive relations of society. In this mode of government, law established procedural norms—such as property rights and rules of market exchange—that allowed individuals to direct the distribution of resources and things.

corporation or the ways that capitalists, through their control of the state apparatus, created a legal form that was beneficial to their class interests. Without denying the validity of those claims, the articulation of the corporation and property was only conceivable through the emergence of new concepts of government based on economy. Nonetheless, these did not entirely eliminate the older problematic that rooted the exceptional privileges of corporations in their commitment to serve public welfare. Instead, they forced a reworking of the nature of these privileges, along with related legal concepts such as police and property, in ways that were consistent with new practices of economic government. The result was that, as the commitment to public welfare was increasingly conceptualized in economic terms, lawmakers admitted a legal embodiment of capital into the political community as a juristic person with *rights held against the state*—and they justified this grant of rights, along with the problems associated with the increasing concentration of corporate economic power, as necessary for economic security.

As a point of historiography, this simply reiterates that when lawyers, judges, politicians, and political activists debated the legal structures of corporations, they did so with an understanding that corporations were part of the social and political order. But this history is also critical to the *genealogical* thrust of this study, which is always a historical critique of the present. Focusing on the tense relations between the corporation and economic government helps us see that corporate capitalism emerged through a series of contingent events and arguments. In important ways, corporations did not fit neatly into the new concepts of government based on economy. Studying the reformulation of this legal and political institution suggests moments in which collective power could have been articulated otherwise. Most important, it provides us with a critical lever on the present, as the logic of capitalism has become even more entrenched as a justification for exceptional corporate rights and privileges.

On Monopolies and Monsters

We can chart the changes in the corporation by looking at its representations. For Hobbes, corporations were worms in the entrails of the body politic, but for nineteenth-century antimonopolists, they were monsters, infections, or uncontrollable growths. In 1835, the legal writer Theodore Sedgwick used the imagery of disease to argue against the rechartering of the Second Bank of the United States (BUS). Its monopoly privileges, he held, made the bank incongruent with free government. Like its predecessor, the BUS was designed to stabilize the national currency and give confidence to the creditors who were funding the national debt.[6] By 1832, when Andrew Jackson delivered his veto of the act to recharter the bank, it was the largest corporation in the country, chartered by the commonwealth of Pennsylvania with a capitalization of thirty-five million dollars.[7] It was also the subject of bitter resentment, primarily among southern and western Democrats, who distrusted paper currency and saw the bank as a tool of eastern capitalists. Sedgwick channeled their ire when he noted that "the revolution of 1776 gave us a free Government, but did not equally emancipate our opinions: in prejudice many of us are still colonists. We received from our English ancestors the legislative practice of creating corporate bodies, and till this day it has passed almost unquestioned."[8] Though Sedgwick recognized that collective action could bring social advances, he believed that corporations and their monopoly privileges threatened to turn back the clock on civilization's progress. Corporations were feudal institutions that subverted popular government with aristocratic privilege. Exemplifying familiar tropes of American exceptionalism,

Sedgwick argued that corporations were anachronistic in a democratic society that lacked the burden of a feudal past. They were a disease inherited from England, and although "great improvements have been made by us on the English system...enough of the gangrene remains to taint the body politic."[9]

For Sedgwick, free markets were necessary medicine. "The science of government, and of political economy, which it is absolutely essential that a free people should understand," provided all one needed to know to render a diagnosis: corporate monopolies departed "from the fundamental maxims of free trade and freedom."[10] Sedgwick worried that the bank would manipulate the money supply as a means of interfering with the value of hard currency. He argued that the proper role for government was only to "fix the standard of money as it does now of weights and measures; then leave the supply to that sovereign equalizer: FREE TRADE."[11] The central problem was the grant of privileges to groups of private individuals. Sedgwick concluded his account by making "a scale of corporate evils, which will give us a more accurate idea of what we have to dread."[12] Banks topped the list, with ferry and water companies, insurance companies, private companies, and incorporated towns following. "Internal Improvement Land Corporations" were the least odious as their "speculative evils are counteracted by the fact, that an object of immense importance can be attained in no other way."[13]

Sedgwick's antimonopoly rhetoric reflected familiar sentiments among the radical wing of Jacksonian Democrats concerning the "monster bank" (see Figure 7).[14] David Henshaw, one of Sedgwick's contemporaries from Massachusetts and a druggist and banker turned Jacksonian Democrat, saw corporations as a sickness as well, but one that resulted from the misapplication of the sovereign power to profit individuals instead of the public at large.[15] His concern was that charters, when treated as vested rights, placed corporations "beyond legislative control, and are thus to become monopolies and perpetuities...and become alarming excrescences upon the body politic."[16] Henshaw, like Sedgwick, argued that the solution was to transform the corporation into a freely available license that set it on par with real individuals. "We may assume this axiom as perfectly sound, that *Corporations can hold their rights upon no firmer basis, nor different tenure, than individuals hold theirs.*"[17]

Unlike Sedgwick, with his free market position, Henshaw referenced the older discourse of sovereignty and its concern with the "*common good.*" Rather than arguing for limited government, he reaffirmed the state legislature's regulatory power over economic exchanges:

GENERAL JACKSON SLAYING THE MANY HEADED MONSTER.

FIGURE 7. "General Jackson Slaying the Many Headed Monster." Famous 1836 political cartoon portraying Andrew Jackson's characterization of the Second Bank of the United States as a hydra-headed monster. The cartoon shows Jackson (left), Martin Van Buren (center), and Jack Downing (right) fighting against a serpent-like bank. Jackson wields a cane marked "veto," while the heads of the monster represent the states. Provided courtesy HarpWeek.

The legislature exercises the undisputed right to regulate the business of individuals, and to define their rights to property. It has first prohibited, then licensed, and then made penal, the selling of lottery tickets. It prohibits the selling of certain articles without a license therefor from designated officers. It forbids the selling of goods at auction without a license and the payment of a tax. It forbids the selling of other articles, except in certain quantities, and with certain brands put upon them by public officers—unwise and vexatious regulations, I grant, but still who disputes the legality of the inspection laws?[18]

Henshaw went on to enumerate other powers of the legislature: the ability to set the hours for markets and business, the prohibition of gambling and swearing, and the setting of rules for inheritance and property transfers. The state legislature had "even affixed a fine to a particular exercise of the liberty of speech."[19] Henshaw was troubled by the notion that the charter, as a contract, prevented the legislature, which otherwise had tremendous power to govern in the public interest, from changing the terms of incorporation. The problem with corporations was that, although created by legislatures, they seemed to take on a life of their own, and one at odds with popular sovereignty. Though the legislature "has a right to take my land or other property for public purposes, paying me therefore a just equivalent," Henshaw wondered, "if railroad, turnpike, canal, and the like corporations, are mere price associations, existing for the benefit of the corporations, and not for the common good, ... what right have they to occupy my land against my consent?"[20]

Despite their similar politics and imagery, Henshaw and Sedgwick emphasized different traditions in nineteenth-century legal and political thought. The differences also highlight ambiguities within the definitions of corporations at that time. For Henshaw, the problem with corporations was the notion that the charter was a contract that created vested rights, allowing members of corporations to avoid legislative controls that applied to other individuals. Henshaw argued, to the contrary, that corporate property was like any other form of property and that the legislature should maintain its ability to take extraordinary measures against individual property if it served the common good. For Sedgwick, however, the corporation was the expression of legislative interference in markets that were better left alone. The problem for Sedgwick was state involvement, and the solution was simply to remove the state from the practice of granting charters in the first place, allowing them to be freely available to any citizen. Arriving at the same conclusion, Henshaw and Sedgwick's arguments were mirror images of one another.

The Police and Political Economy

Chapter 1 explained that police was conceptualized as "the due regulation of domestic order of the kingdom," based on *oeconomy,* and carried out, in part, through the chartering of corporations. By the eighteenth century, liberal thinkers were attacking the concept of police and police science. Adam Smith argued that police constituted one of the "four great objects of law" along with justice, revenue, and arms.[21] Like other sixteenth- and seventeenth-century commentators, Smith connected police to the Greek polis and "the regulation of the inferiour parts of government, *viz.* cleanliness, security, and cheapness or plenty."[22] Whereas European police ordinances treated wealth as a correlate to state welfare, Smith separated wealth from security and connected the former to the division of labor and the market.[23]

By specializing in specific tasks, the division of labor enabled Europe to produce surplus goods and increase its "opulence."[24] It did so because wealth was already immanent to a society of property holders engaged in reciprocal exchanges. Smith explained the power of the market to realize the wealth that existed in society by emphasizing a duality in the concept of price. On one hand, the production of goods entailed a natural price, constituted by what was required to compensate the laborer for the risks and costs of production. Without a natural price sufficient for workers to maintain themselves, no one, in an open and competitive market, would enter a given trade. On the other hand, Smith suggested that goods contained a market price, or exchange value, determined by their supply and demand. Whereas the natural price or value of goods was determined by labor costs, exchange value fluctuated on market conditions. Smith argued that the two prices were actually connected. In markets that were free of regulations, market prices would be driven toward their natural price as laborers shifted to producing goods that were scarce yet desired.[25] The movement in prices and the compulsion it engendered for workers facilitated the self-regulating aspects of the market, which led to general prosperity.

Smith believed that police disrupted this system. Whatever the benefit of police in providing security for person and property, the interference of police in the natural balance of industry was catastrophic. Police represented an artificial barrier in the meeting between natural and market prices that tended "to diminish public opulence."[26] Nowhere was the disruption more apparent than in the monopolies given to corporations and guilds. Corporations destroyed the total wealth of a nation because they "always require a magistrate to fix the prices."[27] Elsewhere, Smith argued that corporations upset the "systems of political oeconomy."[28] In a section of *The Wealth of Nations* titled "Inequalities Occasioned by the Policy of Europe," Smith railed against "the exclusive privileges of corporations" targeting the limits on employment set by guilds and merchant's associations. Corporate towns in the "hands of traders and artificers" also came under fire for preventing "the market from being over-stocked...which is in reality under-stocked."[29] Smith challenged the utility of monopolies in foreign trade as well as those that limited imports to protect domestic production.

Smith argued that the science of political economy provided an alternative means to ensure the public welfare. As Istvan Hont and Michael Ignatieff have argued, Smith reinscribed political economy in the very space that had been occupied by the practices of police and police science.[30] Property, with its reciprocal exchanges and contracts, bound society together, increasing the public welfare unintentionally. The effect of Smith's discourse was to draw a sharp demarcation between a notion of the common good derived from the sovereign's ability to direct the totality of social relations and one connected to a society engaged in exchange.

Yet the hard distinction between police and political economy did not always hold. In revolutionary America, classical liberalism's theoretical commitment to free markets mixed with the needs of colonial government and territorial expansion. Christopher Tomlins has noted that in the United States, the revolutionary emphasis on popular sovereignty in the 1770s and 1780s shifted the connotation of police away from a discourse of security and toward a dynamic logic of "improvement."[31] Early Republican police was a majoritarian discourse that promoted both communal and individual rights and encouraged the participation of "the sovereign people" in shaping "the common good."[32]

Property was paramount to this new configuration of power. William Novak has discussed the early-nineteenth-century police power as the very backbone of early Republican government and regulation. Once again, the legal maxim of *salus publica* was critical, which Novak reads as establishing "that public interest was superior to private interest."[33] The maxim is the same one that grounded the deductive theory of sovereignty discussed in chapter 1, but popular sovereignty gave it a new inflection. Whereas the old model of sovereignty extracted wealth in the interest of the state, the nineteenth-century police power was deployed by state legislatures in the interest of the property holders who composed "the people." Novak references a second maxim, *sic utere tuo ut alienum non laedas* (use what is yours so as not to harm others), which connects police and property. Whereas *salus publica* legitimated an expansive power to promote the common good, *sic utere* was a negative power that limited the ability of the state to act in the public's interest to only those cases in which not acting did harm to others. Harm, however, was connected to ownership—to "what is yours" or "others." *Sic utere* established the protection of property as a guide to when the law could be abrogated.[34]

Taken together, the two maxims challenge the notion that nineteenth-century governance was focused exclusively on either public rights and the police power or the vested rights of individuals.[35] On their own terms, the tensions within the police power suggest a more complicated interaction between public power, private rights, and the people's welfare.[36] More important, the police power highlights a transformation in the ends of sovereignty, as nineteenth-century U.S. police powers connected the public welfare to a general protection of property and propriety. Property, with its etymological links to *proper, appropriation,* and *propriety,* became the basis for political existence (while maintaining all of the racial and gendered exclusions that those terms implied).[37] Treatises, cases, and legislation concerning the police power of the state were one of the central locations for outlining *the content of a life that was proper for the public.* No clearer statement of this intermingling could be found than in U.S. Supreme Court justice Roger Taney's decision from *The License Cases* (1847), in which he argued that the police powers "are nothing more or less than the powers of government inherent in every sovereignty . . . that is to say, the power of sovereignty, the power to govern men and things within the limits of its own dominions."[38] The quotation resonates with Foucault's argument that government concerns "the right disposition of things," but it also complicates Foucault's suggestion that "what government has to do with is not territory but rather a sort of complex composed of men and things."[39] Rather than a smooth transition from sovereign power to government, in the nineteenth-century United States, police power protected property—a set of embodied dispositions and territorial arrangements—as a means of serving the common welfare.

The Corporation's Two Bodies: Police and Property

What made the corporation monstrous, a carrier of disease, and, for all of that, still eminently useful was that it continually blurred the boundary between police and property. As previously noted, the corporation was the institutional structure of colonial government. Many of the colonies themselves were created as corporate bodies, established by royal grants, and regulated through charters. The Revolutionary War and new ideas about popular sovereignty created space for rethinking corporations, but state legislatures after the revolution continued to create corporations with special acts, often granting monopolies or exclusive rights to corporate entities. Legislatures found these monopolies useful for encouraging citizens to undertake costly internal development projects such as canal, bridge, and highway construction. As Pauline Maier has noted, the problem was "to adapt the corporation to American circumstances."[40]

The legal regime that developed had all of the contradictions that commentators like Sedgwick and Henshaw found frustrating and antidemocratic. Though regulation was largely conducted by individual states, and thus the privileges and duties of corporations varied from state to state,[41] an interlocking system of early-nineteenth-century case law established the sources and limits on corporate power. Moreover, because of the ambiguous status of the corporation between property and police, oftentimes, the limits *were* the sources of power, and vice versa.[42]

We can begin with the contract. In 1819, Chief Justice Marshall ruled in the U.S. Supreme Court case of *Dartmouth College v. Woodward* that charters were contracts and corporations should be governed under private law.[43] The case concerned the ability of the New Hampshire legislature to revise the corporate charter of the college granted by King George III in 1769. The question was whether the King's grant was still valid after the Revolution had reconstituted sovereignty on democratic grounds. Marshall's ruling finessed the issue of the validity of the grant by treating the act of incorporation as a private contract between the original members of the corporation and the Crown. As it was a private contract, the new legislature of New Hampshire was compelled to abide by the terms of the charter.

Yet a difficulty remained. Unlike an individual entering into a contract, the corporation was closely connected to government and law: "a corporation is an artificial being, invisible, intangible, and existing only in contemplation of law. Being the mere creature of law, it possesses only those properties which the charter of its creation confers upon it."[44] Corporations were brought into existence at the behest of the sovereign and to serve the ends of government. As Marshall indicated, "the objects for which a corporation is created are universally such as the government wishes to promote. They are deemed beneficial to the country; and this benefit constitutes the consideration, and in most cases, the sole consideration of the grant."[45] If the corporation was chartered for the purpose of government, and had certain similarities to the state, Marshall was also at pains to distinguish the corporation from state authority:

> By these means, a perpetual succession of individuals are
> capable of acting for the promotion of the particular object, like
> one immortal being. But this being does not share in the civil
> government of the country, unless that be the purpose for which it
> was created. Its immortality no more confers on it political power,
> or a political character, than immortality would confer such power
> or character on a natural person. It is no more a State instrument,
> than a natural person exercising the same powers would be.[46]

Subsequent rulings emphasized the role of the corporation as a tool of government and subservient to the state. In the 1839 Supreme Court case *Bank of Augusta v. Earle,* Chief Justice Roger Taney quoted half of Marshall's *Dartmouth* decision, emphasizing not vested rights created by contract but that corporations were "artificial beings ... existing only in contemplation of law."[47] The case considered whether a corporation chartered in one state could do business and enter into contracts in another state. Taney argued that *corporations exist only within the sovereign territory of their charters.* Thus a "corporation can have no legal existence out of the boundaries of the sovereignty by which it was created. It exists only in contemplation of law, and by force of law; and where that law ceases to operate, and is no longer obligatory, the corporation can have no existence. It must dwell in the place of its creation, and cannot migrate to another sovereignty."[48]

Other legal techniques that connected the corporation to the state included the doctrine of ultra vires—literally, "beyond powers of law"—and the general scope of police powers in relation to property. Though both of these have been generally considered limitations on corporate powers, they could also empower corporations to act in the public interest in a variety of ways. Ultra vires required that corporate action stay within the delineated terms of corporate charters. Because many corporate charters were given as special grants by state legislatures well into the mid-nineteenth century, this requirement was nothing other than the negative side of the positive power of the legislature to grant privileges. To say that corporations could not go beyond the power of law reaffirmed that the gifts given amounted to the force of law confirming special status.

As for the police power, corporate property, like all property, was subject to general conditions of the public welfare and *sic utere.* Christopher Tiedeman, the noted laissez-faire constitutionalist, pointed out that "it would be exceedingly liberal, and hence wrongful, construction of the constitutional protection against the impairment of the obligations of contracts, to place corporations above and beyond the ordinary police power of the state."[49] Yet the police power was not just a limit on corporate property, as the power to issue charters was a means by which state legislatures organized the productive relations of society. In undertaking the development of infrastructure—specifically, the construction of transportation and communication networks such as canals, railroads, and telegraphs—corporations had recourse to elemental forms of government power, including the use of property confiscated through eminent domain.

The concerns over the corporation demonstrate neither a society dominated by public law nor a state dominated by private right but rather the tense relations between corporations, property, sovereignty, and development under an incipient form of liberal capitalist government. Because nineteenth-century corporations combined lineages of monarchical authority, religious autonomy, republican government, and liberal critique, they were contradictory objects. Corporations were at times a sovereign grant, at others a vested property right established by contract, or, at still other times, a quasi-public entity with public powers and private control. Moreover, it was through these inconsistent renderings that the corporation derived substantial powers. As a vested right, corporate property was protected from government encroachment; as a public right, corporations were accountable to state legislatures but also entitled to use government power to order the financial, physical, social, and economic relations of society. In addition to possessing the old functions of corporations—managing work, the poor, religion, public charity, and city life—early-nineteenth-century corporations came to be defined by their new roles in canal and railroad construction, banking, turnpikes, communication, and manufacturing. These undertakings formed the basis of antebellum government.[50]

Returning to the mirrored accounts of Henshaw and Sedgwick, we can see how both interpretations present the monstrous figure of the corporation as a "double body" of the political community. Corporations were groups of individuals set out and distinguished from the rest of political community by being granted special powers. The purpose of the grant was the material development of community, which the grant itself undermined. This tension is the very structure of the ban. By granting privileges, monopolies, and immunities to corporations, legislative bodies established the conditions for improvement and development. Chartering corporations was part and parcel of settling and colonizing. At the same time, it was an affront to arguments about popular sovereignty. Henshaw discerned the tension when he noted that the corporation was the indirect means by which the state achieved the public welfare, but only by limiting its own powers to serve the common good. Sedgwick similarly found corporations antithetical to market society, as charters gave corporations special status. But he also conceded space for them to undertake development projects in cases when "an object of immense importance can be attained in no other way."[51] Perhaps the best representation of the doubling, however, is the figure of the monster bank (Figure 7). Not only does the warrior–president (General Jackson) attempt to slay the bank but the monster mirrors political authority, with each of the heads on the hydra adorned with the name of a state that had incorporated the bank (Figure 8). What was monstrous about corporate power was the way it turned sovereignty back in on itself as some kind of foreign creature.

From Police to Administration

Early-nineteenth-century concerns over corporations focused on corporations' legal privileges and monopolies and were treated as political questions.

FIGURE 8. Close-up of "General Jackson Slaying the Many Headed Monster." The largest head belongs to Nicholas Biddle, president of the Second Bank of the United States. His top hat reads "PENN" and "35 000 000," in reference to Pennsylvania's rechartering of the bank against Jackson's wishes. Provided courtesy HarpWeek.

States continued to use the corporate form as a way of carrying out quasi-public works through chartering and, at times, investing in corporations.[52] Critics held that corporations represented the state's undue interference in the market or, alternatively, a particularly onerous version of vested rights that placed unnecessary limitations on public power. By the middle of the century, however, the understanding of both the corporation and monopoly had begun to change. What were previously characterized as pernicious effects of immunities granted by law increasingly came to be seen as effects of the market.

A number of legal changes were responsible for the shift. First, the development of general incorporation laws, which began appearing for religious and scholarly corporations as far back as the 1790s, transformed the privilege of incorporation into a legal norm. The earliest general incorporation laws were individual acts that liberalized the process of incorporation for specific classes of corporations. In 1811, New York passed the first law making general incorporation legal for manufacturing. By the 1830s, industrial and commercial states in the U.S. Northeast had general acts for corporations in business, manufacturing, commerce, and banking.[53] By the 1850s, some form of law permitting general incorporation was standard in many states, and beginning in 1845, provisions for general incorporation were included directly in state constitutions.[54] Andrew Creighton argues that "by the first World War 44 out of the 48 states had enshrined a system of general incorporation at the state constitutional level; all states had systems of general incorporation in force."[55] The proliferation of general incorporation laws increased accessibility to the privileges of incorporation. Moreover, although there was a period of time during which states continued to issue special charters after general incorporation laws had been created, the latter eventually replaced the former, standardizing the grant itself.

Like the provisions in charters issued by special acts, the provisions outlined in general incorporation statutes varied from state to state. The only provision that was uniformly applied was that corporations could act under a common name and seal.[56] Other provisions—the ability to sue and be sued, the power to hold property collectively, stipulations regarding meetings and membership, protocols for choosing directors and setting their powers, the legality of holding companies, questions regarding the liability of shareholders, the assessment of taxes, and issues of interlocking ownership—were the means by which individual states set their corporate policies.[57] But this patchwork system was largely superseded in the late 1880s, when New Jersey passed a series of exceedingly liberal corporate laws. As Morton Horwitz argued with regard to New Jersey's important 1889 Corporation Act, its "major premise was that a corporation could do virtually anything it wanted."[58] More specifically, it legalized the holding company, which made it possible for corporations to own the stock of other corporations, and provided a mechanism for corporations to circumnavigate local corporate regulations. After the passage of the act, so many corporations were chartered in New Jersey that the state government was funded through corporate licensing fees. Other states, such as Delaware and West Virginia, followed suit, passing similarly liberal general incorporation laws. The development of these laws definitively ended the use of the charter as a tool of regulation—ultra vires claims virtually ceased by the 1890s—while simultaneously giving corporations new powers, in terms of ownership, and protections, in the form of limited liability.[59]

The liberalization of state charter policy was radical for two reasons. First, it ended the close relation between the state and the corporation that had characterized early-nineteenth-century charter policy. As discussed in the previous chapter, grants of incorporation often included provisions for property holding, a privilege that went back to the British imperial corporations. But the old grants were designed to benefit the sovereign directly. They were grants at "the mere motion" of the sovereign. Even early-nineteenth-century corporations were intended to directly reinforce the public welfare. By making the charter freely available, states like New Jersey were giving up their claims to directly provide for the common good. It was far different to justify incorporation on the basis of receiving taxes and licensing fees, the only direct benefits to a state from a liberal incorporation policy, than on the basis of the early-nineteenth-century expectation of bridge, canal, and other infrastructure development in return for a special grant of incorporation.

Second, general incorporation laws facilitated the concept of a corporation as a legal person distinct from the state on one side and the members of the corporation on the other. As William Roy has noted, limited liability "depends on treating the corporation as an entity in itself."[60] While limited liability had been granted to specific corporations under the old system of special charters, liberal general incorporation laws standardized it. Instead of encouraging improvement by granting monopolies, general incorporation laws promoted investment by making limited liability a normal aspect of the corporate form. Moreover, general incorporation laws established the corporation as a legal embodiment of capital separate from the state and the stockholders. Implicit in the new policy was the notion that individuals, rather than the state, could better organize the productive relations of society.[61] The state's role was to provide a stable set of legal norms that would enable people to govern themselves economically and through the economy.

The erosion of the regulatory structure for governing corporations locally was accompanied by federal regulations designed to bring corporations, especially their monopoly power, under control. The new forms of administration targeted the effects of corporate consolidation on markets. The events of this story are well known and focus on the railroads, the pivotal industry in nineteenth-century U.S. economic expansion and development. To briefly recount, in the aftermath of the Civil War, the country experienced the beginning of a massive boom in railroad construction in conjunction with westward conquest. The boom lasted through the remainder of the century and was funded by eastern and foreign capital, centralized in New York financial markets.[62] Railroad construction was carried out under state-issued corporate charters and used various public powers of government, including eminent domain, to provide land for the lines. Because of the expense of construction, single carriers served most areas; carriers could charge monopoly rents for the spur lines, while rates on trunk lines were pushed below market cost.

Financial crisis and popular protest over discriminatory rates, most famously associated with the Granger movement, led to a first wave of state regulatory action against railroads.[63] Between 1873 and 1874, Iowa, Illinois, Minnesota, and Wisconsin passed laws to create regulatory commissions that would evaluate railroad rates and set antidiscriminatory rate schedules. Railroads largely resisted these laws as a violation of their property rights. Fighting the regulation in court, the railroads were defeated in the U.S. Supreme Court case of *Munn v. Illinois*. Chief Justice Morrison Waite upheld the legitimacy of legislation against businesses, even private businesses, because they were "affected with a public interest."[64] In short, for Waite, rate regulation was part of the state's police power. Justice Stephen Field, however, issued a strongly worded dissent that challenged the notion that states had unlimited police powers to infringe on private property, even when it was in the public's interest. Instead, he argued for a consistent and federally stipulated set of principles to regulate private property—including corporations.[65]

Though supported by the Supreme Court, the state regulatory agencies did not remain in place for long. All four states abandoned their rate-setting commissions by 1880.[66] But rate setting was reintroduced, seven years later, through the creation of the federal Interstate Commerce Commission (ICC). Whether the ICC pursued a consistent policy (and on what basis and in whose interest) has been an issue of scholarly debate.[67] As with other pieces of controversial legislation, regional politics and interest groups influenced the Interstate Commerce Act. The act was created to establish regulations for common carriers engaged in interstate and foreign commerce, to limit discriminatory rates, and to make pricing "just" and "reasonable." The legislation that created the ICC also outlawed preferential treatment on carriers, standardized long- and short-haul rates, set requirements for the publication of changes in rate schedules, and forbade pooling. Additionally, the ICC was empowered to collect information on the railroads for the federal government by issuing subpoenas for testimony and documents and enforcing the provisions of the act in conjunction with the attorney general. Violations of the act fell under the jurisdiction of the federal circuit courts.[68] Though the act established a broad scope for regulatory action, the U.S. Supreme Court's interpretation stripped the ICC of most of its substantive powers to regulate rates. As Stephen Skowronek notes, the Court "reduced the ICC to a mere statistics gathering agency."[69]

Whereas railroads were the first sector of the economy to come under federal scrutiny for concentration and anticompetitive practices, the Sherman Antitrust Act of 1890 sought to regulate monopolies in other industries.[70] By undertaking regulation at the federal level, the federal government was empowered to follow the common law rules regulating trusts and monopolies engaged in interstate and foreign markets.[71] In the common law, "reasonableness" was determined by whether the action was detrimental to the public. As Martin Sklar has noted, initial enforcement of the Sherman Act adopted the common law understanding of "reasonableness" until 1897, when the Court shifted.[72] The new interpretation, beginning with the Supreme Court's reversal of the Eighth Circuit's common law reading in *U.S. v. Trans-Missouri Freight Association,* read the Sherman Act as outlawing all contracts in restraint of trade, whether reasonable or not. Yet, by 1911, the Court had returned to the more restricted common law ruling in the famous antitrust Rule of Reason decisions in *American Tobacco* and *Standard Oil.*[73] Illegal restraints of trade focused on restriction of competition and illegal use of market power to push out competitors. The post-1911 meaning of *antitrust* had shifted from a general use of law to prevent restraints of trade to a selective use of law to protect markets.

In addition to the Sherman Act and the ICC, the federal government also created a series of administrative agencies to study and create policy on industrial issues. Congress established the Industrial Commission in 1898. Between 1898 and 1903, when the commission concluded, it issued nineteen reports covering a variety of industrial topics, including a massive investigation of trusts and monopolies as well as studies of labor and labor legislation, immigration, foreign combinations, transportation, prison labor, and the conditions of capital and labor in agriculture, mining, and manufacturing.[74] The Bureau of Corporations and the Department of Commerce and Labor were created in 1903. The Bureau of Corporations mirrored the ICC, regulating all corporations (except common carriers) that were engaged in interstate and foreign commerce. Like the other commissions, the Bureau of Corporations had investigative power, which it used for a series of policy studies on key industries, including cotton, beef, lumber, water transportation, steel, and petroleum.[75] The bureau also studied issues of combination, taxation, and incorporation policy.[76] It was supplanted in 1914 by the reorganization of antitrust law through the Federal Trade Commission Act and the Clayton Act.

It has been recognized that the creation of these administrative agencies, along with the court cases that determined the scope of their powers, represented a move away from the local form of government and regulation during the nineteenth century. Some commentators have gone further, provocatively calling the expansion of the federal bureaucracy at the turn of the century the creation of "a new American state."[77] In terms of corporations, the decisive effect of these developments was to further separate corporations from the public power of the states and attempt to regulate corporate power at the federal level and solely in terms of anticompetitive behavior. What, however, did the privatization of the corporation mean in terms of the problematic of government and sovereignty that was already in place in the nineteenth century? How did the new practices of administration transform the old methods of governing through the police and the corporation? And what was the effect of this transformation on both the corporation and sovereignty?

Monopoly and the Market

We can understand the effects of treating the corporation as private, and separate from public power, by considering the way the old figures of monopoly—in the early nineteenth century, the very name of legal privilege and immunity—were reworked by the late nineteenth century. By that time, the "corporation problem" had become the problem of "trusts" and "monopoly," and monopolies were problems of imperfect markets.[78] Though corporations were involved in other controversies (such as railroad rate discrimination, artificially lowered stock values or "watered stock," and political corruption), commentators viewed these issues as manifestations of an underlying tendency toward economic concentration and anticompetitive corporate behavior rather than as autonomous issues in their own right.[79] The first report of the Industrial Commission made the point clear; in response to the question as to the causes of monopoly, its succinct reply was "COMPETITION THE CHIEF CAUSE."[80]

I stress that it was not self-evident even in the 1890s that problems with corporations were economic in nature. The corporation was still primarily a legal device and a property relation. For this reason, texts addressing industrial combinations began with discussions of the corporation's legal status. Yet, contrary to earlier treatises that considered the contradictory rulings that made the corporation both semipublic and private property, by the late nineteenth century, the corporation appeared simply as a legal person or as a device that allowed individuals to organize their property collectively in the form of a legal person.[81] The role of the state was largely removed from the equation. For instance, Walter Noyes began his book on combinations by noting that the corporation is "governed by the general rules of law relating to rights of property, contracts and torts which apply to individuals. Its relations with other corporations, as *persons,* are essentially the same as relations of natural persons."[82] Figured as persons, corporations were placed in a position of formal equality with other individuals in the market.

From the state's perspective, the problem was that if monopoly was no longer the result of legal and political privileges, what were the mechanisms that government could use to bring these economic forces under control? The federal government responded by bringing leading social scientists, such as Jeremiah Jenks, William Ripley, and John Commons, into administrative agencies.[83] Though monopolies were politically unpopular, experts urged the government not to prejudge all of them as threats.[84] Instead, they analyzed the effects of combinations on a variety of industries, on foreign and domestic competition, and for consumers. By considering corporate power as the result of processes internal to the economy, fluctuations in price became an objective way to calculate the impact of consolidation and anticompetitive behavior. According to this metric, some monopolies were reasonable. For instance, proponents of pooling demonstrated that rampant competition depressed prices to such a degree that monopolies were necessary to maintain production. But price also provided a language for claiming that monopolies had negative consequences for consumers or the public at large. In both cases, the statistical and graphic representations of price fluctuations provided a frame of reference for rethinking corporate power in terms of broader social dynamics of the market.

The federal response to the trust problem was thus not political but rather focused on standardizing and making available economic information. For instance, the Industrial Commission advocated for a system of reports of publicly traded firms. The logic was that publicity could "prevent the organizers of corporations or industrial combinations from deceiving investors and the public, either through suppression of material facts or by making misleading statements."[85] In addition to protecting investors and members of the corporation, audits and reports were believed to protect workers and consumers. As the commission argued, "the purpose of such publicity is to encourage competition when profits become excessive, thus protecting consumers against too high prices and to guard the interest of employees by a knowledge of the financial condition of the business in which they are employed."[86] Moreover, with adequate information and publicity, experts could show that some combinations were not really problems at all but merely reflected market tendencies. Because the sovereign was fundamentally incapable of directly managing the economy, the best that the state could do was to exercise oversight and ensure the transparency and veracity of information. Standardized auditing and reports would allow the government to distinguish between combinations that were reasonable for industrial growth and those that were not. Regulators suggested that corporations, however, were better equipped than the state to coordinate the economy, and some reasonable restraint of trade was nothing other than the general evolution of social relations. In an 1894 article, Jenks reiterated these arguments: "it is time that the public, with the economists, give up the idea that free, unlimited competition is the only normal condition of business, so far as fixing prices is concerned, and they recognize the principle of combination and monopoly as equally normal in some places."[87] In his 1900 publication *The Trust Problem,* which included personal reflections on his Industrial Commission work, Jenks reasserted the economic as opposed to political nature of corporate power. "It is impossible to understand why there has been of late so strong a tendency toward the formation of industrial combinations, unless one first sees clearly the economic conditions out of which they arise."[88] Jenks disputed that monopolies develop from "special favors." He argued that monopolies were not exclusive grants and that they did not eliminate all competition. They were simply the result of a rational process by which individuals aggregated their capital and thereby strengthened their position within the market. His chief concerns were for shareholders who often acted without complete information, especially in cases in which companies issued watered stock. Publicity, substantial government oversight, and possibly some form of price control were the answer to the corporation problem, not the unfettered competition promoted by a strong antitrust regime.

In William Rodgers's 1888 cartoon "A Trustworthy Beast," monopolies are presented once again as a many-headed monster (Figure 9). But, unlike the monster bank, these trusts and combinations are not personified. They are represented by Andrew Carnegie, who reassures Uncle Sam that "the public may regard trusts or combinations with serene confidence." Uncle Sam looks on cautiously, but, unlike with Jackson, there is no life-and-death struggle. In fact, there is no indication whatsoever that Uncle Sam or, by extension, the public has any relation to Carnegie's beast. The monstrous hydra remains under the control of the capitalist but separate from both Carnegie and the nation-state.

The difference between these figures gives us some idea of the transformation of the corporation during the nineteenth century in the United States. The new ways of regulating corporations at the end of the nineteenth century remade the corporation, without severing all of its old relations or functions. Both before and after the corporation became understood in terms of the economy, it was presented as a body that was set apart from the normal functioning of state and society. In the case of corporations from the early nineteenth century, I described this process of setting out as a continuation of the exemption first recognized in the old gift of corporate charters. Popular sovereignty, however, redirected the

A TRUSTWORTHY BEAST.

The public may regard trusts or combinations with serene confidence."—ANDREW CARNEGIE, in an interview in *N. Y. Times*, Oct. 9.

FIGURE 9. William Rogers, "A Trustworthy Beast" (1888). The caption reads, "'The public may regard trusts or combinations with serene confidence.'—ANDREW CARNEGIE, in an interview in *N. Y. Times, Oct. 9.*" Provided courtesy HarpWeek.

exception in such a way that it was used for the development of the state, where the state was a reflection of a society of property holders. Through the course of the nineteenth century, the corporation's immunities and privileges, which had connected it directly to the political sovereignty of the state, were removed. New laws and agencies, at the state and federal levels, created a set of procedural norms that facilitated the process of incorporation and made it available to individuals seeking a legal form for organizing capital.

It is tempting to see this process as simply the triumph of the private corporation over the public or semipublic corporation. What I find most vexing, however, is the way the articulation of the corporation to capitalism occurs in the very space that was once structured by the sovereign ban. We might be able to think through this relation and reinscription by asking how the legal embodiment of capital related to and departed from the process of legally suspending the law that we have connected to sovereign power. Much as Adam Smith's political economy developed within the epistemic framework of police, Mitchell Dean explains the way that "economy" has been formulated in relation to governmentality. Dean notes the pivotal role of scarcity in shaping social orders around the market. Once scarcity has been made visible, economy constitutes a mode of power concerned with

> the incessant struggle to bring more lands into cultivation, and to increase the productivity of its labour, so that it can defeat the natural and irreducible ontological scarcity it faces due to the laws of population.... It will balance these considerations against another set of norms, those derived from the delicate, unstable disequilibrium between population and the resources necessary for its maintenance. The discovery of the ontological reality of scarcity means that the administration of life must take into account the means of production of the subsistence of that life.[89]

Late-nineteenth- and early-twentieth-century commentators recognized the corporation as an unparalleled legal form for dealing with the "disequilibrium" between life and the material conditions needed to support it. States, lawmakers, bureaucrats, and experts used the corporation as a tool, enabling the state and individuals to deal with problems of government and regulation under conditions of scarcity. Limited liability and the holding company promised increased profits, which in turn were supposed to support the public welfare. This was the reason why late-nineteenth- and early-twentieth-century commentators suggested not only that corporate consolidation be tolerated but also that it might be necessary for the health of the economy. In the most extreme forms, progressive thinkers like Marx and Veblen argued that the corporation, with its collective forms of property and its ability to protect itself from competitors, prefigured the coming socialized society.[90] Once again, the corporation represented both a mode of power and its negation.

CHAPTER THREE

Personhood

Matt Wuerker's drawing "Corpenstein" can be seen as part of a history of anticorporate rhetoric (Figure 10). Echoing earlier presentations of corporations as monsters, Wuerker draws the corporation as Frankenstein's creature, depicting the act in which the monster's lifeless body is given human form. It is not Doctor Frankenstein coordinating this freakish science project but judges and "big corporate lawyers" with gavels and briefcases in hand, moving the levers of the "Supreme Court," an apparatus that transforms the people's power into its opposite: the living dead monster, "Globomegacorp." Meanwhile, "the people" uselessly grasp the "Bill of Rights," as she is strapped in, seemingly against her will, to this legal contraption. It is a eureka moment for the corporate lawyers, as they applaud the discovery of constitutional protections for corporations by inverting the old royalist proclamation "long live corporate personhood."[1] As the hulking presence of Globomegacorp makes clear, the legal recognition and constitutional protection of the corporation constitute an egregious usurpation of democratic sovereignty by corporate interests.

Recent actions by the U.S. Supreme Court give Wuerker's argument credence. The landmark 2009 decision in *Citizens United v. The Federal Election Commission* expanded the constitutional protections given to corporations as legal persons.[2] That case considered the constitutionality of prohibitions directed at corporate and union participation in elections established under the McCain–Feingold Bipartisan Campaign Finance Act of 2002. In an expansive ruling that overturned long-standing court precedents, the Court held that such limitations on corporate "speech" in elections were prohibited. That the ruling hinged on the treatment of corporations as legal persons was made evident by newly appointed Justice Sonia Sotomayor's comments during the oral presentation of the case. Sotomayor noted that the Court "gave birth" to corporations, endowing "a creature

FIGURE 10. Matt Wuerker, "Corpenstein." Wuerker's cartoon captures the long-standing criticism that the treatment of corporations as persons in Anglo-American law weakens the rights of citizens and undermines democratic government. Image courtesy of the artist.

of state law with human characteristics," and thus "there could be an argument made that that was the court's error to start with."[3]

Indeed, both scholars and activists have looked at the constitutional protection of corporate rights as a great boon to corporate capitalism, and they have adopted a variety of strategies to challenge the conflation of corporate and natural persons within the law. Harvard law professor Morton Horwitz provided the academic statement of this position in his account of the early-twentieth-century development of corporate personhood. "Natural entity theories," he argued, were "a major factor in legitimating big business and . . . none of the other theoretical alternatives [for conceptualizing the legal status of corporations] could provide as much sustenance to newly organized, concentrated enterprise."[4] Nonprofit and political advocacy groups (such as the International Forum on Globalization [IFG], the Community Environment Legal Defense Fund, Ralph Nader's Multinational Monitor, and the Alliance for Justice) reiterate elements of this argument, voicing concerns that legal personhood helps consolidate corporate economic and political power. The IFG has advocated charter reform to end corporate personhood as part of its 2002 report on alternatives to economic globalization, and Nader has recently suggested impeachment of the conservative wing of the Supreme Court as a necessary response to "judicial dictatorship."[5] His imagery is stunningly familiar:

> Inanimate corporations created by state government charters have risen as Frankensteins to control the people through one judicial activist decision after another. It was the Supreme Court in 1886 that started treating a corporation as a "person" for purposes of the equal protection right in the fourteenth amendment [sic]. Actually the scribe manufactured that conclusion in the headnotes even though the Court's opinion did not go that far. But then it was off to the races. These inanimate giants, astride the globe, have privileges and immunities that "We the People" can only dream about, yet they have equal constitutional rights with us (except for the right against self-incrimination (Fifth Amendment) and more limited privacy rights).[6]

Nader, like Wuerker and Sotomayor, focuses attention on the late-nineteenth-century debates that entrenched corporate personhood in U.S. law and, in particular, on the infamous 1886 Supreme Court case of *Santa Clara v. Southern Pacific Railroad Co.*, conventionally credited with granting corporations equal protection of the law and due process rights under the Fourteenth Amendment of the U.S. Constitution.[7] Although the Fourteenth Amendment was passed in the aftermath of the Civil War to protect the rights of freed slaves, early applications of the amendment considered its implications for other legal "persons," including both corporations and aliens. These legal proceedings touched off a wide-ranging discussion among legal scholars, jurists, politicians, and philosophers, resulting in a prodigious outpouring of research and analysis on personhood through the turn of the twentieth century.

Despite these arguments, it remains unclear exactly what it is about legal personhood that, when applied to corporations, is so uniquely empowering. As we have seen, corporations were considered monsters and parasites before they were treated as rights-bearing individuals. For those focused on eliminating corporate personhood, a primary rationale has been that personhood suggests a political commensurability between living persons and corporate entities that corporate wealth and resources belie. Admittedly, the disproportionate political power of large corporations compared to the vast majority of individuals is evident and startling. Yet the same could be said of the relations between the richest individuals and large swaths of the population. In this sense, the monster pillaging democratic politics is the political power of *money*, which the Court confuses with speech. Furthermore, the argument that challenging corporate personhood is neither the paramount issue in corporate governance nor a particularly effective legal strategy has an impressive intellectual pedigree in its own right. John Dewey, the progressive educational reformer, philosopher, and public intellectual, argued in an important 1926 *Yale Law Journal* article that the conception of the corporation as a person does not, by itself, determine the scope of corporate powers. Writing at the height of this earlier debate over corporate personality, he argued that, as a legal category, "'person' signifies what law makes it signify."[8] Conceived as either quasi-public entities created by state power or legal persons, Dewey suggested that resolving problems with the scope of corporate power was a political issue rather than one of legal form. Bringing corporations in line with democracy meant asserting political control over what corporations do, not what they are.

This chapter suggests that although personhood certainly has shaped corporate power, opening legal arguments for corporate interests that would not be available otherwise, it is most usefully understood as a key to the shifting problematic of liberalism. Because corporations were already powerful institutional arrangements for governing the complex of individuals and things before they were given constitutional protections as persons, it is difficult to accept the argument that personhood *uniquely* created and consolidated corporate power. Instead, corporate personhood can be better understood as a retroactive attempt to rationalize an institution closely connected with early modern models of sovereignty and police within the juridical framework of a liberal capitalist political economy—a framework that, by the late nineteenth century, was coming to hinge on concepts of personhood, rights, and citizenship. In doing so, lawyers, judges, and scholars created new meanings and definitions of both the corporation and the political community that redrew the boundaries of political inclusion and exclusion.

Personhood was designed to make the immense value produced by corporations acceptable within a framework of liberal law. It was precisely because corporations had emerged as such effective tools organizing the "complex of men and things" that lawyers and jurists provided a legal framework that enabled broad access to incorporation.[9] To accommodate these institutions, however, lawmakers ceased treating corporations as creatures of positive law, viewing them instead as natural entities that emerged from contracts. Such a transformation did not sit easily within existing theories of sovereignty and government as it repositioned the former grant of the sovereign as a legal entity with a "will" and rights independent from the state, on one hand, and from individual shareholders, on the other. In terms of the structure of the corporation, this effected the separation of ownership from management that scholars from Berle and Means forward have taken as the defining feature of the corporate economy.[10] As such, it fostered the corporate consolidation of industrial capitalism and also transformed the share into a right to future revenue in the form of dividends.[11] This also marked a transition in power relations, emerging at a moment when legal scholars and jurists were rethinking the power of the federal government and the modern state in terms of persons and citizens. The result was a peculiar fusing of a specific form of capitalist value with property as well as with the juridical subject of liberal law. Examined within the historical context of widespread debates about personhood, the contingent articulation of corporations and persons highlights the fact that personhood has never been a self-evident category corresponding directly to living beings. It also clarifies the ways this assemblage of corporations, capital, and personhood refigured the political sphere, treating capital, in this particular legal form, as a qualified life worthy of political recognition and as new modality of the sovereign ban.

Origin Stories

The details of how the corporation became recognized as having personality are well documented. As narrated in chapter 2, attacks on the special privileges of corporations undermined the system of grants that was the source of corporate power. Through the nineteenth century, individual states responded with a range of strategies for regulating corporations. States did not eliminate corporations but broadened the legal process of incorporation in ways that made the privilege increasingly accessible. General incorporation laws, especially those with permissive regulations, were thought to undermine the monopoly power of corporations and to bring corporations in line with democratic forms of government. Though the first state general incorporation laws were established early in the nineteenth century for specific types of corporations, such as religious organizations, the passage of expansive general incorporation laws in the 1880s severely limited the ability of states to regulate corporations through restrictive charters.

By themselves, general incorporation laws did not eliminate the "artificiality" of the corporation. Yet, new conceptions of corporate personality began to emerge within the context of an eroding state-based system of regulation.[12] In addition, the spatial expansion of the capitalist economy made questions about the personality and citizenship of corporations important to a number of jurisdictional issues. If corporations were literally creations of a specific state's sovereignty, as the grant theory suggested, on what grounds could they enter the courts of other states or the federal government? As Gerard Henderson explained, courts had initially answered this question by asserting that corporations were not citizens but that they could still access federal courts based on the citizenship of the individual members of the corporation.[13] Justice Marshall summarized this argument in the 1809 case of *Bank of the United States v. Deveuax*:

> That invisible, intangible, and artificial being, that mere legal entity, a corporation aggregate, is certainly not a citizen, and, consequently, cannot sue or be sued in the courts of the United States, unless the rights of the members, in this respect, can be exercised in their corporate name.... That name, indeed cannot be an alien or a citizen; but the person whom it represents may be the one or the other.[14]

Marshall completely rejected the notion that corporations were human in any sense of the term (they were neither "alien" nor "citizen"). He asserted that corporations were property owned by real people who were citizens of the several states and the United States in general. In essence, when a person brought a suit against a corporation, she was suing the individual investors and shareholders—the real persons behind the artificial being.

Up to 1840, the principle established by *Deveaux* was reiterated in other rulings; soon afterward, the rulings became more contradictory.[15] The 1844 case of *Louisville Railroad Co. v. Letson* directly reversed *Deveaux* when the Supreme Court ruled that corporations were not citizens but should "be deemed to all intents and purposes as a person, although an artificial person" and "capable of being treated as a citizen of that state, as much as a natural person."[16] *Letson* held that citizenship was determined by the state that issued the charter. The Court changed tack almost immediately. First, the Court ruled that citizenship was determined by the location of the president and directors,[17] before reversing the decision again to decide that citizenship was indeed determined by the shareholders, who, for the purpose of jurisdiction, would be assumed to be residents of the state issuing the charter, whether they were so or not.[18]

As the earlier quote by Ralph Nader suggests, *Santa Clara* continues to be treated as clarifying the confusion over the status and citizenship of corporations that existed before the U.S. Civil War by granting Fourteenth Amendment protections to corporations as persons. The amendment, ratified into the Constitution in 1868, emerged out of a flurry of constitutional provisions offered at the end of the Civil War. Nominally, the amendment was intended to reverse the *Dred Scott* decision, which held that African Americans were not citizens and thus had no standing to sue in court.[19] Section 1 of the amendment established a new foundation for citizenship based on birth. It also guaranteed due process rights and the equal protection of law to all "persons."[20] The wording of the amendment—referring to "persons" and "citizens"—left room for judicial interpretation.[21]

Legal scholars have established that the process by which the corporation received the protections of the Bill of Rights was more complicated.[22] Although the Civil War reframed questions of citizenship and personhood, including of corporations, late-nineteenth-century legal rulings on corporate persons were still ambiguous. On one hand, critics attacked corporations as part of the laissez-faire critique of state regulatory power. In the famous 1873 *Slaughterhouse Cases,* the first U.S. Supreme Court case considering the scope of the Fourteenth Amendment, the Court was asked if the creation of a corporation with a monopoly over the location of slaughterhouses in New Orleans violated the rights of butchers under the Reconstruction Amendments. The Court ruled, consonant with antebellum concepts of the police power, that the state could create the monopoly as part of regulating public health. Justice Stephen Field, however, argued in dissent that the Fourteenth Amendment had changed the nature of public power and private right. He suggested that the monopoly was not of a "public character" and thus encroached on the rights of workers to enter into contracts of their choosing, or, as Field put it, "to pursue the ordinary avocations of life without other restraint than such as affects all others, and to enjoy equally with them the fruits of his labor."[23] Although Field's dissent attacked the Crescent City Live-Stock Landing and Slaughterhouse Company, his argument was not directed at all corporations; it only targeted the monopoly grants that had long connected corporations to state police powers.

In the *Slaughterhouse Cases,* the corporation appeared as a state-issued monopoly, an exercise of the state's police powers, and in opposition to butchers both individually and collectively. Nevertheless, the logic Justice Field used in his dissent became the standard interpretation of the Fourteenth Amendment with respect to citizens and was extended to corporations in the guise of private property. Both these applications of the Fourteenth Amendment—protecting individual property from state and corporate regulations, on one hand, and protecting the property of corporations from state regulation, on the other—developed from cases coming out of the Ninth Circuit beginning in the 1870s. Two groups of cases were central: first, a series of suits brought by Chinese workers against discriminatory anti-Chinese ordinances issued by the state of California under its police powers, and second, a group of railroad tax cases questioning the ability of the state of California to levy special taxes on corporate property. At issue in the Chinese civil rights cases were a variety of restrictions undertaken by state and local government in California against the local Chinese population and new Chinese immigrants. The Ninth Circuit was asked to consider whether the Fourteenth Amendment protected citizens along with noncitizens and aliens. As Thomas Wuil Joo has argued in his careful reconstruction of the Chinese civil rights cases, the extension of economic rights to Chinese workers or business owners was not based on a vision of racial equality; rather, it was an attempt by judges to incorporate unenumerated economic and substantive due process rights under the Fourteenth Amendment.[24] What united these cases was that they all concerned "the ordinary avocations of life" that Field had attempted to shield from state police powers in the *Slaughterhouse Cases*. In *Ho Ah Kow v. Nunan,* the Ninth Circuit Court overturned a housing ordinance that applied only to Chinese residents living in dense settlements in San Francisco as a violation of the equal protection clause of the Fourteenth Amendment. *In re Ah Fong* held that a quarantine of Chinese immigrants was a violation of the equal protection clause, which applied to "persons," including citizens and aliens. *In re Quong Woo* and *In re Tie Loy* overturned restrictions on commercial laundries as a violation of the privileges and immunities clause of the Fourteenth Amendment. *In re Parrott* struck down a state law that prohibited corporations from employing Chinese workers as an infringement of both the rights of the workers to choose their employment and the rights of shareholders to deploy their property as they wished. Finally, the U.S. Supreme Court reinforced the interpretation of the Fourteenth Amendment offered in these Ninth Circuit cases in *Yick Wo v. Hopkins,* another case involving prohibitions against commercial laundries in San Francisco. As Joo argues, *Yick Wo* "made clear for the first time that the Fourteenth Amendment 'is not confined to the protection of citizens'... [and] that the Equal Protection Clause and the Due Process Clause are 'universal in their application, to all persons within the territorial jurisdiction.'"[25]

These rulings were vital to the development of constitutional protections for corporations for two reasons: first, they extended the due process and equal protection clauses to noncitizens, and second, because they dealt with immigrants, they reinforced the argument made by Field in his *Slaughterhouse* dissent that the Fourteenth Amendment protected any person—corporate or individual, artificial or real—and his property within the territorial borders of the nation-state. In the California tax cases, the protection of property was extended to corporations, even foreign corporations that were not citizens and had no real legal standing as persons outside the jurisdiction that had issued their charters. The logic was that the corporation was the aggregated property rights of the individuals who made up the corporation, in this case, the shareholders. Justice Field, who wrote the decision in *San Mateo v. Southern Pacific,* stopped short of arguing that corporations were citizens, but he argued that a tax on corporate property was a law that did not operate equally on all persons in the state and was thus a violation of the equal protection clause of the Fourteenth Amendment.[26] Justice Sawyer, in his concurring opinion, stated flatly that the due process and equal protection clauses apply to corporations as "persons" for the purpose of that amendment.[27] This was the principle that was taken up in the headnotes of *Santa Clara,* arguing that the Fourteenth Amendment, "which forbids a State to deny to any person within its jurisdiction the equal protection of the laws, applies to these corporations. We are all of opinion it does."[28]

Rights and the Modern Liberal State

This legal history has been primarily read by critics of corporate power as demonstrating the state consolidation of corporate capitalism. Early-twentieth-century progressives, such as Charles and Mary Beard, claimed that the Fourteenth Amendment had little to do with slavery and was part of a "conspiracy" by the courts to protect business interests.[29] Their argument was that by using the term *person,* the framers of the amendment had intentionally deployed a concept vague enough that it could encompass corporate property. Though popular during the progressive era, the "conspiracy theory" of the Fourteenth Amendment was refuted by Howard Jay Graham, a law librarian, in a series of law journal essays published between the 1930s and the 1960s.[30] Graham noted that the extension of the Fourteenth Amendment to corporate property had tremendous benefits for corporate capital. He argued, however, that "intentionality" on the part of the framers was lacking.[31] More recently, Morton Horwitz has reinforced this view, arguing that the California tax cases did not, in themselves, remake the corporation into a "natural entity."[32] The natural entity theory, as developed in the late-nineteenth-century political thought of Otto von Gierke, and popularized by Frederic Maitland and Ernst Freund, held that corporations and other groups were real people, separate from the property rights of the investors.[33] Horwitz argued that it took another quarter century for the natural entity theory to finally take hold, after the court extended a series of constitutional protections to the corporation that were not associated with the rights of property holders. In *Hale v. Henkel* (1906), the court extended the Fourth Amendment to the corporation, protecting corporations from illegal searches and seizures.[34] By 1900, the directors, as opposed to shareholders, were most often treated as representing the "will" of the corporation. Like Graham, Horwitz argued that the shift to the natural entity theory, while not intended in the 1860s, had important ramifications for early-twentieth-century corporate power. Most important, it helped separate owners and managers, allowing the corporation to limit the liability of shareholders; fostered the growth of monopolies; and encouraged the geographic expansion of a national corporate capitalist economy.[35] Despite their differences on the intentionality of jurists and the importance of the tax cases, both sides of the conspiracy debate stressed that, ultimately, the extension of the Fourteenth Amendment to corporations helped foster the corporate domination of the U.S. economy.

Other scholars, however, have focused more directly on legal reasoning, viewing these cases as nodal points in a shifting debate over the concepts of property and government. Charles McCurdy, for instance, argued in the 1970s that the California tax cases and Justice Field's Fourteenth Amendment jurisprudence should be seen as part of a broader attempt to draw a firm line between the public and the private in liberal law.[36] According to McCurdy, Field was interested in clarifying the distinction between the legitimate use of public power and private rights, which limited that power. The argument concerning the "public character" of corporate undertakings offered in the *Slaughterhouse Cases* was thus the central aspect of Field's jurisprudence as it set up a distinction between property devoted to "the ordinary avocations of life" and property "appertaining to government." Subsequent historians have picked up on McCurdy's theme, focusing on the way Field's decisions structured a new relation between a centralized state power in the federal government and what William Novak has called "the individualization of right" and "the constitutionalization of American law."[37]

Novak describes a new project of state making, with the Fourteenth Amendment and the growth of administration and federal police power at its center. This new state supplanted the local republican nineteenth-century state with a national state, an interest in local self-government with the negative rights of the individual, and the common law foundation of sovereignty with one codified in the Constitution.[38] Novak's central point is that the regulatory state associated with the New Deal and its vision of regulated capitalism did not emerge whole cloth out of the economic crisis of the 1930s. The growth of a modern liberal state and political economy dates back to the Civil War and the constitutional reforms following in its aftermath. Instead of a laissez-faire legal culture limiting the government up to the watershed moment of 1937, when the U.S. Supreme Court finally acquiesced to economic regulation, Novak emphasizes a much longer mutation by which law came to be understood as a tool that the central government could use to provide for the economic security of a nation-state composed of individual citizens (rather than the nineteenth-century conceptions of sovereignty rooted in self-governing associations, communities, and states). Centralization of power in the federal government came at the expense of the states, but it also resulted from the expansion of individual rights against the state, both local and federal.

Analytically, these accounts are sophisticated in their treatment of individual rights. As opposed to considering rights as inherent to the nature of persons, Novak and McCurdy emphasize the sociolegal construction of rights as part of the positive power of the state and law. Unlike conventional left approaches that treat rights as masks of class interests, these arguments show that the transformation in the content of rights was *constitutive of* new concepts of state, nation, economy, and sovereignty. For instance, Novak emphasizes the ways the Civil War set the context for the modern state, placing less emphasis on sovereignty emerging through contract and more on "the overriding prerogative of nation, Union, and national government."[39] This, in turn, implied a reconceptualization of sovereignty as "that power that was 'the source of all law' but 'not itself founded upon law.'"[40] Novak suggests that new theories of positivist and sociological jurisprudence, with their appeals to social science, were part of this transformation—shifts in legal thinking and adjudication deeply concerned with the "pragmatic" use of law to solve practical economic problems.

Yet the political and legal recognition of corporate property as a *person* did not flow directly from the institution of a liberal relation between individual rights and central authority. Taken to its logical extreme, one could imagine the individualization of rights simply eliminating collective institutions. Instead, the application of the Fourteenth Amendment to corporations sought to include within a new liberal order what had been a key, if exceptional, aspect of an older framework of sovereignty that, by the late nineteenth century, was receding. Within this new problematic of liberal government, corporations came to be situated as institutions with a "will" independent from the sovereign power that created corporate personality in the first place. As such, instead of eliminating the logic of the ban inherent in the corporation-as-police, corporate personhood refigured the ban in the form of political rights.

Biopolitics, the Ban, and the Rights of Persons

My claim that sovereignty and the ban are central to the emergence of the U.S. liberal state and its conception of corporate personhood might appear overly schematic, pressing an insight from European political and social theory into a context in which it does not belong. What theory explains (and the historiography occludes) is the shift in power relations that subtends institutional change.

Foucault, too, was concerned with liberalism in both its classical and neoliberal forms, viewing liberalism as a new development in the thought and practice of political reason. This was the core of his argument that modern power is characterized by a historically unique attention to the management, control, and intensification of the power of living bodies. In *The History of Sexuality,* Foucault described two forms by which this power over life developed beginning in the seventeenth century: *disciplines* attempted to supervise, train, and channel the living bodies of individuals, and *biopolitics* were directed at ameliorating the biological life of populations. Foucault located these new techniques of power within social discourses concerning madness, medicine, and sexuality and within social institutions such as prisons, asylums, schools, families, and clinics. He also suggested that by the eighteenth century, these powers to "*foster* life" had been integrated into "the great instruments of the state" as their animating techniques.[41] New forms of power did not signify the end of law, which, for Foucault, "always refers to the sword" and deductive models of sovereignty. Rather, the commitment to intensify life changed the meaning and purpose of law: "It is no longer a matter of bringing death into play in the field of sovereignty, but of distributing the living in the domain of value and utility."[42] Law became concerned with the establishment of norms that allowed institutions to govern by the aggregation of data and information and the targeting, policing, and reform of statistical deviations and outliers.

Normalization thus occurred both within and outside of the judicial system. In this sense, law can be considered as part of a "continuum of apparatuses" directed toward strengthening the makeup of individual and social bodies.[43] Foucault also emphasized that rights were central to law's normalizing power: "We should not be deceived by all the Constitutions framed throughout the world since the French Revolution, the Codes written and revised, a whole continual and clamorous legislative activity: these were the forms that made an essentially normalizing power acceptable."[44] As opposed to Novak, Foucault argued that there was a sharp discontinuity between the old rights of sovereignty and the use of legal rights as *tools* directing individual and social bodies toward desirable ends:

> It was life more than the law that became the issue of political struggles, even if the latter were formulated through affirmations concerning rights. The "right" to life, to one's body, to health, to happiness, to the satisfaction of needs, and beyond all the oppressions or "alienations," the "right" to rediscover what one is and all that one can be, this "right"—which the classical juridical system was utterly incapable of comprehending—was the political response to all these new procedures of power which did not derive, either, from the traditional right of sovereignty.[45]

What Novak presents as the transition from the well-regulated society of nineteenth-century local commonwealths to the twentieth-century liberal nation-state, Foucault shows to be a much broader transition, not just in statecraft or in the location of authority, but in the operation of *power*. Nothing less was at stake than the insertion of "life" as the main object of political control and calculation. Whereas the local commonwealth used state police powers (including the creation of corporations) to pursue the security of a political community of property holders,[46] the modern liberal state deployed new administrative powers along with the Fourteenth Amendment, not to increase the power of the central government alone, but to strengthen the *salus* of individuals and populations. And not just individuals with the political status of citizens but individuals *as such by virtue of their status of living beings.* In this sense, Novak's emphasis on the state as generative of modern power is misplaced, taking what was a *response* by legal and state institutions to new biopolitical questions— which had their origins in diverse configurations of power and knowledge across both state and society—as its cause.

Once law and administration focus on governing life, however, old legal concepts take on new meanings and establish new criteria for deciding which lives will be "fostered" and which will be "disallowed" to the point of death.[47] Foucault had recognized as much in his 1975–76 lecture series at the Collège de France, when he explained the ways race and, in particular, "state racism" drew a fissure in the political community between lives that must be saved for the defense of society and those whose death can be demanded in the name of "security." In that context, it was not just broad ideologies about race and eugenics that led to state racism but the incorporation of these ideas into racialized legal codes and policies that came to structure citizenship, work, political participation, sexual relations, and so on. For this reason, scholars concerned with the persistence of sovereignty in biopolitical regimes have focused on rights as a vital condensation point where biopolitical management intersects the sovereign ban. Agamben, for instance, argues that the referent of rights, even modern liberal rights, continues to be the banned subject of bare life. His genealogy of rights runs from the 1679 writ of habeas corpus (*"Corpus is a two-faced being, the bearer both of subjection to sovereign power and of individual liberties"*) to the 1789 French Declaration of the Rights of Man and Citizen, in which "the principle of nativity and the principle of sovereignty... are now irrevocably united in the body of the 'sovereign subject' so that the foundation of the new nation-state may be constituted."[48] In each instance, the subjects of rights take on the cast of a double body that is both "at the mercy of" sovereign power and also "free."[49] Agamben's central claim is that the politicization of bare life sets off a series of demarcations within the political sphere that continually draw lines between lives that are recognized as worthy of political recognition and those that can be exposed to death, or, more simply, between human and citizen. Agamben names this demarcation the "camp" and, taking the Nazi concentration camp as his paradigmatic example, shows the ways the suspension of law enables a demarcation of space where legally designated bare life may be killed.

Roberto Esposito echoes these claims about rights in his examination of biopolitics, with special emphasis on the way this division is established within the liberal *dispositif* of the person.[50] Whereas Agamben locates the life that may be killed in the space of the camp brought into being through the legal exception, Esposito suggests that this sacrificial relation is found within the very concept of personhood in Western thought. Reaching back to classical and early Christian concepts of the person, Esposito notes that personhood continually produces divisions between that part of the person recognized by law and the animal part of the human that is depersonalized and simply a living being. Situated in hierarchical relations to one another, Esposito shows the different ways the living body is exposed to death to strengthen those aspects of the person recognized by law. Esposito traces the persistence of this "immunitary paradigm," where life is preserved by its exposure to death, through modern political forms. Under Nazism's radicalization of the Hobbesian framework of sovereignty, the body in question becomes linked directly to the social body of the state, and racialized biology and eugenics govern the immunitary paradigm. But Esposito also contends that an immunitary dynamic structures liberalism more generally. Liberal immunity resides within the right to property, where ownership of one's own body *by the person* becomes the grounds for rights over, first, the objects of labor and, eventually, through the convention of money, the world.[51] This gives liberalism its biopolitical dimensions, as liberal law and right focus on governing the biological substrate of the person that produces the conditions necessary for both individual and social life.[52]

This theoretical excursus highlights two aspects of the problematic structuring personhood and right that have remained obscure. First, a transformation in power associated with the increased centrality of biological life or simple human existence as an object of political calculation exists below the institutional changes giving rise to the liberal state. Shifts in the state apparatus, in this sense, are better conceptualized as retroactive effects of changes in the organization of power that occur both within and beyond state institutions. Second, these scholars suggest that rather than being a simple transition from sovereign to biopolitical orders, modern liberal rights reactivate and intensify the sacrificial logics of abandonment and immunization that Foucault locates within an older deductive model of sovereignty. It remains to be seen, however, what uses these theories have for explaining the extension of rights to corporations on the basis of their personhood.

Legal Persons

To reassess the biopolitical underpinnings of corporate personhood and corporate rights, consider the amazing outpouring of scholarship on questions of corporate personality at the end of the nineteenth century.[53] This literature responded to questions concerning corporate citizenship raised by the case law, but its immediate origins were in the writings of German political theorist Otto von Gierke, whose work was translated into English and enthusiastically promoted by prominent Anglo-American legal scholars such as Frederic Maitland and Ernst Freund.[54] If instrumental theories about the role of capitalism in structuring corporate personhood were correct, Gierke's omnipresence in these debates would be strange, as his focus was not on modern capitalist companies but on ancient German associations and fellowships. Gierke argued that associations were real entities that had a concrete existence rooted in the social reality of group life and independent from both the individuals who composed corporate bodies, on one side, and the state, on the other. He outlined this theory in a series of works written in the 1870s and 1880s, which culminated in the four-volume study *Das deutsche Genossenschaftsrecht* (The German Law of Fellowship). A point often noted but rarely expanded on is the radically different nature of Gierke's arguments from those that would dominate discussion of corporate personality in the United States. Whereas U.S. scholarship focused on liberal property rights, Gierke's thought was concerned with the role of groups in the formation of the state. In other words, Gierke's concept of group personality was not just translated from one context to another;[55] it articulated a defense of corporate legal personality within a radically different problematic from that which would come to preoccupy U.S. corporate lawyers and legal theorists.

Gierke's ideas on group personality emerged within a philosophical and legal culture dominated by historicism and romanticism and the figures of Hegel and Savigny.[56] Hegel discussed corporations *(korporation)* in his *Philosophy of Right,* presenting a narrow understanding of the concept relative to Gierke's expansive one. The problem for Hegel was to articulate a theory of the state that could unify the disparate interests of individuals in civil society. Hegel's account of right presupposed this unity as always already internal to human reason, which was fundamentally social and intersubjective. Yet, the dialectical movement from the particularity of individual interests to the ultimate unity of reason in the state required intermediary institutions. Corporations, in Hegel's account, played an integral part in that process, functioning as the "second ethical root" that, along with the family, mediated individual interests to establish the universal basis of the state.[57]

Like Hegel, Gierke emphasized the social and historical development of groups, but Gierke's concept of *genossenschaft* was distinguished from the Hegelian corporation by its autonomous existence, which was not dependent on the state's legal recognition.[58] This wider notion of group personality was the very essence of the historical development of the law. Offering a critique of Savigny's reliance on Roman law, which treated corporate personality as fictional, Gierke argued that groups were real legal entities linked to the historical development of Germanic communities.[59] Gierke's early work actually inverted the relation between state and corporation, suggesting that the state itself was derived from associational life as one group among many. He characterized the history of the relations between the state and society as a struggle in which constituted political authority attempted to limit the rights of competing groups. Volume 1 of the *Genossenschaftsrecht,* which focused on the historical development of association law, began with an account of two groups engaged in dialectical conflict, with the "freedom of the people" to engage in fellowships opposed to the "principle of lordship and service" from which the state emerged. Through a series of five historical stages—from "the earliest history" to the nineteenth century—Gierke narrated attempts to suppress group life and make the sovereign territorial state the unified and sole possessor of law and moral right.[60]

But to what ends? Maitland, among others, suggested that Gierke sought to limit the influence of Roman law in the codification of the German Civil Code and replace it with what he understood as an authentic expression of the history and spirit of German life and culture. It is thus hard to consider Gierke's critique of the state as one that broke with the juridical logic of sovereignty and right. In fact, Gierke's argument, quite clearly, was that if the goal of the state was to embody the moral and ethical dispositions of the people—to embody Right in the fullest sense of that term—then the state had a much weaker claim as a representative institution than the authentic, spontaneously formed, and essentially timeless communities and associations that were, by his definition, the essence of German law. Rather than a Hobbesian biopolitics of the state or a Lockean biopolitics of the individual, for Gierke, the life at stake in politics was social and communal. This included and gave meaning to modern economic cooperatives and corporations as well. Gierke argued that associations based on capital and property were spontaneous formations that gained legitimacy as counterweights to the centralizing economic policy of German police states. Economic corporations were legitimate because they were expressions of the interaction of interests in society, not because they provided a more efficient or rational form of production or exchange.[61]

Gierke's thought remains important for a genealogy of political reason because it theorizes sovereign right not as a property of the state but of the community. Displaying the ambiguous position that constitutes the very structure of corporate sovereignty, Gierke presented fellowships and associations as living entities that, through their historical development, come to be the sources of state and legal power, while also marking a challenge to and freedom from centralizing authority. This is the double body of the corporate sovereign. Moreover, Gierke's argument can be understood in relation to those aristocratic histories of the French nation that Foucault locates as pivotal to justifying later arguments about state racism.[62] Precisely because Gierke gives the community precedence as the life force and fount of right and state power, the life of the community becomes that which "must be defended" by the state. It is thus not hard to see the short distance between Gierke's ode to authentic German fellowship as an expression of the people and the corporatist legal doctrines that would be critical to the ideology of fascism.

But this characteristically ambiguous doubling also enabled others to appropriate Gierke's thought. British pluralists, including the Anglican John Neville Figgis and socialists like George Cole and Harold Laski, drew on Gierke's ideas of real personhood to theorize the diffusion of sovereignty throughout society. In his youth, Laski found corporate doctrines "a powerful weapon in the hands of those who viewed, in any but a formal sense, the claim of the state to sovereignty as a dangerous threat alike to peace and freedom."[63] Unable to separate the discourse of real personality from "that German romantic nationalism,"[64] Laski eventually abandoned his position on corporate persons, but this issue was less troublesome for Frederic Maitland, who translated and popularized Gierke in Anglo-American legal circles. Maitland, a legal scholar and historian whose intellectual work focused on the development of law in England during the Middle Ages, found Gierke's ideas useful in justifying the historical common law privileges of groups and individuals such as the borough or the parsonage.[65] The real entity theory could be used to legitimate a liberal–pluralist form of sovereignty, while also making legal theory correspond to a history of decentralized political development in England.

In the United States, however, questions of corporate personality were shaped by a different problematic. Whether or not Gierke was historically accurate in his description of German fellowships as timeless and spontaneous communities, it was absurd to conceptualize corporations in the United States on these terms. Thus history did not figure prominently in arguments for organic conceptions of corporations in the United States. The real entity theory was offered as an analytical description of law and a technical resolution to problems of regulation in a federal system that was increasingly asked to decide questions concerning the liabilities and finances of corporations. The debate over corporate personality in the United States was devoid of claims about the rights of communities; much less was it concerned with Maitland's parsons. Its primary mode of analysis was to examine the relation between the signifying function of legal concepts and their correspondence with legal practice and the world of corporate capitalism.

Ernst Freund, a law professor from the University of Chicago, drew on Gierke's ideas in his 1897 essay *The Legal Nature of Corporations*. Yet Freund shunned the historical aspects of Gierke's thought, suggesting that corporate personality should be conceptualized in ways that facilitated corporate governance. For Freund, the corporation had an interest or "will" that could not necessarily be defined in terms of individual members of the corporation. "The law does not create the corporate person," he wrote, "but finding it in existence invests it with a certain legal capacity. The corporation rests upon a substratum of physical persons, but it is not identical with them, for out of the association of the individuals the new personality arises, having a distinctive sphere of existence and a will of its own."[66]

Unlike Gierke's concerns with communal life, the concept of "will" connected corporations with liberal theories of property and thus with the individual at the core of liberal legal thought and capitalist markets. Freund argued that individual interests, rather than group life, were the foundation for the rule of law. "The rule of law arises out of the conflict of human interests, which it tempers and regulates in accordance with the necessities of social existence."[67] In other words, law was not the command of the sovereign but a framework within which individuals could pursue a multiplicity of ends and desires. Law facilitated the process by translating interests into rights. Referencing the legal thinker Rudolph von Jhering, Freund noted that "every right is a legally protected interest."[68] But Freund also suggested that exercising a right required "control." Rights were a complex of individual desires and the legal means or force to achieve them. Property rights were thus "the most important and familiar of all rights" because they combined interest and control in one person. In recognizing property rights, the state provided the means of control by which an individual could direct an object toward a desired end. Freund established two conditions for rights: first, they must be transferable to others; second, they "must belong to some definite human person capable of exercising control."[69]

The juristic person emerged as a way of bringing interest and control together in cases in which they might be formally separated. Freund used the example of an abstract ideal such as science or art, in which an infinite and indefinable number of people are "interested" in the desired ends, but do not have the legal means to control property dedicated to those ends. Thus a building dedicated to the promotion of science can have rights vested in a person separated from those who have interests in the desired ends of scientific advancement.[70] The business corporation was an extension of this principle. By recognizing it as a legal entity, separate from its members, interest and control were identified in one legal body. Many individuals could have interests in making profits through a particular enterprise, while lacking the control necessary to carry out the enterprise successfully. But the corporation, recognized as autonomous from both the state and the shareholders, could direct all those assets toward a desired end. Moreover, the principle of limited liability flowed directly from these assumptions. If the interest represented in the corporate body was only the sum total of the aggregated capital each member contributed, then the corporation could only be responsible for the amount of capital it controlled.[71] In asserting the reality of corporate personhood, Freund sought to unite the interests of the corporation with the controlling agents, giving rights to the body in its entirety. This distinction separated corporations from partnerships, whose actions could be directly linked back to the individuals whose interests were legally represented in the enterprise.

U.S. jurists who accepted these arguments did so to solve practical problems. Their perspective was less concerned with squaring contemporary law with that of Coke or Blackstone than with recognizing corporate interests and easing the process of representing aggregated capital within the legal system. Dwight Jones, a lawyer and legal writer on municipal corporations, summarized the perspective when he wrote in 1892,

> Corporations stand in the community as vigorous facts.
> They possess powers held by no individuals. They acquire
> property in their own right, which is subject to no debts of
> their shareholders. . . . It is essential for the rights of the public
> that the personal responsibility of this entity should always be
> recognized, for it is this body that controls the property, it is
> this body that enters into the life of the community as one of
> its members. . . . Any mingling of corporate existence with the
> existence of the shareholders will weaken corporate rights.[72]

This is not to say that the organic or real entity theory was universally accepted. Many thought it was a ridiculous abstraction.[73] The issue under debate was how to best solve contemporary problems involving corporations such as those concerning taxation, jurisdiction, and liability.

As the debate continued, jurists could acknowledge that the terms were somewhat fungible because both sociological and nominalist interpretations had already seeped into the law. Unmooring law from its formalist precepts, lawyers expressed the sentiment that the debate over personhood was really just confusion over the meaning of words. University of Texas law professor Bryant Smith repeated an oft-voiced sentiment:

> The voluminous arguments about whether corporate personality is
> real or fictitious, are, for the most part, to no purpose, chiefly for
> lack of a definition of terms. One man's reality is another man's
> fiction. In a sense, every idea that enters the human mind is a fact
> and has reality. . . . In either case it is an abstraction, one of the
> major abstractions of legal science, like title, possession, right and
> duty.[74]

Max Radin, echoing John Dewey, made the point clear when he noted that corporate personality was a verbal and fiscal convenience but also "an important merchantile device rendered necessary by a credit economy, that is, by a system of economic organization that involves speculation to any degree whatever."[75] Moreover, this implied that the problems with corporations were not problems in their legal definition, much less in the relation between law and right, but in the social relations that occurred under the guise of that legal name: "The real danger that lies in the corporate organization is the fact that the great accumulations of capital are by their very mass, tremendously powerful—and consequently capable of much mischief. Obviously, however, that is an incident of our economic structure and not a consequence of the corporate entity."[76]

Speaking for the Liberal State

In showing that the law was a socially constructed set of ideas, norms, and rules that should be judged in terms of their practical effects, the legal realist response to the problem of corporate personhood was to write it out of existence. This argument, in turn, required accepting certain assumptions about both the corporation and the relations between law and society. When Radin suggested that corporate power was a problem of the accumulation of capital, he asserted the private nature of corporations. More important, he made it seem as if the law were merely recognizing a set of socioeconomic relations that were relatively autonomous from state power. This was certainly a departure from Gierke's social theory, in which corporate personhood posed fundamental questions of legal right and state legitimacy. It also departed from nineteenth-century understandings of the corporation in the United States, in which the corporation had been a technique of government—an artificial entity chartered to achieve some ends that were beneficial to both the members of the corporation and the public at large.

Whether this caused the rise of corporate capitalism is thus an interesting question but is also somewhat beside the point. What the shifting positions in the debate over corporate personality explain is how U.S. jurists and scholars conceptualized the relation between state and persons and the particular role of economic interests in conjoining the two. Though the claims for corporate personhood were couched in the language of rights and citizenship, the justifications were concerned with harnessing the productive capacities of corporations without disturbing a legal and economic system structured around individual right. Even before the organic theory was adopted in law, Justice Field advocated extending protections to corporate property based on its seemingly unlimited potential for social development. In the *Railroad Tax Cases* (1882), he described corporate power in almost theological terms, accentuating the capacity of corporations to undertake the tasks of government and sovereignty:

> As a matter of fact, nearly all enterprises in this state, requiring for their execution an expenditure of large capital, are undertaken by corporations. They engage in commerce; they build and sail ships;

they cover our navigable streams with steamers; they construct houses; they bring the products of earth and sea to market; they light our streets and buildings; they open and work mines; they carry water into our cities; they build railroads, and cross mountains and deserts with them; they erect churches, colleges, lyceums, and theaters; they set up manufactories, and keep the spindle and shuttle in motion; they establish banks for savings; they insure against accidents on land and sea; they give policies on life; they make money exchanges with all parts of the world; they publish newspapers and books, and send news by lightning across the continent and under the ocean. Indeed, there is nothing which is lawful to be done to feed and clothe our people, to beautify and adorn their dwellings, to relieve the sick, to help the needy, and to enrich and ennoble humanity, which is not to a great extent done through the instrumentalities of corporations.[77]

Rather than presenting corporate power as the creation of law, Field suggested, like Abbé Sieyès's famous claims on behalf of the Third Estate, that the law could only legitimate a power that guaranteed the material existence of society and the state.[78] Corporations, he argued, provide the basic care of the public, thereby rendering them "people" in a double sense: as those with formal legal rights and as the group within society ("the people") who provide the material support and conditions of possibility for the state's existence. Of course, the correlate to this is that once the corporation was qualified as a life worthy of political existence, its interests became important in the legal and technical calculations aimed to provide for the population.

In terms of the genealogy of political reason, such developments could be taken as evidence of a shift away from deductive sovereignty toward more positive conceptions of power. To do so, however, is to lose track of the strange doubleness clinging to corporate institutions. Like "personhood" for Esposito or "the people" for Agamben, the corporate person also has been rife with semantic ambiguity, referring to both the collective efforts that supply the material needs for society and the peculiar ways collectivities are recognized by law as individuals dedicated to property and profit.[79] The fissure internal to the corporate person is not between law and biology, politics and bare life, but rather between the possibilities enabled by collective action and the singular ends of economic security recognized by liberal law.

CHAPTER FOUR

Territory

Within Western modernity, sovereignty has implied territorial control.[1] Max Weber made territory fundamental to his "ideal typical" definition of state sovereignty, as "a characteristic of the state." His argument that states claim monopolies on the legitimate use of physical force explicitly stated that this power was exercised "within a given territory." State legitimacy and right therefore depended on territorial boundaries. And politics, which Weber defined as the struggle over "the distribution of power, either among states or among groups within a state," was a similarly territorial concept.[2]

If territory is literally the ground of sovereign power, and if corporate power was founded in sovereign power, how do we conceptualize the ways corporations seem to free themselves from the territorial boundaries of nation-states? This is no idle theoretical question. Today, the most pressing issues in corporate governance concern a kind of deterritorialization in which political boundaries have a difficult time containing corporate capital. And these issues have entered public consciousness. In the United States, for instance, capital flight, the location of corporations with respect to taxation, and the global interconnections of the financial system are critical political issues.[3] How are the spatial dynamics of corporations related to the distribution of power that Weber identifies with politics? What are the practices within sovereign power that create and maintain these spatial distributions? How do these practices change our understanding of sovereignty and territory?

To answer these questions, this chapter examines the regulation of foreign corporations. Because corporations emerged within the complex of territorial sovereignty, there has been a long (yet, today, largely unrecognized) history of debate over the rights and privileges of corporations beyond the boundaries of the territories that issued their charters. These conflicts persist in such disparate discussions as those concerning trade disputes, the nationalization of foreign corporate assets, and the liabilities of corporations under public international law. To situate these debates historically, this chapter examines the conflict of laws, which are the political customs that determine the system of law in force when jurisdiction is in dispute. Comity, or the deference one sovereign shows another, was one of the key concepts in conflict of laws thinking. Historically, it also provided an early legal framework for the regulation of foreign corporations, resolving disputes over the legal status of corporations from the colonial trade wars of the seventeenth century to the corporate-led territorial expansion of the U.S. railroad system in the mid-nineteenth century.

In the late nineteenth century, however, lawyers began to question the usefulness of comity as a mechanism for regulating a corporate capitalist economy that frequently crossed political boundaries. Within U.S. law, as I described in the preceding chapters, lawyers, academics, and bureaucrats responded by streamlining and standardizing corporate regulations between jurisdictions within the United States as part of a wider effort to make the law into a set of predictable norms necessary for business calculations. Reorganizing law at a national level harnessed the corporate management of life for a liberal capitalist order. But this national regulatory framework was insufficient once businesses began to move not only across jurisdictions within the United States but internationally as well. Like the earlier attempts to normalize corporate power in a national context, advocates of an international corporate law hoped to replace national regulatory systems with what they called a "liberal system" of administration that treated corporations as "natural persons" in international law.[4] Through the 1910s and 1920s, commentators and international commissions, including those within the League of Nations, attempted to standardize legal controls over foreign corporations.[5] These attempts never achieved the force of law and thus left a great deal of ambiguity in the transnational regulation of corporations. This ambiguity persisted even after World War II, when international economic regulation was taken over by the Bretton Woods institutions and their concerns with monetary regulation and capital flows.[6] It remains a source of corporate power today.

Recognizing the attempt and failure to create an international legal framework for corporations allows us to make two important points. The first concerns the spatial dynamics of law. Whereas law is usually taken as the link between sovereignty and territoriality—as the discourse that legitimates the use of force over a specific area—examining arguments over the international status of corporations highlights the role of law in *establishing* borders and *territorializing* space. Although war and international relations are certainly important to the production of state territoriality, the legal framework for economic regulation also constitutes an arena in which territory is produced, maintained, and contested. Though at times, the space of law corresponds with state territory, it can also take other spatial forms. Thus my second claim is that the nation-state is one particularly powerful territorialization of sovereignty but not the only one. Sovereignty defines territory and binds it to a system of law. In doing so, sovereign power produces both an inside and an outside to the constituted order. However, what is outside of the law still bares a relation to sovereign power. This history of the regulation of corporations through international law demonstrates the importance of the spaces outside of the law for the distribution of power that Weber noted as foundational to politics.

Comity and Territory

To study comity is to address sovereignty at and beyond its territorial limits. As creations of law, corporations were linked to specific territories. Comity served as a legal remedy that allowed corporations to take actions in territories other than those that had issued their charters. Though the origins of the doctrine can be found in Roman law, seventeenth-century Dutch legal writers, such as Christian Rodenburg, Paul and Johannes Voet, and Ulrich Huber, developed the concept of comity that governed foreign corporations.[7] As with legal devices like extraterritorial jurisdiction and private international law, comity was important in establishing a European state system in the aftermath of the Holy Roman Empire, and it was based in theories of territorial sovereignty articulated by Jean Bodin and Hugo Grotius. Comity provided a way to decide disputes between sovereigns over the application of territorial laws in an international context.[8]

Comity balanced the territorial aspects of sovereignty with social relations that went beyond jurisdictional boundaries. As such, the development of the legal doctrine responded to both intra-European questions of jurisdiction—which could involve cases as varied as torts, marriages, or the laws of agency—and imperial concerns over trade and commerce. In each case, fundamental issues about the existence of law beyond territorial borders were in dispute. For instance, Grotius's early investigations into international law concerned disputes over trade routes in India. In *De Jure Praedae*, Grotius defended the Dutch East India Company's prize wars against Portuguese traders who were protecting their trade monopoly. Though Grotius acknowledged Vitoria's principle that Christians "may not deprive infidels of their civil power and sovereignty merely on the ground that the latter are infidels,"[9] Grotius viewed the freedom of the sea as essential and argued against Portuguese attempts to appropriate trade

routes as private property.[10] Grotius's support for Dutch commerce relied
on the assertion that the seas, as the open space necessary for exchange,
could not be appropriated and that individuals encountered one another in
these spaces as sovereigns in the state of nature. Commerce and trade were
natural rights, and he argued that any infringement on trade legitimated
the private war of the Dutch East India Company against the Portuguese.
The legal question that remained was what law would govern contracts
made in spaces like the seas that, through their connection with trade and
exchange, were deemed open and free to all. What laws governed spaces
lacking a sovereign authority or where sovereign power was in dispute?

The articulation of a legal discourse on conflict of laws provided an
answer, although the Dutch writers were divided over whether comity
implied formal legal requirements or simply established customary rules.
Comity signified courtesy and friendship, and it implied a kind of courtesy extended from one autonomous or sovereign entity to another. Dutch
writers, such as Paul and Johannes Voet, treated comity as custom and not
law. They rejected Grotius's assertion that the *ius gentium,* or "law of nations," could compel sovereigns to carry out foreign laws. As a customary
norm, comity did not imply enforceable legal obligations. Foreign laws
were followed "for comity and equity," but it was left to the discretion of
territorial sovereigns to decide the force of law within the state.[11] Ulrich
Huber, however, followed Grotius in asserting that comity was part of
the law of nations, implying an indirect legal obligation on all sovereigns
to follow foreign laws when it did not harm citizens. As the comparative
legal scholar Hessel Yntema noted, Huber's intention, stated in *De Jure
Civitatis,* "was to supplement the epoch making treatise of Grotius in the
field of international law with a counterpart dealing with the principles
of public law applicable within each State."[12] Huber gave a much stronger meaning to comity as not only a customary deference one sovereign
showed another but a legal doctrine that entailed duties and obligations.
Moreover, for Huber, comity was a legal system governing conflicts in the
colonies and on the seas, in addition to those within a sovereign territory.[13]

The debate over whether comity constituted custom or law was fundamentally a debate about the territorial limits of the sovereign exception.
Viewing comity as law meant a different type of global order than treating
comity as a customary right. In both instances, comity implied that sovereigns were subject to *no* law. Of course, the very essence of sovereignty
is the way it founds law within a given territory. Comity extended this
principle into places where a sovereign's law was not in force, including
other states, the colonies, and the seas. If this immunity was conceptualized as a custom, it implied that deference was shown at the behest of

the sovereign power exercising territorial control. Comity-as-custom reinforced the notion that sovereignty was the power to decide the application of law *within a given territory.* As a legal norm, however, comity implied an overlapping form of sovereignty that extended each sovereign's ability to grant legal exceptions and immunity beyond the borders of her own territory. The notion that comity was obligatory meant that the sovereign exception was not geographically bounded but something that inhered in the personality of the sovereign in all parts of the world.

These issues were particularly important with the spatial expansion of capitalism, as comity brought together and attempted to resolve conflicting ideologies of sovereignty, capitalism, and law. Debates about comity reappear in moments when socioeconomic relations transgress political boundaries. Thus, in addition to its role in seventeenth-century trade wars, comity was central to the creation of nineteenth-century U.S. federalism. The comity doctrine entered U.S. law in the 1797 U.S. Supreme Court decision of *Emory v. Grenough*.[14] A lengthy note attached to the decision appended a translation of a section of Huber's *De Conflictu Legum.* The axioms suggested that comity was a *legal obligation*:

1st. The laws of every empire have force within the limits of that government, and are obligatory upon all who are within its bounds.

2d. All persons within the limits of a government are considered as subjects, whether their residence is permanent or temporary.

3. By the courtesy of nations, whatever laws are carried into execution, within the limits of any government, are considered as having the same effect every where, so far as they do not occasion a prejudice to the rights of the other governments, or their citizens.[15]

Samuel Livermore, who published the first American text on the conflict of laws in 1828, decried Huber's notion of comity as an unsound principle for clarifying cases involving jurisdictional disputes.[16] For Livermore, the application of foreign laws depended on the nature of the object and obligations in question. Going back to Roman law, Livermore drew a distinction between statutes that were personal and those that were real, in which "the effects of the former were bounded by no territory, while the effects of the latter were circumscribed within the limits of the territory subject to the power of the legislature."[17] The distinction had wide import in the nineteenth-century United States, most notably in determining the status of slaves when they or their owners were in states that had abolished slavery. According to Livermore, northern courts recognized slavery as a property right, not because of comity, but because slavery was considered a form of personal property under the U.S. Constitution.[18] Huber's doctrine threatened to undermine the distinction: "the capacity of a person will not be fixed by the laws of his domicil; but will depend upon the positive laws of the different places, in which he may casually be."[19] Livermore argued that the Roman distinction, strictly applied, was sufficient for managing conflict of laws cases.

Joseph Story's *Commentaries on the Conflict of Laws* popularized Huber, although classical legal scholar Alan Watson has argued that Story interpreted Huber incorrectly, treating comity as a custom instead of a legal obligation.[20] Rather than an international system of private law that was enforceable irrespective of location, as Huber suggested, Story made comity a decision every sovereign makes in every issue involving the conflict of laws.[21] Nevertheless, it was Story's concept of comity that influenced the development of conflict of laws doctrines. For instance, the famous German jurist Savigny (already mentioned as an important predecessor to Gierke) cited Story's reading of Huber approvingly in his work on the conflict of laws, though he also believed that comity was insufficient for deciding many cases.[22]

Corporations quickly emerged as an important area for the elaboration of conflict of laws rulings. Created through the police powers of states, corporations in the early American republic were closely connected to specific territories through the charter. Questions as to the extraterritorial powers of corporations were not very important when the corporations were towns, churches, or hospitals—entities firmly located in specific places. As the corporate form was increasingly used for commerce, trade, banking, and transportation, lawsuits began to appear challenging the ability of a corporation to engage in business outside the territory in which its grant of incorporation was issued. The legal question was whether these transactions were ultra vires and thus beyond the force of law. Comity doctrines were used as a way of regulating these extraterritorial or transjurisdictional business practices. Like the charter more generally, the application of comity to the corporation reflected the close link between corporations and sovereign power.

The doubling of corporate sovereignty runs throughout nineteenth-century case law on comity, as jurists attempted to reconcile corporations' close links to territorial sovereignty with the promotion of capitalist relations that transgressed boundaries. The 1839 case of *Bank of Augusta v. Earle* made comity the controlling doctrine in cases concerning corporate domicile until after the Civil War.[23] Justice Taney sided with earlier precedents that viewed corporations as expressions of sovereign power and rooted them within territorial borders:

> A corporation can have no legal existence out of the boundaries of the sovereignty by which it is created. It exists only in contemplation of law, and by force of the law; and where that law ceases to operate, and is no longer obligatory, the corporation can have no existence. It must dwell in the place of its creation, and cannot migrate to another sovereignty.[24]

A case in which all parties appealed to Story, Taney's decision in *Bank of Augusta* rendered comity a custom, not a legal obligation. Yet if corporations were truly limited to the jurisdictions in which they were created, it would have jeopardized the circulation of money and commodities, which was an increasingly important part of the corporation's reason for being. Opponents argued that any extension of legal privilege outside of the state issuing the charter constituted an ultra vires expansion of corporate power and was thereby prohibited.

This respected the sovereignty of individual states but threatened commerce and therefore, potentially, the common good. Taney responded to this concern by referencing the long history of legal thinking designed to facilitate extraterritorial commerce:

> The cases of contracts made in a foreign country are familiar examples; and Courts of justice have always expounded and executed them, according to the laws of the place in which they were made; provided that law was not repugnant to the laws or policy of their own country. The comity thus extended to other nations is no impeachment of sovereignty. It is the voluntary act of the nation by which it is offered; and is inadmissible when contrary to its policy, or prejudicial to its interests. But it contributes so largely to promote justice between individuals, and to produce a friendly intercourse between the sovereignties to which they belong; that courts of justice have continually acted upon it, as part of the voluntary law of nations.[25]

This led Taney to rule that "adopting, as we do, the principle here stated, we proceed to inquire whether, by the comity of nations, foreign corporations are permitted to make contracts within their jurisdiction; and we can perceive no sufficient reason for excluding them, when they are not contrary to the known policy of the state, or injurious to its interests."[26]

"Interest," in this case, was the interest of the sovereign. Taney's use of the comity doctrine allowed him to incorporate the sovereign decision into law under that term. Taney did not specify a system or institution that would decide which corporate actions violated principles of territorial sovereignty; instead, his ruling that the actions of corporations were lawful as long as they corresponded to the sovereign's interests left the sovereign with the power to pursue a range of policies. Though states could conceivably exercise power to restrain corporations chartered in other states, the system was designed to *facilitate,* not *limit,* the expanding geography of economic transactions. As legal historians have argued, nineteenth-century law was not tradition's last line of resistance against new forms of economic organization but an active participant in that transformation.[27]

By the early nineteenth century, comity was regularly applied to cases that concerned mundane business matters. For instance, the issue involved in *Bank of Augusta* was whether a bank chartered in Georgia could purchase bills of exchange through its agents in Alabama. The question before the court concerned both the effect of these transactions on Alabama banks and the standing of foreign corporations engaged in commerce in the state. Though the ruling asserted that corporations have no extraterritorial existence, the real point of the ruling was that the monopoly privilege could not erect territorial boundaries on commercial exchanges that were important to the welfare of many states and the nation as a whole.[28] The ruling meant that in Alabama, agents from banks in Georgia could make the same purchases as agents from the local banks. Yet because the commercial transactions of most corporations were carried out through agents, the ruling, while seeming to assert territorial limits on corporations, in essence allowed corporate agents to transact business anywhere. Comity, as rendered by Taney, meant that only an explicit legal act forbidding a certain type or class of extraterritorial transaction could be prohibited as ultra vires.

The Limits to Comity in National Economic Space

The application of the comity doctrine to corporations was meant to expand commerce within nineteenth-century assumptions of local state sovereignty. But comity was less than ideal as a legal tool to promote capitalism. Many lawyers in England and the United States argued that comity, along with the conflict of laws and private international law more generally, was too abstract for the pragmatic needs of commercial transactions.[29] Reflecting the ideological shift, both British and American jurists tended to view these issues as unfitting for the "commonsensical school" of

Anglo-American law, highlighting the inability of theoretical legal reasoning to provide a consistent set of normative rules for business.[30] A. V. Dicey, the famous British jurist, summed up this sentiment in a nationalist tone: "no Englishman is surprised that any German should muddle his head over a futile controversy, for we all know that the Germans of today and above all German professors, always think wrongly, and act wrongly."[31]

Lawyers in Britain and the United States defined their concerns as "pragmatic"; they sought the most efficient means for liberalizing the regulation of corporate business at a time when transactions were expanding across individual states and international borders. Yet their arguments against comity contained some sleight of hand. In essence, they implied that the law had not kept up with business and should therefore be changed to reflect the "reality" of both the corporation and an economy that was increasingly national and international in scope.[32] This failed to note all of the ways that comity, like most corporate regulations, was designed to promote business and economic expansion. Taney's decision in *Bank of Augusta,* which viewed corporations as creatures of local state power, had already bent comity toward the presumption of recognition of foreign corporations engaged in commerce. In basing the regulation of foreign corporation on comity, however, Taney's ruling still permitted states to act against foreign corporations in a variety of ways.

For instance, in the mid-nineteenth century, states restricted foreign control of banks and insurance companies. As Gerard Henderson, an advocate for the standardization of corporate law, noted, the restrictions were designed to ensure that corporations transacting business in the state did so under its laws and not under another state's more permissive incorporation laws.[33] The U.S. Supreme Court declared that these regulations were lawful in *Paul v. Virginia,* a case involving a Virginia act prohibiting foreign insurance companies from transacting business in the state. The court ruled that corporations were not citizens of the United States and thus not protected under Article 4, section 2 of the Constitution, which provided that citizens recognized in one state would be recognized as citizens of the several states and the United States.[34] Justice Field, who wrote the opinion, argued that corporations were special privileges created by individual states and that other states were only bound to recognize those privileges extraterritorially on the basis of comity. Citing Taney's ruling in *Bank of Augusta,* the Court asserted that corporations were not citizens and that insurance did not constitute commerce under the definition of the commerce clause of the U.S. Constitution. Instead of taking jurisdiction over foreign corporations engaged in insurance, *Paul v. Virginia* supported the older doctrine that left regulation to the states.[35]

It was only by pointing out the way that comity could potentially hamper the growth of capitalism, and thereby the public welfare, that lawyers made their case for abandoning the concept. In what amounted to a fundamental reformulation of corporate sovereignty, the British politician E. Hilton Young summarized the problems with comity. He described this approach to regulating foreign corporations as "the restrictive system," in contrast to the newer "liberal theory" of regulation he advocated.[36] The restrictive theory rested on territorial principles. Because a juridical person could have no being outside of the law that produced it, business that crossed multiple jurisdictions did so only on the deference and goodwill of each sovereign. This was the definition of comity originated by the Voets, found in Story, and reasserted by Taney in *Bank of Augusta*. In a profound reversal, Young argued that leaving the courts to decide whether a corporation was a person subverted the law and was therefore "a mere negation of law."[37] Law, for Young, was a system of standardized norms corresponding to observable facts; law was not a system of sovereign decisions. With respect to the obligation to recognize corporations extraterritorially, however, Young defined law as the very thing that an older generation of legal thinkers had considered ultra vires, beyond the power of law.

In mounting his critique of comity, Young appealed to the language of the emerging capitalist order: fact, efficiency, pragmatism, and science. The restrictive system's chief limitation was that it was "in variance with fact" and "would be an incalculable injury to civilization in general and commerce in particular."[38] The fact in question was not the ability of the sovereign to take action in the name of public welfare but commerce, which Young repeatedly presented as a universal benefit to all parties. Though he noted that "the primary purpose in the creation of commercial associations is not the public welfare, but private gain," he quickly reasserted the link between capitalism and a global *salus publica*. "It is in the interest of all nations alike to promote international commercial intercourse. Capital is cosmopolitan, and commercial associations are associations rather of capital than men."[39]

Young also asserted that the restrictive system threatened corporations' abilities to carry out the missions for which they were chartered. Young distinguished two types of powers in all juristic persons. *Civil capacity* included the standard rights to sue, contract, and hold property. Young contrasted this with *functional capacity,* which encompassed the corporation's reason for being: to "educate, heal the sick, insure lives or mine gold."[40] Functional capacity was nothing other than the biopolitical power of the corporation to govern life in the terms dictated by their incorporation, the old exemption from law. Though Young argued that corporations maintained their functional capacity only within the territory in which they were chartered, he also claimed that limits on civil capacity—such as on the ability to contract and sue in foreign jurisdictions—constituted a limit on the functional capacity of the corporation. When other states limited the range of actions corporations could take abroad, they also limited a corporation's ability to carry out the duties for which they were chartered at home. Moreover, the law could not prevent agents or representatives of the corporation from suing and contracting in foreign jurisdictions in their civil capacity as real persons. This undermined the notion that comity could keep a corporation out of a territory. With limitations that did not limit and restrictions that did not restrict, Young argued that comity was a cumbersome fiction that achieved no practical benefit. "No comity is necessary to confer upon an agent an attribute which he enjoys like any other natural person."[41]

The liberal theory solved these difficulties by treating the corporation as a natural person. Its goal was to use law to facilitate the expansion of capital beyond territorial boundaries. Legal realists and advocates for sociological jurisprudence took the lead in championing the liberal theory, arguing that law should be more attentive to its political and social effects. In addition to Young, realist scholars, such as Gerard Henderson, Walter W. Cook, Wesley Hohfeld, and Ernst Lorenzen, promoted an experimental, scientific, and pragmatic approach to issues involving foreign corporations and the conflict of laws.[42] Cook, for instance, framed his approach to the conflict of laws as a complete rejection of the "theoretical method" associated with "'territorial' theories" and sought to ground his analysis on "the observation of concrete phenomena" modeled on the physical sciences and John Dewey's experimental philosophy.[43] Henderson, whose study of foreign corporations in U.S. constitutional law was structured around Young's distinction between liberal and restrictive theories, simply dismissed the older practice of judges for newer sociological methods. "It is now recognized that most rules of law represent a rough compromise between those economic and social needs of the present which are able to make themselves felt, and the formulas and doctrines of the past, a compromise constantly being worked over and readjusted, all the while striving towards logical consistency merely because inconsistency means litigation and waste of effort."[44]

Within the United States, new approaches to the regulation of foreign corporations were able to circumvent the older discourse of comity by shifting power to the national government. Although judges and legislatures did not abandon the language of comity and local territorial sovereignty, in practice, national regulation enabled corporations to engage in business practices beyond the territory of their incorporation. Though Story and Taney had already transformed the more rigorous understanding of comity offered by Huber, the liberal theory articulated by realists was a direct and thorough attack on territorial restrictions to capital accumulation. Through the first decade of the twentieth century, comity retained nominal importance, but most of its substantive features had been abandoned.

To understand this process, we can return to the changes in both state and federal law discussed in chapter 2, noting their impact on foreign corporations. First, liberal general incorporation laws, like New Jersey's Corporation Act of 1889, essentially ended the practice of special incorporation laws. Individual states also passed laws that required foreign corporations to register papers.[45] While registration reiterated the state's control over corporate regulation in a particular jurisdiction, the practical effect of these regulations was to allow businesses chartered in other states to conduct business on the same grounds as domestic corporations.[46] Second, federal agencies worked to standardize the treatment of corporations across jurisdictions. For instance, a 1915 report by the Bureau of Corporations focused on the various state laws regulating foreign corporations. As with the general project of these administrative agencies, the Bureau's report was primarily a fact-finding study that put a concise review of state corporate laws in one place as an "aid to business."[47] The report also stressed the importance of a unified system of state laws for business practices, lamenting that the Commissioners on Uniform State Law had unsuccessfully attempted to pass a draft law standardizing business regulations four times between 1910 and 1914.[48]

The assertion of federal jurisdiction in cases involving corporations—up to their protections under the Constitution—constituted a powerful limit on the notion of territorial control residing in individual states. Though *Paul v. Virginia* reiterated the old comity theory by upholding local state regulation of insurance, it did so only under the condition that *insurance* was distinct from *commerce* under the commerce clause of the U.S. Constitution.[49] The federal government maintained power over interstate commerce and, by 1910, began to exert it in the interest of securing equality of access and limiting discrimination of business corporations by individual states. Though we associate the terms *equality* and *discrimination* with civil rights cases, in the early twentieth century, they were applied to corporations as part of their due process protection through the Fourteenth Amendment.

In a series of 1910 railroad cases, the Supreme Court invalidated a fee imposed by the state of Kansas on foreign corporations as a violation of the federal government's power to regulate interstate commerce.[50] The fee was assessed on the total capital stock of the corporations, meaning that the fee took into account corporate income and assets located outside of Kansas. Whereas Justice Holmes dissented to the ruling, arguing that states had the power to exclude foreign corporations and that the fee constituted merely a limited exclusion, Justice Harlan, writing for the majority, argued that the state had no power to regulate an interstate corporation.[51]

These issues were reviewed again in the debates over antitrust legislation. As already mentioned, antitrust was a new assertion of power by the federal government. One of the questions in antitrust legislation was the extent to which the federal government could challenge state economic regulation in the context of interstate commerce. In early antitrust suits, most notably *United States v. E.C. Knight Company* (1895), the Court limited the federal application of antitrust legislation.[52] Though the case concerned sugar refining, the Court held that manufacturing, like banking and insurance, did not constitute interstate commerce and was therefore solely subject to state regulation. Although *E.C. Knight* asserted the older power of the states to regulate noncommercial interstate business, subsequent antitrust cases asserted federal jurisdiction. By the time of the famous 1911 antitrust cases of *US v. Standard Oil* and *US v. American Tobacco,* which returned antitrust to its common law construction as prohibiting not all but just "unreasonable" restraints of trade, the commerce clause was being used to protect national markets and competition.[53]

In terms of the U.S. context, then, a liberal theory of sovereignty and corporate regulation was able to take hold at the turn of the twentieth century because it had a federal system able to step into the space occupied by the states under the territorial theories of comity. Comity became less important when most corporate business involved interstate commerce, when business corporations were chartered under the liberal provisions of New Jersey, and when federal agencies were attempting to standardize corporate regulations across the country. The transformation of corporations from expression of local police powers to private legal persons was contingent on the development of a national regulatory structure. As both the case law and the writing of legal scholars indicate, the creation of a national regulatory structure for corporations was a new assemblage of power, which refigured sovereignty as well as the logic of the ban. The ability of individual states to direct the exceptional powers of corporations toward the promotion of the common good was curtailed, while the national government solidified its power over corporations that were, by the beginning of the twentieth century, treated as persons under federal law.

Simultaneously, jurists promoted personhood and the geographic mobility of corporations under the argument that the territorial expansion of capitalism was necessary for securing public welfare.[54]

The Limits to Comity in International Economic Space

In the international context, Anglo-American legal scholars also desired a liberal theory of corporate regulation, although it was more difficult to implement. After all, the distinction between the restrictive and liberal systems outlined by Young, while influential among realists in the United States, was written to clarify the role of foreign corporations in British law and to contribute to wider European discussions on international law. With the consolidation of national economic space by the late nineteenth century, there was little "foreign" about a company chartered in New Jersey doing business in New York. Internationally, however, definitions of corporations varied from legal system to legal system, thus making basic regulations, such as the assessment of liability, the levying of taxes, the enforcement of contracts, or the policing of monopolies, difficult.[55] Moreover, when discussing relations between nation-states or between nation-states and corporations (whose "nationality" was often in dispute), both national and international law had to mediate the demands of foreign policy and interstate conflicts, in addition to legal concerns with commerce, private right, and public law. Unlike the federal structure of the United States, in international law, there was no global sovereign who could simply define the corporation as a subject of rights and, thereby, a natural person in the law. Instead, the regulation of corporations in the international economy was left to a patchwork of bilateral treaties and national laws, along with international laws, customs, and norms that largely lacked force.

The discrepancies that vexed advocates of federal regulation—specifically concerning the nature of corporate personality, its property, domicile, and nationality—were equally confounding in this patchwork structure. In the nineteenth century, U.S. law followed principles of international comity and adhered to the territorial basis of sovereignty implicit in that doctrine when ruling on cases with international significance. For instance, a series of late-eighteenth- and early-nineteenth-century cases concerned insurance claims for impressed ships during wartime.[56] The courts sought to promote trade without extending the jurisdiction of U.S. courts beyond the territorial boundaries of the nation-state or violating the sovereignty of European states and their colonies. *Vasse v. Ball* concerned an insurance claim on an American brig, the *Salmon,* which carried cargo from Haiti to Philadelphia at the behest of the French minister in Haiti.[57] On the return trip, a British privateer captured the ship as a French vessel and took it to Bermuda. The main issue before the Court was whether the insurance claims had to be paid (they did), but the case also raised a secondary issue of the neutrality of the American ship engaged in trade. On this count, the Court was emphatic in protecting the right of Americans to trade with both parties without violating American neutrality. Yet when it came to reversing the decision of the Court of Admiralty, the Supreme Court was more deferential: "We cannot presume that the Judge of a foreign court has perjured himself, by declaring that property to be French, which we know to be American; and, of course, we must assume the position, that his decree proceeded upon the other allegations of the libel. Those other allegations do not furnish any cause for canceling the policies in the present case."[58]

In *Murray v. The Schooner Charming Betsy,* the ship of Jared Shattuck, a natural-born American citizen but a longtime resident and real property holder on the Dutch island of St. Thomas, was captured by French privateers.[59] While sailing to Guadeloupe, the ship was overtaken by the American ship *Constellation* as violating the Non-Intercourse Act passed in the United States against France. At trial, the central issue was the prize money for the American captor and the insurance claim of Shattuck. The Court held that Shattuck's citizenship was irrelevant. Carrying armed French soldiers, the Court ruled that the American captain was fully justified in seizing Shattuck's ship. But the Court also suggested that the American law should not interfere with Dutch neutrality unless expressly stated by Congress and that Shattuck, having lived his entire adult life under Dutch authority and sailing under the Dutch flag, was not in violation of U.S. law by having his ship captured by the French. Chief Justice Marshall stated, "An act of Congress ought never to be construed to violate the law of nations if any other possible construction remains, and consequently can never be construed to violate neutral rights, or to affect neutral commerce, further than is warranted by the law of nations as understood in this country."[60]

These cases focused on property or insurance contracts. When it came to business corporations, the deference of U.S. courts to other sovereigns enabled corporations working transnationally to avoid regulation. Sometimes the refusal to take jurisdiction could be directly attributed to the sovereignty of the corporation. In *Mason v. Intercolonial Railway of Canada,* a suit was brought to the Supreme Court of Massachusetts concerning a Canadian corporation whose sole owner was King Edward VII of England. Though the stock was owned by the King, the business itself was controlled by a private group of directors and engaged in for-profit enterprise. The court ruled, citing *Schooner Exchange v. M'Faddon,* that it had no jurisdiction to hear a civil case involving a foreign sovereign.[61] *Mason* followed the doctrine set in *Bank of the United States v. Deveaux,* looking beyond the corporate legal form to the individual investors as a means of determining the nationality of the corporation.[62] But this went against Taney's ruling in *Bank of Augusta v. Earle,* which treated citizenship as based on the location of incorporation. For Taney, foreign corporations enter other states on principles of comity, allowing them to be subjected to local law.[63] The practical effect of the decision in *Mason* was to make the entire company impervious to suit outside of the British Commonwealth. Nathan Wolfman, the counsel for the plaintiff in the case, published a response to the decision in the April 1910 issue of the newly formed *American Journal of International Law.* In it, he attacked the concept of comity, arguing that "international comity is simply a subservient and related part of the network of principles which make up the law of nations, principles based exclusively upon sound reasoning and justice."[64] Wolfman appealed to the private nature of the railway business to encourage the extraterritorial reach of American law. "It is a main purpose of the writer to show that when such foreign government conducts an undertaking commercial in its character and not in its strict capacity as a sovereign government the law of nations should permit suit to be brought against such government providing property belonging to it may be found within the jurisdiction of the home courts."[65]

In *Mason,* the corporate device and the deference shown to sovereigns cloaked a company in sovereign immunity. The same principles also allowed extremely powerful corporations and combinations to exercise de facto sovereignty abroad by working through client states. The most famous example of this form of corporate sovereignty was chronicled in *American Banana v. United Fruit Company.*[66] The case involved an American banana exporter by the name of Sam McConnell. McConnell had once been an associate of the United Fruit Company, but in 1903, he bought a plot of land in Panama, which at the time was still part of Colombia. McConnell began construction of a railroad to bring his bananas to market, but the United Fruit Company, seeking to maintain its monopoly of the banana trade, ordered McConnell to sell his land. The governor of Panama interceded on United Fruit's behalf by petitioning Colombia to abrogate its rights to McConnell's land, thereby relinquishing it to Costa Rica, which had close ties with United Fruit. In September 1903, the government of Costa Rica and the United Fruit Company sent Costa Rican troops to take McConnell's land, but in November of that same year, Panama revolted and established an independent republic with

McConnell's land as its northern border. McConnell sold the plantation to American Banana Company, a U.S. multinational, in June 1904, which was shut down a month later by the Costa Rican military and United Fruit.

The suit claimed that United Fruit was engaged in a conspiracy to corner the banana market and was a monopoly under the Sherman Antitrust Act. Justice Oliver Wendell Holmes, who delivered the opinion on the case, recognized that United Fruit had trespassed on the rights of McConnell and American Banana, not to mention on the rights of the new state of Panama. But in his decision, he argued that the U.S. courts had no jurisdiction based on either the Sherman Antitrust Act or tort law more generally for the contracts made in Colombia, Panama, and Costa Rica. These could only be adjudicated by the sovereign power where the act was undertaken, whomever that may be. "A seizure by a state is not a thing that can be complained of elsewhere in the courts. The fact, if it be one, that *de jure* the estate is in Panama, does not matter in the least; sovereignty is pure fact."[67]

We should recognize the porous border here between fact and law in relation to sovereignty.[68] The "fact" of Costa Rican sovereignty—made evident through military control—was nothing other than a legalization of the United Fruit Company's coercive attempts to maintain its monopoly. Holmes could have referenced a variety of truths on the ground—most notably the company's control over Costa Rica and the U.S. military presence in Panama. While the ruling appeared to merely acquiescence to a powerful corporation, it also reflected the interests of the U.S. State Department and the new secretary of state, Elihu Root.[69] Thus the decision deferred not only to the sovereignty of a company-backed military occupation but also to the interests of the executive branch of the United States. By clinging to the absolute and indivisible notion of state sovereignty, Holmes's ruling supported the corporation in its drive for economic and military control of both the banana trade and the territory.

With U.S. economic and imperial expansion, treatises and executive orders could be used to gain legal standing for corporations in colonized countries. For instance, in the aftermath of the Spanish American War, U.S. corporations interested in trade with Cuba needed recognition under the Cuban Commercial Code, which was still organized under Spanish law derived from the French Napoleonic Codes.[70] U.S. business corporations entering Cuba did so by filing copies of their charters and bylaws through Cuban consular offices. They also required authorization from the secretaries of state of the individual U.S. states that issued their charters as well as certification of their tax status from the Treasury Department, all of which was then entered into the Mercantile Registry of the Cuban

Commerce Department. Although the Cuban system was fairly open to foreign corporations, the actual adjudication of claims was substantially determined by politics. The Platt Amendment, which granted the United States the power to intervene in Cuban affairs, also ensured preferential treatment in disputes concerning U.S. companies. As Gordon Ireland put it in a 1927 article, "it is pretty well understood that a third nation pressing beyond diplomatic measures in support of claims of her nationals, such as Societies or Corporations claimed not to be Cuban citizens in spite of registration there, would not be dealing with Cuba, alone: while corporations of the United States able to convince their State Department of the justice of their claims are in specially preferred positions regardless of their technical citizenship rights."[71]

In international law, legal theory blurred with economic policy and sovereign decisions. The lawyer Ernest Schuster argued in 1916 that "reciprocal recognition of corporate bodies is frequently secured by international conventions" before listing agreements Britain had with France, Italy, Belgium, Spain, and Greece.[72] Reciprocal recognition with Germany, however, ended at the outbreak of World War I. Although the United States had entered into commercial treaties in the nineteenth century, the treaty of 1911 with Japan marked the first time a clause was inserted into a commercial treaty directly relating to corporations.[73] The clause allowed corporations organized under the laws of one of the signatory countries to sue and be sued in the courts of the other as well as to maintain their rights to conduct business and enter into contracts. It reappeared in a 1921 treaty with Siam and was elaborated in a 1925 treaty with Germany.[74] By 1934, the United States had entered into commercial treaties with clauses pertaining to the reciprocal recognition of corporations with the states of Austria, El Salvador, Estonia, Finland, Hungary, Honduras, Latvia, Liberia, Norway, and Poland as well as agreements with Greece and Turkey.[75] In addition, many countries, including Austria, Belgium, Bolivia, Colombia, Denmark, France, Germany, Italy, Japan, Mexico, Uruguay, and Venezuela, passed laws that required foreign corporations—U.S. or otherwise—to register with the host country and submit to the host country's laws. Shareholders in these foreign companies could be foreigners, but once registered, the company itself could be considered to reside in the territory for purposes of national law.[76]

In the 1910s and 1920s, resolving questions about the nationality of corporations became even more pressing because international conflicts increasingly involved transnational business interests. During World War I, concerns over the enemy status of foreign corporations became central to various legal communities. The issue was raised in the famous British case of *Daimler Company v. Continental Tyre Company* but had international implications.[77] The case involved a bill of exchange owed by the Daimler Company to Continental Tyre, a British corporation whose ownership was largely German. The question was whether Continental Tyre could sue to recover the funds in British courts or whether the company was an enemy under the provisions of the Trading with the Enemy Proclamation of 1914.[78] The initial ruling was in favor of Continental Tyre but was reversed on appeal to the House of Lords. Lord Parker's majority opinion asserted that it was neither shareholders nor the location of the company that was critical for determining the citizenship or the enemy status of the company; rather, it was the citizenship of the persons in de facto control of the corporation.[79] In looking beyond the corporation to shareholders, *Daimler,* like *Mason,* rejected more liberal theories that considered corporations within national law irrespective of ownership or control.

The *Daimler* case concerned the legal claims that enemy corporations could make in a host country's court, but corporate domicile and nationality were also important in cases involving the nationalization of corporate property in a foreign country. Following the Russian Revolution, a number of cases emerged concerning the validity of confiscating property owned by Russian corporations chartered under the tsar but held abroad as well as claims from owners and debtors seeking to recoup property and money confiscated by the new Soviet government.[80] Resting on comity grounds, as well as precedents set in South and Central American cases, including *American Banana,* U.S. courts held fast to the argument that although the Soviets could confiscate property within their territory, they had no power against the competing claims of owners in the United States for property held in the United States.[81]

The results of each line of cases did not amount to a systematic application of international law. Each selectively considered national policies and diplomatic concerns. Though many recognized the problems that the growth of international business created for territorially based regulation, there was no universal agreement that the liberal theory would solve the problems of international economic regulation or that it could resolve the tension between national regulation and international law. Ernst Feilchenfeld, a consultant for the League of Nations who was later a law professor at Georgetown University, suggested that although international law contained elaborate rules governing sovereignty and jurisdiction over property, there was no ground for treating corporations as citizens in international law.[82] His summary of the subject was taxonomic. First, he challenged the distinction in international law between territorial sovereignty and personal sovereignty. Feilchenfeld argued that international law only dealt with state sovereignty that is, at times, restricted when other sovereigns exercise authority over foreign persons in their territories. While one sovereign could restrict the sovereignty of another over a citizen who had left home and entered the host state, the host state could not alter the original legal relation that another sovereign created. The critical question was whether corporations were "persons" or "citizens" in international law. Could corporations absolve themselves from their legal requirements by moving to another territory? Or were corporations legal relations—a nexus of individual owners, property rights, and privileges to contract and control territory—that were subject to a body of territorial law?

Feilchenfeld did not equivocate:

> This opinion, which tries to solve the problem [of sovereignty *in personam*] by analogies between "natural" and "artificial" persons, seems to mistake the facts. Such an analogy is based either on the assertion that a corporation is a living body, or on the assertion that a corporation is a fictitious person. The first assertion is a rather poetic way of comparing one thing to another by a figure of speech [rather] than a scientific analysis of facts. . . . As to the second assertion, it may or may not be that a corporation, although not a living person, is treated like or considered as a person by some systems of municipal law; but—and this seems to be generally admitted—a system of law can make a corporation a living person no more than it can make any other dead thing alive.[83]

Instead, Feilchenfeld argued that corporations were a "legal entity of rights and legal capacities which are impressed with a special character derived from the objects of the corporation."[84] Dealing with the nationality of the corporation should be the same as dealing with each of its constitutive parts, and thus a state should be able to assume sovereignty over the individual investors, the work of the corporation, and real property if it falls within the territory of the state. Legal relations were territorial; the corporation, as a living body or a fictitious person, was "stateless" but largely irrelevant.

Feilchenfeld's critique of the liberal theory suggested that states were neither obligated to recognize foreign corporations nor obliged to defer to the home country when a foreign corporation was within the jurisdiction of a host country. The rules of international law only permitted continuing the systems based on territorial sovereignty. Feilchenfeld suggested that treatises and executive decisions were thus a "highly desirable" way of mediating the tensions in international economic regulation, but a more robust system, such as that offered by the liberal theory, could not be founded in the norms of interwar international law.[85]

There was no resolution during the interwar period, though in the late 1920s, the League of Nations attempted to address issues of corporate citizenship and domicile through its Committee of Experts for the Progressive Codification of International Law.[86] The committee noted that although most legal systems generally adhered to territorial notions of nationality based on the location of incorporation and headquarters, there was no customary agreement on the determinations of nationality for corporations before World War I. The war, with its emergency measures against enemy corporations, had challenged territorially based concepts of nationality with the control doctrine outlined in the *Daimler* case. Although the committee viewed the control doctrine as "pathological," they lacked a means to reconcile the territorial basis of sovereignty and liberal theories that treated corporations as juristic persons.[87] The committee advocated a middle way that would keep regulation within national territories, while adopting a conception of corporate nationality connected to the country issuing the charter for purposes of international law. This left substantial room for individual states to structure policy, but it definitively separated investors, shareholders, and directors from the legal nationality of the corporation.

As late as 1947, Sigmund Timberg of Columbia University and the Antitrust Division of the U.S. Justice Department lamented the way that "international law still resolutely disclaims any real responsibility for the regulation of international economic affairs" and that this shortcoming was the result of an "antiquated conception of the sovereign equality of states" and reflected the "disparity between the territorially fragmented nature of legal systems and the integrated nature of business organization and economic practice."[88] In an account that seems strangely prescient today, Timberg noted that predicating the international regulation of corporations on territorial sovereignty empowered corporations. His own account focused on the abilities of corporations to evade regulation, submerge facts about corporate business, and take advantage of more amenable government policies through territorially based systems of regulation.

The project of international economic regulation remains incomplete. At the end of World War II, the mantle of international economic regulation fell to Bretton Woods institutions.[89] Yet national corporate regulations could still shape transnational business, provided that they had the geopolitical power to give those laws force abroad. For the United States, that power was primarily directed at the protection of markets (along with accessing low-cost labor and resources). While *American Banana* argued that the enforcement of U.S. antitrust laws was geographically contained within the nation-state, the recognition that anticompetitive behavior abroad could have important effects at home caused a shift in regulation. As Jonathan Turley has noted, through the mid-twentieth century, the U.S. courts applied antitrust laws extraterritorially for the protection of markets, while being considerably more reticent about extending jurisdiction over cases focused on environmental or labor protection, which, without explicit congressional statements to the contrary, were assumed to be only binding within the nation-state.[90]

Corporate Sovereignty and the Space of Law

It is hardly controversial to say that sovereignty relies on territory. Understanding sovereignty as a practice, we can see that sometimes sovereignty is best characterized not by the space of the nation-state but by what the nation-state leaves out. Michael Hardt and Antonio Negri have argued that sovereignty in Western political theory has been structured by a juxtaposition between a space in which law was valid and an outside space where law lacked force.[91] This relation was central to juridical theories based on the social contract, in which the space of law depended on the temporal movement from nature to society.

The distinction between the inside and the outside of law was also incorporated into the state system of international law that proved to be so ineffectual in standardizing corporate controls. National corporate regulation in the United States marked a shift in political rationality from sovereignty to government, although it was a shift that preserved corporate immunities in the form of private rights subjected to national administration. Though administrative norms did not eliminate the exceptional powers of the corporation, they justified them in economic terms and attempted to make them work for the public welfare. Internationally, however, there was never the kind of resolution between sovereignty and government that characterized the U.S. domestic compromise. Through the twentieth century, corporations that were created by territorially based systems of law became increasingly powerful in the international economy by distancing themselves from territorial modes of regulation while maintaining some of the old deference afforded by comity. The story of comity, conflict of laws, and the regulation of foreign corporations explains how companies carved out legal autonomy by inhabiting the negative spaces of the international state system.

It also clarifies the importance of the ban in establishing the geographies of sovereign power. Theorists such as Schmitt and Agamben, who have situated sovereignty within the state of exception, emphasize space as constitutive of sovereign power. In concrete terms, the exception creates spaces outside of the constituted order that ensure the order's ability to exist. Both Schmitt and Agamben recognize that this space is also conceptual, as space is internal to the very concept of law. Schmitt, for instance, emphasized the relation between space and law in his discussion of the *nomos,* which names not only a legal order but the act that establishes the relation between a legal order and a determinant localization.[92] Agamben, too, has recognized the important relation between space and the law when suggesting that the camp constitutes the "*nomos* of the modern." The figure of the camp marks the space that law defines as outside of the legal order to establish its own being. For this reason, he terms the camp a "dislocating localization":

> The political system no longer orders forms of life and juridical rules in a determinate space, but instead contains at its very center a *dislocating localization* that exceeds it and into which every form of life and every rule can be virtually taken. The camp as dislocating localization is the hidden matrix of the politics in which we are still living, and it is this structure of the camp that we must learn to recognize in all its metamorphoses into the *zones d'attentes* of our airports and certain outskirts of our cities.[93]

We can see in these changes in the conception and regulation of the corporation the trace of the ban and the double body of corporate sovereignty. Not only does the corporation continually get defined in terms of its privileges and immunities (established either by the gift of the sovereign or by natural right) but also—and especially in global economic space— the corporation internalizes the state of nature and its relations of force within the political order. Comity, after all, was a doctrine designed for the state of nature. The deference a corporation was shown under doctrines of comity was directly related to the geopolitical relations that governed the international sphere. When commentators like Timberg noted the failure to move past comity in terms of international economic regulation, they were noting the persistence of relations of force in a part of social life (the economy) that, Timberg argued, should be governed by law and standardized legal relations—at least, according to the ideology of legal liberalism. Though we have seen that standardized legal norms do not eliminate sovereign immunity, the uneven and patchworked regulation of corporations internationally leaves every question of the applicability of the law up for decision.

CHAPTER FIVE

Responsibility

By the first decades of the twentieth century, lawyers, jurists, and political thinkers had created a form of corporate sovereignty that supported a powerful assemblage designed for the production and realization of capitalist value. Within the context of U.S. national law, this assemblage depended on a direct rendering of the subject of rights in terms of its productive capacity, extending constitutional rights and privileges to those lawmakers viewed as providing for the material basis of national life, including corporations. In the international context, the failure to ground an increasingly global capitalist order in a corporate subject of liberal law left corporations open to navigating a pockmarked system of national regulation and geopolitical power. Neither regime—which were two sides of the same legal–economic–territorial structure—was detrimental to corporate capitalism, and both worked on a biopolitical paradigm that set aside spaces and structures for investing in life as well as abandoning it in the name of capitalist value.

The vacuum left by the failure of liberal theories of corporate regulation did not eliminate the restless attempts to order and territorialize the world. As early as the 1960s and 1970s, activists, politicians, lawmakers, diplomats, academics, and corporate marketing departments were generating new visions of corporate capitalism, its regulatory frameworks, and its social duties, obligations, and privileges. By the 1990s, responsibility and citizenship had moved from debated terms to semiformal, quasi-legal regulatory regimes, coalescing into corporate social responsibility (CSR) and corporate citizenship (CC). In response to the pressure and campaigns of activists, policies on CSR and CC have now become increasingly important for companies as well as states and transnational institutions such as the United Nations (UN), the World Bank, and the European Union. This in turn has generated something of a cottage industry among scholars who promote, analyze, and critique CSR and CC.

CSR and CC are thus complex processes, open to investigation from a variety of angles. What interests me about them is the specific domain Sadler and Lloyd identify as "the wider implications of CSR as a set of activities in its own right, in terms of the re-drawing of the boundaries between corporate- and state-centered regulation that CSR represents."[1] As opposed to the numerous empirical assessments of CSR (that analyze the diverse strategies by which CSR regimes are implemented by companies and political organizations; the effects of these policies on corporate profitability, shareholder value, and corporate structure; or the impact of CSR on social issues such as working conditions, environmental governance, and human rights), Sadler and Lloyd consider CSR as a framework of economic government, one that rearticulates the balance between the political and the economic or public and private power.

As with other progressive critics of CSR, Sadler and Lloyd treat CSR as part of the market-led and privatized forms of governance associated with neoliberal globalization.[2] Although they note the emergence of CSR as a response to the more radical claims of anticorporate activists seeking to hold corporations accountable for the inequalities structuring the global political economy, they suggest that the current manifestations of CSR and CC embodied in regulatory frameworks like the UN Global Compact (GC) or the World Economic Forum's Global Corporate Citizenship Initiative are business driven, relying on voluntary forms of assessment that lack the force of law. Current projects of CSR share "a recurrent theme that left to their own devices, global corporate citizens can evolve and broaden the sphere of what is seen as being appropriately beneficial behavior for the greater social and environmental good."[3] As such, CSR replaces formal politics and civil action with individualized and voluntary choices in private markets as a way of securing social welfare. Moreover, Sadler and Lloyd suggest that the prevalence of CSR initiatives also limits the ability of nongovernmental organizations and civil society groups to press for more radical forms of public corporate responsibility through formal legal accountability.

A number of responses can be made to this account. Clive Barnett offers one of the most sustained engagements with discussions about neoliberalism, directly challenging the notion that the rise of regimes of responsibility equals the depoliticization of society.[4] He suggests that analytical accounts using "neoliberalism" to explain contemporary politics risk homogenizing social struggles by presenting responsibility as a coherent and seamless political project orchestrated in the interests of a capitalist class. This narrative, in which elites push consumer choices in markets as a substitute for collective political action, fails to grasp the central insight of Foucauldian scholarship concerning the ways "consent is actually secured" and "anchored at the level of everyday life."[5] Instead, Barnett suggests in his collaborative work with Paul Cloke, Nick Clarke, and Alice Malpass that new regimes of responsibility have to be understood as shifts in political rationality, where a variety of actors come to problematize their political participation and daily practices in new ways.[6] On this read, responsibility is not only about a global struggle for the hegemony of market-based regimes or the forced depoliticization of civic life; rather, responsibility names a shift in political rationality made manifest through embodied practices and social mobilizations, where diverse individuals consider themselves, their conduct, and their interrelations with others and the world in new politicoethical registers. Lest we fail to grasp the implication, Barnett has put it bluntly: "there is no such thing as neoliberalism!"[7]

Barnett's reformulation usefully points out some problems in using neoliberalism as a catchall explanation for contemporary politics. As I have repeatedly argued throughout this genealogical account, any attempt to approach corporate power through the dichotomies of state and economy or public or private misses the ways that both corporate and state power emerge at, construct, continually transgress, and occasionally consolidate the blurred boundaries of these social spheres. Quite simply, for all their sophistication, accounts of contemporary politics that hinge on neoliberalism are already framed by a state–economy dichotomy that implicitly suggests that the resolution to current problems is the reassertion of (good) state power and (good) formal law. This makes it hard to account for the ways that law has been instrumental in the production of these seemingly deterritorialized, privatized, and market-led forms of political rationality in the first place. Sadler and Lloyd, for their part, are sensitive to these problems but nonetheless insist that there are coherent elite political projects that must be considered as such. True enough. But in emphasizing the contemporaneity of neoliberalism, critics on the left obscure the long history by which the law has consolidated private power in corporate institutions. Put another way, corporate power has always been articulated within the context of responsibility. Discourses of responsibility, citizenship, and commitments to serve public welfare (in however strange or dreadful ways) are the very ontological root of the corporation and its legal justifications for existence. Corporations and their advocates have long made the legal argument—recognized by state authorities and incorporated into the apparatuses of corporate regulation and administration—that their exceptional status is warranted because they carry the responsibilities of serving society and public welfare.

Conversely, attention to the diffuse ways individuals, groups, and social networks use responsibility to problematize political participation seems inadequate to confront configurations of power that, however varied and micropolitical in origin, seem to have taken on relatively stable institutional forms. Focusing on daily practices and political rationalities of ethical self-reflection emphasizes the ways diverse subjects and social networks constitute themselves, their politics, and their normative practices. Certainly these processes are critical to the ways power and knowledge are retroactively stabilized in new forms of political reason, but as the previous chapters should make clear, corporations, too, are constituted as subjects within liberal law. New regimes of CSR and CC are as much about realizing the responsibilities and citizenship of corporations as they are about flesh-and-blood human beings. Focusing on the way ethical consumption and responsibility are problematized by subjects as they constitute themselves and their politics elides the ways that this reflection also occurs within institutions like corporations and the international legal frameworks that shape and channel corporate power.[8]

Taken together, these insights suggest problems with engaging "corporate social responsibility" as either another example of neoliberalism or as part of a process of ethical self-reflection by spatially and socially dispersed individuals and groups. Responsibility emerges as part of the problematization of political reason, not only by individuals reflecting on their conduct. Instead, responsibility can be better understood as part of an ongoing transformation in sovereignty, but one that remains ensnared within the logic of the ban. Contrary to arguments about neoliberalism that read responsibility as a shift in state power, viewing responsibility in terms of the problematic of sovereignty maintains the focus on responsibility as a political strategy or technique, which Barnett usefully emphasizes. It also considers the ways these rationalities are institutionalized not simply in structures of states and law but in different configurations characterized by the *extension, withdrawal,* and *diffusion* of legal authority. Through this process, the potentialities opened by new conceptions of responsibility are actualized into technical and legal apparatuses. Thus the problem with responsibility is not that it fails to achieve its stated goals; rather, the problem is that the dominant formulation of what those goals are, along with the modes of analysis used to calculate, adjudicate, and institutionalize responsibility and citizenship as quasi-legal categories referring to both individuals and corporations, already presupposes and *justifies as necessary* the two forms of government we have been charting: the government of life by capitalist value and capitalism, in its collective, personified form, as a form of life worthy of political existence. It is because the institutionalized visions of responsibility and citizenship take their warrant from a relation to both sovereignty and capitalism—and thus are always already constituted by and through the fissure between qualified life and abandoned life, or the differential renderings of life in terms of value—that they are unstable as a foundation for a just legal, economic, and social order.

This chapter explores two different formulations of responsibility in corporate regulation. Both cases emerged from a sense that something had gone dreadfully wrong with the corporate economy, producing a new set of corporate monsters. In each instance, responsibility was posited as the solution for realigning the actions of corporations with the welfare of communities, societies, and nations. The first section focuses on responsibility in the context of U.S.-based legal debates over the social and political effects of economic concentration. This discussion of CSR examines the responsibilities managers and shareholders have to both corporations and society. Though the debate came to fruition in the 1970s and continues to shape discussions of CSR today, its origins date back to the 1930s and concerns over the responsibilities accompanying corporate property. The second section considers the attempts, also emerging in the 1970s, to make transnational corporations behave responsibly through international legal frameworks and voluntary agreements. Owing to the geographic dimensions of international business, involving different systems of national and international law and corporations operating across multiple legal jurisdictions, responsibility came to be formulated not in terms of property rights but rather in terms of the responsibilities states and corporations had to each other, the international community, and the welfare of specific populations. In both cases, the debates channeled potentially radical questions about corporate power into legal and distributional questions about the extent to which corporations can be made legally responsible for social welfare and the legal mechanisms for doing so. Framed in this way, responsibility retraced the old terrain of corporate sovereignty as it became an instrument for balancing the legal privileges of incorporation and the benefits of those privileges for economic development against the destructiveness of global capitalism and antidemocratic tendencies of corporate power. The chapter concludes by considering other potentials that continue to reside within the concepts of responsibility, a proposition that is more fully explored in the succeeding chapter.

Responsibility and the Biopolitical Economy of Corporate Property

In the September 13, 1970, issue of the *New York Times Magazine*, Milton Friedman published a polemic, brusquely titled "The Social Responsibility of Business Is to Increase Its Profits."[9] Rehashing for a broader audience the arguments put forward in his 1962 text *Capitalism and Freedom,* the Friedman doctrine articulated what has come to be the classic free market argument against corporate social responsibility. Today, this argument for shareholder primacy has been incorporated into the mainstream of corporate law and regulation.[10] Friedman contended that managers, as agents of shareholders, had fiduciary duties to undertake actions solely intended to increase profits for the company and, by extension, dividends for shareholders. Friedman contrasted this vision of corporations with social responsibility, equating the latter with a "socialist view" in which "political mechanisms, not market mechanisms, are the appropriate way to determine the allocations of scarce resources to alternative uses."[11] Although Friedman's argument relied on simple dichotomies between political mechanisms and market mechanisms for resource allocation, or more directly, between government and business, he also recognized that both politics and markets were forms of organization in which "political principles" were at stake. Echoing the classical economic arguments of Adam Smith, Friedman emphasized that market mechanisms worked by individuals disposing of their property as they deemed fit, whereas political mechanisms required the "conformity" of individuals to "serve a more general social interest."[12] Friedman thus presented CSR as a form of political coercion that was not only economically inefficient but, more gallingly, an inappropriate restraint on liberty within a free society.

Although today Friedman's arguments about the legal requirement for corporate profit maximization are taken for granted, seen in context, they were a departure from the long history of corporate law that we have been chronicling. In particular, Friedman's polemic was directed at two different ways of reasoning about the responsibilities of corporations, one that was gaining importance in political discussions about corporate power in the 1970s and another that constituted the mainstream understanding of corporate law for the bulk of the twentieth century. The 1970 article responded directly to a wave of direct-action campaigns advocating for corporate social responsibility at shareholder meetings of major U.S.-based corporations. Most notable of these attempts was Campaign GM, in which activists attempted to install more socially minded public interest directors onto General Motors's board. Although the impulse behind Campaign GM concerned issues including weapons production for the Vietnam War, urban race relations, and environmental degradation, the actual content of what constituted responsible behavior took a backseat to the focus on institutional reform through proxy voting.[13] Friedman thus mentioned the "GM crusade" as an example of a misguided strategy for corporate governance—photographs of the leaders of Campaign GM accompanied the *New York Times Magazine* essay—without having to deal with the substantive claims about what constituted responsible behavior and whether the actions of GM and other major corporations were socially beneficial.

Of far greater concern for Friedman, however, were corporate law scholars and business leaders, the latter of whom he presented as the "unwitting puppets of the intellectual forces that have been undermining the basis of a free society these past decades."[14] In this sense, Friedman was attacking the notion that corporations were a unique form of socialized property, a position that had been dominant among legal thinkers and policy makers since Adolf Berle and Gardiner Means's pivotal 1932 text *The Modern Corporation and Private Property.* Friedman, for his part, was correct to present Berle as an intellectual forbearer to the movements for social responsibility of the 1970s. Douglas Schwartz, a Georgetown law professor and lawyer for Campaign GM, situated the public interest proxy fight as part of the general social upheaval of the late 1960s. But the specific strategy of shareholder activism rested on the analogy of "corporations to the state, and saw them as the makers of economic policy."[15] Schwartz noted, "There is nothing original in this idea. The position that there exists in the United States a private economic state was expounded as early as 1932 in A. Berle and G. Means, The Private [*sic*] Corporation and Private Property."[16]

The pivotal issue for both Friedman and the social activists was Berle's famous argument[17] that corporations entailed a new type of property relation in which ownership and control were not centered in the same person, effecting a split between the property used to manage an undertaking and the "passive property" that was directed toward producing returns to investors. Taking on this claim in *Capitalism and Freedom,* Friedman wrote,

> A major complaint made frequently against modern business is that it involves the separation of ownership and control—that the corporation has become a social institution that is a law unto itself, with irresponsible executives who do not serve the interests of their stockholders. This charge is not true. But the direction in which policy is now moving, of permitting corporations to make contributions for charitable purposes and allowing deductions for income tax, is a step in the direction of creating a true divorce between ownership and control and of undermining the basic nature and character of our society. It is a step away from an individualistic society and toward the corporate state.[18]

Like Friedman, Berle, too, had advocated shareholder primacy as the solution to the problems of control with corporate property, treating managers as agents who are duty bound to carry out the operations of the corporation in the shareholders' interests. Berle first articulated this argument in his famous debate with Edwin Merrick Dodd in the pages of the *Harvard Law Review* during the early 1930s.[19]

If Freidman's philosophy of shareholder primacy has become the baseline for today's mainstream corporate law, Berle and Dodd seem like progressive alternatives for CSR. For instance, William Bratton has argued that scholars "could remain here for an indefinite period debating the question whether something concrete can be done to make corporations more responsible, and I suspect little more would be accomplished than a restatement of points made by Berle and Dodd."[20] Berle initiated the debate, arguing for the centrality of shareholders' interests in governing corporations. He opened his 1931 *Harvard Law Review* article with the declarative proclamation that "all powers granted to a corporation or to the management of a corporation, or to any group within the corporation, whether derived from statute or charter or both, are necessarily and at all times exercisable only for the ratable benefit of all the shareholders as their interest appears."[21] The statement suggested that the fiduciary obligations of managers would prevent them from running powerful corporations for their own personal benefit. For Berle, shareholding was a means of recognizing broad social concerns against the narrow, short-term interests of managers, but this conceptualization, in turn, rested on the empirical claim that stock ownership had become both separated from management and increasingly diffused throughout society.[22]

Dodd's response echoed Berle's argument that property must be deployed in the interests of shareholders and reaffirmed the commitment to "giving stockholders much-needed protection against self-seeking managers."[23] Dodd also suggested that the business corporation was increasingly an "economic institution which has a social service as well as a profit-making function."[24] Dodd justified the social responsibilities of business by emphasizing the legal rulings that treated corporations and corporate property in terms that I connected with the police of society in chapters 2 and 3. This included cases dealing with public utilities, railroads, and, increasingly by the 1930s, labor legislation that placed restrictions on private property under the argument that certain types of corporations had social obligations extending beyond the responsibilities entailed by shareholders' proprietary claims. For instance, Dodd referenced the public use argument from the landmark case *Munn v. Illinois* as "having the merit of emphasizing the fact that business is permitted and encouraged by the law primarily because it is of service to the community rather than because it is a source of profit to its owners."[25] In particular, Dodd stressed the connection between economic planning and a broad social conception of economic security. He was careful to distinguish this vision from communism, arguing that the importance of economic planning "is no longer confined to radical opponents of the capitalistic system."[26] Thus, while reasserting the link between corporations and public welfare, Dodd argued that managers, with their tools of economic planning, played a unique role in pushing corporations to address social needs.

Although recent scholarship positions Berle's vision of CSR as more progressive than Dodd's "business commonwealth camp"—particularly as Berle advocated for more expansive government regulation during the 1930s—we should also recognize that Berle's advocacy of CSR was less a critique of corporate capitalism than an elevation of the role of corporations in economic governance.[27] Even as he grew circumspect of corporate economic concentration, he continued to look for solutions that would maintain corporate economic power and the general structure of U.S. corporate law. During the 1930s, his earlier arguments for shareholder primacy gave way to a commitment to technocratic economic planning by both corporations and the state that could balance the interests of competing groups. As Berle and Means argued in the last chapter of *The Modern Corporation and Private Property,* "it is conceivable,—indeed it seems almost essential if the corporate system is to survive,—that the 'control' of the great corporations should develop into a purely neutral technocracy, balancing a variety of claims by various groups in the community and assigning to each a portion of the income stream on the basis of public policy rather than private cupidity."[28] Bratton and Wachter suggest this constitutes Berle's "corporatist vision" of the economy, linking it with policies such as the National Industrial Recovery Act, which Berle helped draft.[29] Yet Berle's commitment to technocratic planning and his analogy of the corporation to the state suggested that corporations could become, like states, politically neutral economic actors. Rather than offering a progressive critique of state and corporate power or articulating an alternative vision of the economy, by the 1950s, he was arguing for a kind of joint economic governance in which "the state would join corporations and their constituents in a special regulatory apparatus" to both provide social welfare and maintain efficient production.[30]

There is without doubt a difference between Friedman's and Berle's positions on shareholder primacy, as Berle treated corporations as a uniquely socialized form of property, whereas Friedman viewed them as entities governed by iron laws of profit maximization rooted in the property rights of individual shareholders. Less commented on, however, is the problematic structuring these more progressive articulations of responsibility—a problematic, I argue, that reiterates the biopolitical logics of corporate sovereignty. Responsibility emerged as such a vexing problem for U.S. corporate law precisely because it was the hinge by which corporations have been empowered to govern, discipline, and extract value from the lives of individuals and populations under liberal forms of rule. To wit, the charters and statutes that Berle mentions in initiating his argument for shareholder primacy were always already conceptualized in terms of responsibilities, but, as narrated in chapter 1, they were the responsibilities due to the sovereign in exchange for the privileges and immunities of incorporation. As this framework was rethought within a newly emergent national system of liberal law and economy at the turn of the twentieth century, corporations remained institutions connected with governing life. Severed from public power and treated through new concepts of property and personhood, the corporate government of life was increasingly focused on its commodification, economizing existence and valuing individuals in relation to the total process of production, circulation, and consumption of commodities.

This was a biopolitical economy through and through, as the ability to put bodies to work was central to the new justifications for corporate personhood and property. One need only think of the emergence of scientific management as a tool for directing the laboring body in the industrial labor process or the concern of scientific managers with disciplinary control of the minutiae of bodily comportment and the ethnonational classifications used to organize the labor process.[31] Corporations also translated the bodies of workers into management problems, rendering the collective potentiality of humans within the language of efficiency and costs. The eminent legal philosopher Morris Cohen grasped the dramatic shift in forms of rule when he argued that, with the emergence of the corporate economy, the employer was no longer concerned with "the health and morals of his apprentice" because "the human element is thus completely subordinated to the profit motive."[32]

The trade-off for accepting the reduction of life to capitalist value was that it enabled a form of corporate property that promised to provide the material existence of daily life for the mid-twentieth-century, U.S., middle-class male stockholder, worker, and, above all, consumer. Berle and Means accepted the importance of these institutions, noting at the beginning of *The Modern Corporation and Private Property,*

> The great companies form the very framework of American
> industry. The individual must come in contact with them almost

constantly. He may own an interest in one or more of them, he may be employed by one of them, but above all he is continually accepting their service. If he travels any distance he is almost certain to ride on one of the great railroad systems. The engine which draws him has probably been constructed by the American Locomotive Company or the Baldwin Locomotive Works; the car in which he rides is likely to have been made by the American Car and Foundry Company or one of its subsidiaries, unless he is enjoying the services of the Pullman Company. The rails have almost certainly been supplied by one of the eleven steel companies on the list; and coal may well have come from one of the four coal companies, if not from a mine owned by the railroad itself. Perhaps the individual travels by automobile—in a car manufactured by the Ford, General Motors, Studebaker, or Chrylser [sic] Companies, on tires supplied by Firestone, Goodrich, Goodyear or the United States Rubber Company. He may choose among the brands of gas furnished by one of the twenty petroleum companies all actively seeking his trade. Should he pause to send a telegram or to telephone, one of the listed companies would be sure to fill his need.[33]

Berle and Means go on to describe in exhaustive detail the way large corporations, from General Electric and Westinghouse to the Radio Corporation of America and Warner Bros., shape daily existence for someone who "stays in his own home in comparative isolation and privacy" as well as for someone who "seeks amusement."[34] They also touch on the indirect ways corporations were integrated into daily life through "the production of most of the bread that the American eats, to much of the cotton he wears and to many of the other agricultural produces he consumes."[35]

In many ways, the account is similar to Justice Field's panegyric to corporate personhood in the *San Mateo* case. But unlike Justice Field's writings, Berle and Mean's were suffused with an immunitary dread in which empowering corporations led to economic concentration. This threatened, on one hand, the political subject at the center of democratic rhetoric in the United States and, on the other, the property rights so important for maintaining that subject's political and economic status and the social hierarchies of which it was a part.

It was this dread that "responsibility" was meant to abate. Responsibility reconnected the production of value in the corporation with the language of property rights that the corporate economy was, in fact, radically transforming. Distancing himself from any critique of capitalist social relations and its biopolitical logics, Berle shifted the immunitary problem without grasping its ontological root. Rather than somehow deactivating or rearticulating the link between sovereignty and capitalism in the double body of the corporation, Berle sought to fully reanimate the sovereign power at the core of corporate property, presenting first shareholders and then technocratic planners as the figures who could decide whose welfare the corporate production of value would serve.[36]

The Global Politics of Responsibility

Advocates for CSR in the United States turned to shareholder democracy and managerial discretion because of the centrality of property rights to definitions of corporations in U.S. law. Property provided a legal basis for attempting to resolve the productive capacity of corporate capitalism with social interests, desires, and wants. In the international context, there was no universal structure establishing the legal meaning, power, and responsibilities of shareholders and managers or even a single legal definition of corporate entities that could ground debates over responsibility. Concerns over corporate power at the global scale were linked with the growth of multinational corporations (MNCs) and foreign direct investment (FDI) in the late twentieth century and the unique problems MNCs posed for nation-states—particularly developing states—and national markets. As corporate activities increasingly spanned multiple political jurisdictions, involving complex interrelations between parent and subsidiary companies, they were (and continue to be) perceived as difficult to control through political institutions. Consequently, the initial attempts to make corporations behave responsibly focused on the creation of transnational codes of conduct.

As with many aspects in the genealogy I have been charting, the rise, fall, and transformation of transnational codes of corporate conduct is well documented. It is narrated as a shift from "code to compact," a story that begins with the global economic crisis of the 1970s.[37] The decades following World War II saw the emergence of an international capitalist political economy based on U.S. political hegemony and the United States' support for economic internationalism. Agnew and Corbridge have usefully termed this the "liberal international order," noting that it was a geopolitical configuration that assumed a "transcendental identity between the American and world economy. The expansion of one was seen as good for the other."[38] This order was anchored in the growth and development of U.S. military power but was also institutionalized in postwar global economic and political governance through the UN, the International

Monetary Fund, and the International Bank for Reconstruction and Development (later to become the World Bank). FDI by corporations was also vital. As John Dunning noted, "the thirty-five years since the end of the Second World War have been ones of almost uninterrupted growth" in FDI, with investment originating from U.S.-headquartered firms alone rising from 7.3 billion dollars in 1938 to 162.8 billion dollars in 1978, a more than twentyfold increase.[39]

By the 1970s, however, the system was beginning to fray from both tensions internal to that model of capitalist accumulation and new political and economic challenges. Here, too, the international investment decisions of corporations were critical. For instance, in the United States, the growth of FDI by U.S. firms undercut the socioeconomic relations that anchored mid-twentieth-century U.S. economic growth. As Agnew and Corbridge argue, "by the late 1960s, as domestic technology and management followed capital abroad, traditional exports were replaced by the foreign production of US affiliates to the detriment of employment in the United States. American mass consumption was no longer fully supported by the relatively high wages of its workers in mass production."[40] This change was expressed geographically. In the early twentieth century, U.S. and Western European firms invested in the developing world to control primary commodities. Post–World War II FDI was increasingly concentrated between advanced capitalist states, along with the development of significant flows of outward FDI emerging from Japan and newly industrialized countries in Asia by the 1960s.[41] The macroeconomic changes were thus potentially unsettling for workers and industries in both home and host countries of MNCs as well as for industrialized and developing states. In addition, these changes occurred at the same time that MNCs were coming under political pressure for a number of high-profile scandals. Chief among these was the role of the International Telegraph and Telephone Corporation, working in conjunction with the U.S. Central Intelligence Agency, in overthrowing the democratically elected Allende government in Chile.[42] Within this tumultuous context, national governments and international institutions began to investigate the political and economic impacts of MNCs and FDI from a variety of angles. In the United States, hearings were held in both Congress and the Securities and Exchange Commission, but considering the international scope of the corporate economy, the UN became an important venue for discussing and potentially regulating transnational corporations.[43]

Even before the 1970s, the UN had a history of taking up questions of international business regulation. As early as 1948, the UN addressed restrictive business practices in the Havana Charter for an International

Trade Organization, an issue that was subsequently addressed by the UN Economic and Social Council (ECOSOC) and the UN Conference on Trade and Development (UNCTAD).[44] In July 1972, in response to complaints from the Chilean delegation, ECOSOC passed resolution 1721(LIII), which authorized the secretary-general to appoint a Group of Eminent Persons (GEP) "to study the role of multinational corporations and their impact on the process of development, especially that of developing countries, and also their implications for international relations."[45] The secretary-general appointed twenty men to the panel, with backgrounds in government, academics, banking, and industry. Geographically, representatives hailed from both advanced industrial and developing countries, with more limited representation from the Soviet bloc.[46] To help the GEP with its deliberations, the UN Department of Economic and Social Affairs published a report, titled *Multinational Corporations in World Development,* that provided data on the activities of transnational corporations (TNCs) and set the initial framework for the GEP's analysis. During fall 1973, the GEP held hearings in both New York City and Geneva, where policy makers, academics, representatives from business, and political advocates (including those critical of MNCs) expressed their views on corporate regulation. This process resulted in a second publication, *The Impact of Multinational Corporations on Development and on International Relations,* which included policy recommendations. The primary request was for the creation of a commission on TNCs (later formed as the UN Commission on Transnational Corporations, or UNCTC) that could inform policy as well as a permanent research, information, and data collection organization (the UN Centre on Transnational Corporations) to empirically study the issue. A secondary recommendation was for the establishment of a code of conduct, but the content, legal status, applicability, and enforceability of such a code remained ambiguous in the 1974 report.[47]

Scholars have presented the code of conduct as emerging from the demands of developing states, which, during the 1970s, were becoming increasingly powerful at the UN.[48] Through the establishment of the Group of 77 (G-77) at the UNCTAD meeting in 1964, the resolution for the creation of a New International Economic Order (NIEO) at the Sixth Special Session of the UN in 1974, and the establishment of the Charter on the Economic Rights and Duties of States (CERDS) passed that same year, developing countries advanced a series of arguments about the importance of national sovereignty for developing states in international economic affairs and the need for redistributive policies to redress colonial exploitation. As Jennifer Bair has persuasively argued, these actions by the G-77 "sought to make explicit the link between political freedom and economic independence, arguing that the anti-colonial struggle would continue until the sovereignty of Third World states over their national economies was realized."[49] The agenda of the G-77 and the vision of a redistributive NIEO fundamentally shaped the discussion of corporations at the UN in the 1970s. Indeed, the report of the first session of the Commission on TNCs opened by situating the actions of the commission within the framework of the NIEO resolutions and the CERDS.[50] Discussion of the potential regulations was also shaped by the model of the Andean Pact, whose Rule 24 represented "the most far-reaching measures" for protecting host countries from the actions of foreign firms.[51] José Campillo Sáinz, undersecretary for industry and commerce of Mexico, asserted Mexico's support for a code of conduct that would complement CERDS.[52] Furthermore, during the first meeting of the commission, Argentina, Barbados, Brazil, Colombia, Ecuador, Jamaica, Mexico, Peru, Trinidad and Tobago, and Venezuela submitted a paper to serve as a "basis for preliminary work for a code of conduct to be observed by transnational corporations."[53]

Such support for legal codes could break in multiple ways. Although developing states advocated for legally binding codes on MNCs that respected host country sovereignty and economic priorities, others more favorable to MNCs saw the code as a vehicle for creating legally binding obligations for states about the treatment of business in their countries. During the GEP hearings, Gilbert Jones and Jacques Maisonrouge, on behalf of IBM, noted the difficulty in producing a commonly agreed on and legally enforceable code but nonetheless supported the effort. They advocated for a code that could guide both firms and countries on issues of employment, stock ownership, transfer pricing, and "the judgment of a company's performance, particularly in a developing country ... in the area of social responsibility."[54] Irving Shapiro of DuPont suggested that "a common code of behaviour for multinational—and, for that matter, national—business would be a logical and constructive step so long as it was accompanied by parallel standards for other parties to the arrangements—Government and labor."[55] And Thomas Murphy, vice-chairman of the board for GM, suggested that a code might function similarly to the recently agreed on General Agreement on Tariffs and Trade, as "a companion agreement—a General Agreement on Investment."[56] Even the International Chamber of Commerce (ICC) "welcomed" a code of conduct, humbly offering its own guidelines as a model and "probably the only existing comprehensive series of proposals in this area."[57]

The annual reports submitted by the commission to ECOSOC between 1975 and 1994, along with Centre on Transnational Corporations publications specifically addressing codes of conduct in 1976, 1986, and 1990, attest to the difficulties in generating a code.[58] From the outset, there were significant conflicts over the method for establishing a code, its specific content, the legal or voluntary status of its provisions, and its applicability to both states and corporations, yet the reports consistently stressed the unanimous support for the formulation of a code and the expectations of its immanent completion.[59] In 1976, the commission established an intergovernmental working group to lead the effort.[60] The working group reported on the growing points of agreement in the formulation of a draft code, but during the late 1970s, nationalization; respect of the economic sovereignty of developing countries; the relation between the code, the NIEO, and CERDS; and changes in the global economy reemerged as points of contention within the commission reports.[61] By the early 1980s, the draft code was almost finished. Sten Niklasson, the chairman of the working group, reported in 1982 that two-thirds of the code was agreed on and stated that "the areas of serious difficulty were few—approximately five or six."[62] A full draft of a code was presented to ECOSOC in 1983, although no final resolution was made.[63] In a retrospective assessment of the negotiations, the UNCTC reported agreement on a wide range of issues, including "TNC adherence to the development goals of host countries; observance of domestic laws of host countries; respect for fundamental human rights; adherence to socio-cultural objectives and values; abstention from corrupt practices; co-operation among entities of a TNC to meet their responsibilities in their host country; promotion of exports and imports; avoidance of restrictive business practices; consumer and environmental protection; disclosure of information on TNC structure, policies and activities; and observance of fair employment and labour practices."[64]

Nevertheless, by the late 1980s, negotiations stalled irreversibly. Reports continued to indicate broad support for a code in the abstract, but tensions remained, particularly over the status of the code as international law and the ability of a single code to deal with the complexity and dynamism of global economic relations.[65] In 1992, at the Forty-sixth Session of the General Assembly, the ECOSOC report argued that "no consensus was possible on the draft code at present" and suspended negotiations.[66] The next year, the information-gathering functions of UNCTC were transferred to UNCTAD's Division on Information, Technology, and Enterprise Development. Business scholar Sagafi-nejad has argued that the conflict over the code was "the lightning rod" precipitating the move and reorganization of the UNCTC, thus linking the failures of the code to "radicalism" associated with the history of North–South conflicts at the UN and the intransigence of the United States to the UNCTC.[67] A similar sentiment was expressed in the 1990 UNCTC report, *The New Code Environment*, which argued that restarting negotiations required the abandonment of the "heavy emotional baggage of early controversies" and a turn from "conflict to co-operation."[68] Capturing the mood with respect to the code of conduct, the report from the seventeenth session of the UNCTC in 1991 noted that "one delegation expressed the view that the tone and approach of the draft code belonged to an era when many host Governments mistrusted transnational corporations and sought to limit foreign investment flows."[69] The statement also reflected the different economic circumstances of the era, in which many developing states were actively seeking FDI as a path to economic development.[70]

By the late 1990s, the UN renewed a commitment to a code of corporate conduct in the guise of the UN GC, encouraging business leaders to participate in ten principles based on "universal consensus" in areas of human rights, labor standards, environment, and anticorruption. The principles, in turn, derived from existing international agreements, including the Universal Declaration of Human Rights, the International Labor Organization's (ILO) Declaration on Fundamental Principles and Rights at Work, and the Rio Declaration on Environment and Development.[71] UN secretary-general Kofi Annan announced the initiative to global elites at the World Economic Forum in Davos, Switzerland, in 1999, emphasizing that the GC was designed to save the "vulnerable" global economy from the "backlash from all the 'isms' of our post-cold-war world: protectionism; populism; nationalism; ethnic chauvinism; fanaticism; and terrorism."[72] Thus the compact from its inception was not meant to radically alter global economic relations but rather to "find a way of embedding the global market in a network of shared values."[73] Annan presented the compact as a choice between "a global market driven only by calculations of short-term profit, and one with a human face."[74] Moreover, this language of choice has been central to drawing a distinction between the conflicts surrounding the first code under the auspices of the UNCTC and the voluntarism of the GC.

Voluntarism is also at the core of apprehensions that the GC lacks the power to compel good corporate behavior. This concern has been exacerbated by the treatment of human rights obligations for transnational corporations at the UN generally and under the GC specifically. International human rights law has had difficulties addressing violations committed by corporations because the human rights regime that developed through the twentieth century primarily aimed to protect people against states. Owing to the centrality of corporations in managing economic and social life, the UN Commission on Human Rights began to consider the human rights responsibilities of transnational corporations through the creation of a working group in 1998. Between 1999 and 2003, the same years during which the GC was coming to fruition, the working group was crafting a Draft Code of Conduct for Companies that, by 2003, had emerged as the Norms on the Responsibilities of Transnational Corporations and Other Business Enterprises with Regard to Human Rights, or more simply, the UN Norms.[75] The Norms analogized corporations to states and sought to hold corporations accountable for human rights violations as "the most powerful nonstate actors in the world." Although recognizing that many corporations conformed to international standards, the Norms targeted companies and businesses "implicated in abuses such as employing child laborers, discriminating against certain groups of employees, failing to provide safe and healthy working conditions, attempting to repress independent trade unions, discouraging the right to bargain collectively, limiting the broad dissemination of appropriate technology and intellectual property, and dumping toxic wastes."[76] Situating the Norms in the lineage of the failed UNCTC code effort as well as the successful 1976 Organization for Economic Co-operation and Development's Guidelines for Multinational Enterprises and the ILO's 1978 Tripartite Declarations of Principles Concerning Multinational Enterprises, David Weissbrodt, a member of the working group, and Muria Kruger presented the Norms as the "first nonvoluntary initiative accepted at the international level."[77]

Clearly the genesis and content of the Norms reflected the notion that corporations pose specific threats to public welfare that require not only the action of individual states but international law and governance as well. As with much of the discussion of transnational corporations at the UN, the response to the Norms was mixed, with human rights advocates, primarily represented by nongovernmental organizations, supporting the document and business interests, such as the ICC, opposed.[78] In 2005, the secretary-general appointed noted international relations scholar John Ruggie as a special representative (SRSG) to study the existing obligations of TNCs under international human rights law, develop methods for conducting "impact assessments" of TNCs' human rights activities, and "compile a compendium of best practices of States and Corporations."[79] The connections between the SRSG and the GC were clear. Between 1997 and 2001, Ruggie served as UN assistant secretary-general for strategic planning, playing an important role in initiating the GC.[80] Moreover, the resolution creating the SRSG instructed the office to work closely with the special adviser to the secretary-general for the GC, in addition to a wide variety of governmental and civil society groups, including states, employers, workers, and indigenous communities. Although Ruggie indicated that groups like Amnesty International and Human Rights Watch encouraged him to "endorse" or "build upon" the Norms, he ultimately decided not to, abandoning the Norms as a mandate for the SRSG's activities.[81]

In making his case against the Norms, Ruggie provided a wide-ranging critique. Similar to the earlier code debates at UNCTC, Ruggie focused on problems with the definition of transnational corporations used in the Norms and the attribution of human rights obligations to TNCs within their "spheres of influence."[82] Finding that term ill-defined, Ruggie argued that there was no way to clearly distinguish the responsibilities of TNCs from those of states, and thus the Norms, if enacted, would lead to "endless strategic gaming and legal wrangling on the part of governments and companies alike."[83] In addition, the emphasis on direct obligations for corporations might limit or conflict with state enforcement of human rights, given that states rather than corporations have the primary duty to protect individuals under international law. The loose definitions of the Norms could potentially exacerbate the complexity of international human rights law, which he characterized as a "fluid area, but one in which significant protection gaps remain."[84] For Ruggie, closing the gaps meant building up the institutional capacity of states to effectively enforce human rights law. Thus, instead of holding TNCs directly responsible for human rights obligations, Ruggie advocated "expand[ing] the international regime horizontally, by further clarifying and progressively codifying the duties of states to protect human rights against corporate violations: individually, as [sic] home as well as host states, and collectively through the 'international cooperation' requirement of several UN human rights treaties."[85] Finally, Ruggie argued that increasing the ability of states to make corporations accountable for their human rights violations required "soft law hybrid arrangements" as well as many strategies that "lie beyond the legal sphere altogether."[86] By moving beyond a focus on simple legal compliance or on legal liability, Ruggie hoped to foster a wider capacity for governing companies in the sphere of human rights law.

Reiterating Responsibility

Considering the institutional resistance to formal legal strategies at the UN, it is understandable that critical scholars have focused on legal enforceability as central to the creation of an effective global corporate social responsibility regime. Weissbrodt, responding to Ruggie's criticism, made the case that compulsory rules were necessary to guide global business practices. "Beyond the voluntary human rights principles that the SRSG prefers, however, there is a tremendous demand in civil society for a comprehensive set of standards governing the conduct of international business, which go beyond voluntary codes of conduct like the Global Compact."[87] More critically, political scientist Susanne Soederberg has argued,

> The intended effect [of the GC] is not only to legitimize market-led, voluntary forms of CSR as the only viable alternative, thereby discrediting alternative forms of governing corporations primarily through regulatory standards, but also to promote the common-sense understanding that states and societies should seek to enter a compromise with TNCs—witnessed by Ruggie's insistence . . . that social actors strive to graft their pursuit of broader social agendas onto the "global reach and capacity" of corporations. The point that Ruggie, like many mainstream global governance theorists, tends to ignore is that the "global reach and capacity" of corporations is not a natural occurrence driven by the unstoppable forces of globalization, but instead a social construct authored and legitimated by bourgeois states across the globe to serve particular class interests.[88]

This argument, however, raises questions that require careful consideration. If, as Soederberg correctly suggests, the capacities of corporations are produced and legitimated by bourgeois states in service to class interests, what is there to suggest that "governing corporations by regulatory standards" is not only distinct from but a radical alternative to bourgeois law? To put it another way, if the power of corporations has been created through legally authorized exemptions, privileges, and immunities (as this genealogy has attempted to demonstrate), what sense do we have that legally enforceable codes constitute a decisive break from corporate power? Why make legal enforceability contra voluntarism the object of struggle when both have proven effective at consolidating the corporate government of and reduction of life toward capitalist value?

As these questions indicate, the argument reaches a troubling limit. Even the most far-reaching propositions for legally binding codes—by the G-77 in the UNCTC debates of the 1970s or, more recently, in the UN Norms—failed to break with the doubling that characterizes corporate sovereignty. In fact, these codes were written within its topology. To be sure, the NIEO and CERDS offered a political critique of the existing international economic order from the perspective of decolonized states. But the strategy of pursuing codes of conduct, while associated with that critique, could not challenge the viability of capitalism, corporate or otherwise; rather it demanded a different model of capitalist development based on the economic sovereignty of developing states. As Bair points out, "the Code of Conduct, and the broader NIEO agenda of which it was part, was an effort by the G-77 to define development as the politics of recognition and redistribution."[89] This is not to suggest that the broader oppositional politics of developing states in the 1970s did not have the potential to proliferate new "regulatory ideals about a 'better life' (or freedoms) within specific time-space contexts," which might continue to truck under the "placeholder" of "development."[90] But it does mean that the particular strategy of legal codification of rules for TNCs at the UN was an effort to institutionalize at the international level the regime that Joel Wainwright has described as "capitalism qua development."[91] Although both attempts to produce legal codes for TNCs in the 1970s and the 2000s ultimately foundered, there were significant areas of agreement across the participants involved in these efforts, including representatives of TNCs and capitalist states, that legal codes could be useful. By the 1970s and 1980s, advanced capitalist states experiencing deindustrialization and capital flight were becoming equally concerned about the regulation of TNCs. As international legal scholars such as S. K. Chatterjee have argued in making the case for supporting CERDS, much of the content of the charter and the NIEO "reiterated a number of established principles of international trade, commerce and economic relations generally."[92] Similarly, the UN draft Norms went far beyond the GC in establishing direct obligations for corporations under international law. Even though they have not been enacted, the UN Norms continue to provide another avenue for arguments seeking legal redress for corporate abuses. We should also recognize, however, the ways the Norms codify rather than challenge the corporate government of life by making corporations, no less than states, responsible for enforcement.[93]

Thus we can interpret debates over global codes of conduct as depoliticizing not because they opted for voluntary as opposed to legal mechanisms of enforcement but because they are framed in a way in which the distinction between voluntarism and legal enforcement becomes the paramount question for transformative political projects. This is true of the advocates for the GC, who tout voluntarism as the key to effective regulation, but it is also true of the critics who hold out legal enforcement as a radical alternative. This preoccupation with law connects the discussions of responsibility through international codes with the U.S. legal discussions on CSR that look to property law as a foundation for realigning corporate and social interests. In both the United States and the global context, responsibility names the attempt to bring the power, rights, privileges, and immunities of corporations within a constituted political order, not by eliminating them, but by accommodating them, making their power over life and death tolerable. For Berle, Dodd, and the UN Norms, this means laying bare the sovereignty over life that corporations effectively exercise and attempting to find various legal mechanisms to both maintain and circumscribe that power. For the G-77 and, in a different way, Ruggie, Annan, and other supporters of the GC, it means reaffirming the sovereignty of states up to and including the power to maintain corporate privileges and immunities in the name of state power. Either way, responsibility, in these formulations, redounds to sovereign power.

There are other alternatives. We can find a different iteration of responsibility by following Ruggie's invocation of the work of noted political theorist Iris Marion Young in his defense of the GC. In the early 2000s, Young began to systematically address responsibility as an outgrowth of her long-standing interest in social justice. Writing in response to a series of events, including the September 11 attacks on the World Trade Center and the Pentagon, the U.S. wars in Iraq and Afghanistan, and inequalities associated with and exacerbated by contemporary economic globalization, Young posed the question of what responsibilities people have to others in a globalized world.[94] Young began by challenging the concept of personal responsibility, which seeks to hold individuals alone responsible for their own actions. Showing how proponents of neoliberalism have elevated personal responsibility into the governing logic of contemporary policy, Young faulted advocates of personal responsibility for failing to grapple with the structural causes of injustice. In particular, Young reserved the term *responsibility* for structural problems, distinguishing it from *liability, fault,* or *guilt,* terms most often associated with personal culpability.

The problem for Young was that liability and guilt are legal and moral concepts that require demonstrating causal connections between the person assigned responsibility and the events or actions for which she is being held responsible. Although Young argued that there are cases in which legal liability should be pursued—her example is the owner or manager of a factory violating local labor laws[95]—liability differs from political responsibility in important respects. The first difference is the aforementioned distinction between personal and political responsibility. Liability references legal individuals (including corporations), but Young also noted that this serves to single out bad actors while exculpating the structural conditions producing injustice. Yet structural injustice, by its nature, involves diffuse social practices reproduced by myriad individuals following what are defined as "normal" social protocols. Young thus argued, "While it is usually inappropriate to *blame* those agents who are connected to but removed from the harm, it is also inappropriate ... to allow them (us) to say that they (we) have nothing to do with it."[96]

In response, Young advocated for a *social connection* model of political responsibility. This model implies relations of responsibility on individuals who participate in structures that produce unjust outcomes, or as Young put it, "all who dwell within the structures must take responsibility for remedying injustices they cause, though none is specifically liable for the harm in a legal sense."[97] Young went on to outline five features of the social connection model: it "does not isolate perpetrators. It brings background conditions under evaluation. Its main purpose for assigning responsibility is forward looking. Responsibility under the social connection model is essentially shared. It can therefore be discharged only through collective action."[98] She also identified a practical example of a global political project that conceptualizes responsibility in these terms through the global antisweatshop movement. Young found promise in the ways activists connected spatially diffuse consumers and retailers with the conditions of production in sweatshops. And unlike theorists who ground political responsibility in national communities, Young emphasized that because the economic structures producing injustice are today global, so, too, is the responsibility that such injustices compel.

Ruggie invoked Young's argument against liability as a justification for "soft law" approaches to the role of transnational corporations in securing human rights. His misreading is highly self-serving, rationalizing the GC's relatively toothless vision of CSR and evacuating much of Young's trenchant criticism about the structural production of global inequality and injustice—the very unequal structure that the GC maintains and attempts to legitimate. But Young was not criticizing legal codes in favor of voluntarism; rather she was critiquing legal liability for taking individuals rather than the structures themselves as the subjects of justice. This difference is even more clearly expressed in Hannah Arendt's formulation of political responsibility, on which much of Young's theory is based. For Arendt, political responsibility was grounded in collective political life based on two conditions: "I must be held responsible for something I have not done, and the reason for my responsibility must be my membership in a group (a collective) which no voluntary act of mine can dissolve."[99] In this way, Arendt clarified the distinction between the personal and private moral and legal relations of guilt and the public and political concept of responsibility. For Arendt, who always sought to maintain the specificity of politics as a realm of collective action, the blurring of public responsibility with personal guilt threatened to debase political claims for justice with private resentments.[100] In an account that echoes Nietzsche's discussion

in *On the Genealogy of Morals*, Arendt locates the blurring between guilt
and responsibility in the shift away from the ancient Greek and Roman
treatment of ethics and morals as a discourse on the conduct of citizens
in public. In particular, Arendt notes that "with the rise of Christianity,
the emphasis shifted entirely from care for the world and the duties connected with it to care for the soul and its salvation."[101] But the private
responsibility one had toward the salvation of souls was grounded in
transcendental religious truths. "The rules were *absolute* because of their
divine origin, and their sanctions consisted in 'future rewards and punishments.'"[102] Arendt sought to restore a properly political conception of
responsibility because divinely ordained moral and ethical rules for the
salvation of souls are inadequate for responding to the world in a desa-
cralized age. As she argued, "in the center of political considerations of
conduct stands the world."[103] Arendt compels us to take up politics as a
way of excising the political theology that undergirds modern legal thinking about guilt and responsibility.

Responsibility to the Vicariously Innocent

To what ends is a politically responsible engagement with the world directed? Much of Arendt's argument links responsibility to national collectivities, a relation that Young is at pains to break. Moreover, because
everyone lives within society, Arendt sees that living in the world—by definition—imposes responsibilities: "we can escape this political and strictly
collective responsibility only by leaving the community, and since no man
can live without belonging to some community, this would simply mean to
exchange one community for another and hence one kind of responsibility
for another."[104] It is our position in social life that gives us our responsibility. But a paradox emerges. As Arendt noted, the world has its "refugees and
stateless people." "It is true that the twentieth century created a category of
men who were truly outcasts," she wrote, "belonging to no recognizable
community whatever ... who indeed can not be held politically responsible
for anything. Politically, regardless of their group or individual character,
they are the absolutely innocent ones; and it is precisely this absolute inno-
cence that condemns them to a position outside, as it were, of mankind as
a whole."[105] Presumably, given Arendt's own interests in the assessment of
guilt and responsibility in relation to these very same stateless people and
refugees, political responsibility requires finding some way of attending to
these individuals. But Arendt gave little direction into how a responsibility
to this "category of men" might look, given that responsibility is connected
precisely to the collectivities from which these individuals are excluded.

For this reason, I conclude this chapter with one other formulation of responsibility. Though less philosophically rigorous than the arguments of Young and Arendt, it has direct resonance with the questions at hand. In November 1973, at the second session of UN hearings on multinational corporations, the GEP invited radical political economist Stephen Hymer to comment. Hymer's statement to the committee began by admitting how differently he viewed questions concerning MNCs in international relations and development from the approach taken at the UN. "It is an honour to be able to address you," he began, "although I must confess that I am not exactly sure what I can say that might be of any use to you."[106] Hymer's disagreement stemmed from the way the first UN report, *Multinational Corporations in World Development,* framed its questions, focusing on "ways to minimize abuses while maintaining the flow of private foreign investment."[107] He characterized this as a "limited approach" that was "myopic" in simply accepting "the current structure of the world economy as given and concentrat[ing] on how life could be made easier within it."[108] Instead, Hymer stressed the inability of private multinational capitalism to provide a world of peace and prosperity and offered an alternative socialist model of socioeconomic organization.

Given that the statement was made in 1973, his analysis of the problems with multinational capital was quite prescient. In particular, Hymer focused on two processes of division associated with global capitalism: one that occurs within the corporation and another that occurs in the world. The first concerned the divisions of labor within firms, "between capital and labour, between management and operations, between the head and the hand."[109] Hymer argued that corporations function by separating production from planning within the vertical structures of companies so that a worker at the bottom "supervises a few people, remains rooted in one spot, and deals with narrow specialties," whereas those at the top control "tens or hundreds of millions, the time horizon covers decades, and vision covers the world."[110] This vertical division in the firm also gets translated into spatial divisions in the landscape, in a "spatial distribution of employment and earnings."[111] Deploying the Marxist concept of uneven development, Hymer argued that economic control becomes spatially concentrated in large cities. This produces what Hymer called a "world hierarchy of cities," in which the vertical divisions between planning, management, and production within the corporation are translated into uneven relations between places. World cities become centers of high-level planning, negotiations with government and media, and finance, whereas more peripheral locations become centers of daily management and work. In this way, "this imperialistic tendency of multinational corporations is a geographical reflection of the hierarchical and authoritarian structure of corporate organization."[112]

Hymer's theory of uneven development was part of the early work on spatial divisions of labor that radically transformed the field of economic geography in the 1970s and 1980s. Subsequent industrial and corporate geographers have continued to develop his insights on the spatial dynamics of MNCs, and his arguments about economic centralization prefigure much later research on global cities.[113] More interesting for my purpose is the alternative Hymer offered in his oral statement. There Hymer distinguished his vision of the global economic order from that which characterized debates at the UN, including a trenchant critique of capitalism as development. "What I should like to see is a study made in which the goals for the developing countries are changed, and the goal does not become development, a very ill-defined policy which in fact over the last 25 years has meant integration into the world economy, but rather the removal of misery. We talk, maybe not of developing countries or underdeveloped countries, or less developed countries, but of the miserable sectors in the world population." Clarifying what responsibility to the "miserable sectors" entails, Hymer continued, "We would all agree, for example, that penicillin would have to be made available on a very wide-scale basis so that everybody in the world should have access to this and other necessary drugs. We would also have ideas on minimum standards of food, clothing, housing and communications which we agree would give everybody a basic standard of living and get them out of the sea of misery."[114] Providing such basic goods would require little assistance from multinational corporations, as "the multinational corporation's strength does not lie in basic goods for minimum standards of living, but rather lies usually in very highly advanced products for the consumption of the middle class and the upper middle class."[115] Moreover, it would have little to do with the global capitalist system that the UN negotiations attempted to preserve. Thus the UN discussion

> does not give us such a report or such a knowledge of what are
> the possibilities of attacking misery. The multinational corporation
> and the system that is envisaged in this report gives us the
> possibility of spreading industry at a fairly rapid rate to the under-
> developed countries to take advantage of cheap labour.... But
> we know that the process of industrialization... based on cheap
> labour, is one which is accompanied by a great increase in
> misery not a decrease. A certain group, a small element of the
> population—perhaps 5 or 10 per cent—who become employed

in the modern sector have their standards of living improved. But the rural areas deteriorate and the city fills up with large numbers of people who are under-employed and live in a very deprived state.[116]

Hymer's statement rejects the problematic structuring the other discussions of responsibility. His is not an immunitary politics in which we empower corporations by delimiting the precise ways their exploitation can ensure our salvation through legal or voluntary codes. Hymer is not interested in meting out toxic dosages. His position, rather, is what we might call, following Roberto Esposito, an affirmative biopolitics aimed at proliferating the possibilities and capacities of human bodies. In particular, Hymer focuses on those figures that are continually ascribed within capitalism as being devoid of value—not the small group that gets at least temporary employment through the continual process of investment but the "miserable sectors" who are included within capitalist development only inasmuch as they are disused and inoperative. Discussions of corporate responsibility focused on making corporations accountable—to shareholders, managers, stakeholders, citizens, state sovereignty, legally enforceable codes, or even international human rights—have no way of addressing the miserable sectors, except through corporate sovereignty's own logic of capitalist development, in which corporations govern life toward the production of capitalist value. These miserable sectors constitute the "category of men" Arendt calls the vicariously innocent and that Agamben examines as *homo sacer*. Attentiveness to this figure is the essential starting point for taking political responsibility to the world.

CHAPTER SIX

The Corporate University

The preceding chapters have argued that corporate power and political sovereignty are genealogically linked and therefore unintelligible without one another, and they have explained the political implications that follow from such an argument. In particular, I have set out to demonstrate that the problem of sovereign abandonment reappears not only through the exercise of corporate power but even, and more alarmingly, in some of the best attempts to limit corporate power and redirect corporations toward more socially beneficial ends. Readers might understandably take from this the politically paralyzing notion that corporations or corporate power are somehow impervious to social control, destined to regulate life itself in particularly nefarious ways. In truth, my argument runs precisely in the other direction. Approaching corporate power genealogically shows the true *tragedy* of corporate sovereignty[1]—a tragedy inherent in the double nature of corporations as collective institutions. Although corporations continually pose questions about being in common and political autonomy, these potentialities are for the most part unrealized in the particular renderings of corporate power in modern Western political and legal thought. Nonetheless, the problems of collective action and autonomy remain internal to the articulation of sovereignty and capitalism that structures corporate institutions.

In this final chapter, I would like to show the *nonnecessity* of this articulation by thinking through one specific issue: the corporate university. As an academic who has spent a large portion of my life institutionalized, so to speak, in the university, current questions about the social functions and governance of universities play an outsized role in my own concerns. The claim, however, that universities are ivory towers and that what happens in these institutions is only of narrow academic interest fails to grapple with the important role of universities in contemporary political economy.[2] Regional scientists and planners have examined the roles of universities in the development of regional innovation centers, such as Silicon Valley and the Route 128 corridor in Massachusetts, which are presented as the leading edge of today's "knowledge economy."[3] Similarly, the creation of higher education markets, transnational research collaborations, and the importing and exporting of researchers, students, and physical university assets have become important avenues by which states promote and profit from foreign direct investment.[4] Scholars have also documented the use of university-led development as a strategy for industrializing states in the context of contemporary globalization.[5] In the United States, public research institutions, cognizant of these changes, justify public support in the language of jobs and economic growth, while also attempting to profit from university research, on one hand, and increasing tuition, on the other.[6] Students are well aware that academic credentials are a necessary precondition for entering global labor markets and are taking on unprecedented levels of indebtedness toward that end.[7] Meanwhile, the sectors of for-profit and online universities are rapidly expanding, with even worse results for student finances.[8] In response, universities are re-emerging as one of the primary locations for political activism and opposition, as these transformations, along with more localized policies such as department closings, labor struggles, and fee increases and tuition hikes, have set off protests at universities across the United States but also in many other parts of the world.[9]

Contrary to the ivory tower image, then, universities already are an integral part of the world and central to new circuits of capital accumulation. Yet the connections between universities and contemporary global political economy have many activists and scholars concerned. A growing chorus has come to fret about the corporatization of the university. Rather than being a clearly articulated concept, the corporate university stands in with a series of other terms—including the neoliberal university, the military–industrial–academic complex, knowledge factories, academic capitalism, diploma mills, and the commodification or commercialization of higher education—for the ways that universities and the business world bleed into one another.[10] In this sense, identifying the troubling changes confronting higher education as *corporatization* is accurate but also leaves underexamined the question of what corporatization actually entails. The great irony of contemporary discussions on the corporate university is that universities have always been corporations. In fact, universities are one of the primary institutions on which the legal form of incorporation is modeled. This includes not only the power of collective representation for aggregate forms of capital that characterizes modern business corporations, along with many aspects of the contemporary university, but, more important, the claims to autonomy and freedom that make corporations so troubling for constituted political orders.

There are thus vital stakes in how we think about and engage the corporate university. This chapter offers a response to corporatization that is quite different from the current talk of "dismantling" these institutions.[11] The first section begins by reviewing the structural transformations commonly referred to as the corporatization of the university. This is a large and ever-growing literature, and the central concept of "corporatization" remains somewhat ill defined. My purpose is not to provide an exhaustive empirical account of the changes across a wide variety of institutions of higher learning in different geographic settings but rather to provide a general overview of the concerns critics have associated with the corporatization of the university. Scholars have argued that corporatization is changing the institutional *practices* of universities as well as the *content* of university teaching and research. One of the notable aspects of these arguments is the way they have congealed into an interdisciplinary discussion, if not a full-blown field, of "critical university studies."[12] The second section examines the way that the corporate university and corporatization are constructed as objects of disciplinary reflection in this emergent field and advocates a different way of approaching research, thinking, and reading about the corporate university that is not interdisciplinary as much as it is antidisciplinary.

The third section considers the corporate university from an antidisciplinary perspective by examining two texts: a pamphlet written by the noted medievalist Ernst Kantorowicz (who we met in chapter 1), titled *The Fundamental Issue,* and Ernst Freund's short 1897 text (which we encountered in chapter 3), *The Legal Nature of Corporations.* Although there are many troublesome arguments in both of these documents, I suggest that they allow us to envision an alterative formulation of the corporate university, one that is oriented not around an anticorporate capitalism (which maintains the production of capitalist value while lashing out at the corporate legal form) or a corporate anticapitalism (in which global businesses market to consumers reified inversions of their revolutionary desires) but rather an anticapitalist corporatism, where corporatism stands for an autonomous politics of being in common.[13]

The Corporate University

The corporate university thesis is an account of economic restructuring. Although critics note long-standing concerns about the influence of business in university education (dating back at least to Thorstein Veblen's

1918 tract *The Higher Learning in America*), they equate the corporatization of the university with a series of macroeconomic, institutional, and ideological shifts that began in the 1970s and 1980s, primarily in U.S. public universities and, to a lesser extent, at other institutions of higher education in the Anglophone world. At its heart, then, corporatization is an Anglo-American story, with U.S. public institutions at its center. Recognizing this specificity is important, as there are certainly other dynamics reshaping universities beyond U.S. political borders or even the U.S. sphere of influence. Nevertheless, critics also suggest that the corporatization of the university, if not a global process, at least has global relevance, as the U.S. model of higher education has been exported abroad in conjunction with economic globalization, and many states now view the tertiary education sector entrepreneurially, as a critical component of national, regional, and urban development. In this way, corporatization of the university mirrors the corporate legal form itself, which came to dominate business organization in the United States and England before becoming a more globally available institutional form put to different historical and geographical uses.

The narrative of university restructuring begins with the broader transformation from Fordist industrial development and social regulation to neoliberal globalization.[14] Scholars, however, pay far less attention to what the university was like in the heyday of mid-twentieth-century Fordism, as the narrative depends on establishing a dramatic rupture between past and present. This transition has been variously characterized as a "wholesale culture shift [that] is transforming everything from the way universities educate their students to the language they use to define what they do" or as a "sweeping set of economically driven changes steadily transforming academic institutions around the world from the 1980s onwards."[15] On this read, the post–World War II increases in public spending on higher education were part of the commitment by advanced industrial states to social reproduction and welfare. In the U.S. case, the state (both the federal government and individual states) supported university research, particularly research in the sciences that promised technological and military applications, but also broadened access to higher education through programs such as the 1944 Servicemen's Readjustment Act (the GI Bill). Thomas Bender has argued that "it is difficult today to grasp the magnitude of the infusion of new funds into the university, especially the most select research universities, in the quarter-century following World War II" and notes that government funding for higher education in the United States rose from 2.2 billion dollars in 1950 to 23.4 billion dollars in 1970.[16]

The commitment of the state to university research and education shaped scholarly work in a number of academic disciplines. Postwar state funding was instrumental in the development of large scientific projects, such as the Manhattan Project and the Radiation Lab at the Massachusetts Institute of Technology, many of which incorporated university research directly into the activities of government agencies.[17] The funding of basic science was deeply connected with the development of weapons for the Cold War, but so, too, was research in international relations, area studies, and the social sciences more generally. We now have numerous accounts of the roles that the academic social sciences played in the Cold War and in the construction and maintenance of U.S. economic hegemony and the liberal international order.[18] In my own discipline of geography, scholars have shown the tight interrelations between the academic production of geographic knowledge and both state–military and imperial projects.[19] Humanities education, too, took its bearings from the nation-state. Bill Readings has described how the humanities functioned to socialize students into national culture and citizenship, with literature, in particular, tasked with educating the student, as a political subject, into the ethical development of the state.[20]

Scholars emphasize a turn toward corporatization in the 1970s. The fraying ideological linkage between universities and national culture was already evident in the global student protests of the late 1960s, which challenged the cultural authority of academic institutions.[21] By the 1970s, policy makers in a number of advanced capitalist states, but primarily in the United States, began to alter spending priorities with regard to public education. Slaughter and Leslie have logged the sharp decreases in funding for U.S. public universities during the 1980s and 1990s, along with more moderate cuts in education spending in the United Kingdom, Canada, and Australia. More significantly, they establish that cuts were directed at undergraduate and graduate education by eliminating block grants, which allowed universities to direct spending, and replacing them with targeted research funds. Concomitantly, the U.S. Congress's 1972 amendment to the Higher Education Act changed the disbursement of government financial aid, shifting it away from universities and toward students in the form of grants and loans.[22] Slaughter and Leslie argue that the economic pressures flowing from these policy shifts forced universities to adopt more market-oriented strategies, but they, along with many other critics, suggest that the relation between corporatization, public funding, and higher education was recursive, with spending cuts and entrepreneurial strategies for university funding reinforcing one another. Moreover, scholars connect reduction in state support to economic globalization and the development of new telecommunications technologies as other drivers of university change.[23]

Whereas critics identify multiple causes of corporatization, the accounts of what constitutes it are fairly uniform. We can note at least six overlapping processes. First, corporatization is equated with universities attempting to directly market and profit from research. This is the phenomenon that Slaughter and Leslie identified as "academic capitalism." Of course, a central justification for the importance of public research institutions has always been based on their ability to transfer technological and scientific developments to society. Contemporary university practices differ in that universities are increasingly involved directly with the commercial aspects of development, often in partnership with industry. Roger Geiger has chronicled an increase in university ties to business beginning in the 1980s in the United States. The 1980 Bayh–Dole Act granted universities ownership of patents stemming from federally funded research, and both individual states and the National Science Foundation created programs to promote collaboration between university researchers and industry. These policies established the conditions in which university patent offices, research parks, public–private partnerships, and independent research units proliferated through the 1980s and 1990s.[24] David F. Noble has described the extension of the university–business nexus from research into teaching and instruction through the commodification of online education and distance learning.[25] This logic culminates in the for-profit model of university education, in which universities themselves are the direct mechanisms for returning dividends to investors.

Two primary concerns are raised by the attempts to profit from university research. The first involves the potential for business ties to disrupt scholarly research. This has become a pressing issue for biomedical and biotechnology fields, in which industry funding and conflict of interest controversies have been prevalent.[26] The second concern is that areas of research without direct transfers to the market go unfunded. The commodification of the university thus poses special problems for the humanities, which are increasingly asked to provide economic justification for their existence, as well as for units that take critical stances with respect to dominant institutions. A number of recent cases have highlighted the precariousness of humanities and critical research such as the closing of Middlesex University's philosophy department, which specialized in European continental thought and critical theory; the slow institutional elimination of the heterodox economics program at the University of Notre Dame; or the shuttering of humanities departments, including French, Russian, theater, and classics, at the State University of New York, Albany.[27]

The second component of the corporatization of the university concerns its management along business lines. As the aforementioned cases suggest, departments are continually evaluated for the returns they bring. These calculations are at once financial but also involve jobs, prestige, or the further development of institutional capacities. Managerial assessments depend on data, and the rise of a continual stream of audits—the tabulations of grant moneys and publications, the measuring of impact factors, quantitative student evaluations—provides administrators the information that makes managerialism possible. The result of these exercises in quantification is readily apparent in the proliferation of university rankings and research assessments that both governments and individuals use to evaluate universities. Managerialism also has gone hand in hand with the expansion of a new class of administrative professionals on campus. A 2010 report from the conservative Goldwater Institute recorded a dramatic rise in the number of administrators and the financial resources flowing into administration in U.S. universities between 1993 and 2007. Using U.S. Department of Education data, the report registered a 39 percent increase in administrative employees relative to an 18 percent increase in employees involved in teaching, research, and service. They also reported a 61 percent increase in inflation-adjusted spending on administration per student relative to a 39 percent increase on instruction.[28]

Third, running universities on a business model has transformed labor relations within these institutions. U.S. institutions have significantly eroded the tenure system, replacing tenured faculty with a variety of contingent workers, ranging from adjunct professors on non-tenure-eligible lines to graduate student instructors. The 2006 American Association of University Professors Contingent Faculty Index, based on U.S. Department of Education data, detailed a drop in full-time tenured or tenure-track faculty from 56.8 percent of all faculty at U.S. degree-granting institutions in 1975 to only 35.1 percent in 2003.[29] Jack Schuster and Martin Finkelstein provide further documentation of this revolution in academic labor. Drawing primarily on information from the National Center for Educational Statistics, they show not only the rapid growth of contingent and casual labor but also the gendered gap in tenured appointments. Whereas women made up under one-third of tenure or tenure-track appointments in both 1992 and 1998, they made up more than half of non-tenure-track appointments in those same years.[30]

Marc Bousquet has demonstrated that this casualization of academic labor is not a crisis, as it is so often characterized, but rather "a smoothly functioning new system with its own easily apprehensible logic, premised entirely on the continuous replacement of degree holders with nondegreed labor."[31] Although graduate education was originally conceptualized as an apprenticeship into academic life, unionization efforts of graduate students and contingent faculty have demonstrated that these labor processes primarily benefit universities, their administrators, and private corporations. Rather than graduating into academic appointments, the unsecured positions of these workers in flexible labor markets allow universities to profit from low wages and corporations to subsidize their employee training. Bousquet explains that this shift to casualization is not a result of glutted job markets but rather of a conscientious shift in hiring practices by university administrators, which remains unchecked by complacent and distracted faculty—or, as he pithily puts it, *"we are not 'overproducing Ph.D.s'; we are underproducing jobs."*[32] In this sense, the deprofessionalization of the professoriate mirrors other processes by which the university promotes and profits from low-wage labor, including outsourcing and subcontracting much of the nonacademic work on campus.[33]

Fourth, labor relations are changing not only within academic institutions but also between universities, states, and global labor markets. I have already noted the ways the global "knowledge economy," which depends on the commodification of knowledge, information, services, and communication, has put a new priority on university education as an anchor of industrial growth. Organizations such as the World Bank have focused on "knowledge" as a key element of social and economic progress and have emphasized the importance of tertiary education to the development of technical and professional workers as well as national economic survival.[34] For students, then, university education is increasingly important as a gateway to employment. Even the World Bank argues that limited access to higher education poses a risk for developing countries of "being further marginalized in a highly competitive world economy."[35] Bousquet describes the ways this has turned "the student" into a distinct category of laborer, specifically designated as "not workers" and, in U.S. law, deprived of labor rights.[36] Similarly, Ross Perlin has examined the role of colleges and universities in fostering the unpaid labor of students through internships that students view as necessary for securing future job prospects.[37]

Fifth, declining state support has encouraged not only the transfer of research to the market but also the commodification of the university itself, along with its academic credentials, as a consumer good. Branding is evident, from the glossy publications of university public relations departments to the shifting language in which students become "consumers" or "clients." Many have examined the ways high-level collegiate athletics have reshaped the university into a commodity. Derek Bok has suggested that athletics represented the first foray into commercialization for many universities and examines the costs to both universities and student athletes for fielding highly competitive sports programs.[38] Samantha King

and Sheila Slaughter studied the ways corporations seek to profit by signing "all-school contracts," in which "companies such as Nike and Adidas
endorsed entire schools rather than individual coaches or teams."[39] They
also chronicle the registration of university names, logos, and mascots as
trademarks and the billions in revenues these trademarks generate.[40] Student and labor activists associated with the global antisweatshop movement have in turn successfully targeted the conditions of production of
university apparel as a threat to university brands.[41]

University brands have also gone global in the construction of satel-
lite campuses. Andrew Ross, among others, has reported on the attempts
to incorporate higher education into global trade liberalization through
the World Trade Organization's General Agreement on Trade in Services
(GATS).[42] Although university associations from Canada, the United
States, and Europe jointly opposed the inclusion of higher education in
GATS, they have failed to stem the global trade of university services.[43]
Ross estimates the global market for trade in higher education services at
between forty and fifty billion dollars and focuses on the expansion of U.S.
universities abroad—what Tamar Lewin in the *New York Times* called "a
kind of education gold rush"—best exemplified by New York University's
expansion into Abu Dhabi.[44] In addition to the direct expansion of U.S.
institutions internationally, Kris Olds has documented the Singaporean
state's efforts to produce a "global schoolhouse" that will attract universities, capital, and researchers from various parts of the world, while also
restructuring the local economy.[45] These processes of internationalization,
in turn, have created new scales of regional and transnational regulation
for higher education governance.[46]

Sixth, corporatization changes the content of university education. Undergraduate courses in business management and professional master in
business administration (MBA) degrees have expanded rapidly since the
1960s, both in terms of total numbers of programs and the countries offering credentials. Business schools and MBA programs were late arrivers
to the modern university, appearing formally within university curricula
only in the first decades of the twentieth century.[47] Hyeyoung Moon and
Christine Min Wotipka report dramatic growth in the number of countries offering professional managerial education from approximately fifty
countries in the late 1970s to more than one hundred by the end of the
1990s. Moreover, they argue that roughly 14 percent of university students worldwide were enrolled in business or administration programs
by the end of the 1990s, surpassing enrollments in traditional disciplines,
including humanities, law, natural sciences, and engineering.[48]

Corporatization also changes the content of university research and teaching in less direct ways. For instance, Bill Readings has emphasized a shift from the University of National Culture to the University of Excellence. Whereas the disciplinary formations that emerged in the ninetieth-century German research university were directed at fostering the ethical development of the nation-state, Readings argued that the corporate university has at its center an abstract concept of "excellence" divorced from specific content. As a sign lacking any concrete referent, "excellence" can function as a simple unit of accounting and administration to which all work in the university can be directed. This in turn indicates that "excellence is not a fixed standard of judgment but a qualifier whose meaning is fixed in relation to something else."[49] Metrics, rankings, and assessments function as the "something else" to which excellence refers. Readings also shows the illogic and arbitrary nature of these comparisons, as excellence "allows the combination on a single scale of such utterly heterogeneous features as finances and the make-up of the student body."[50] Thus the only real function of excellence is that it allows the formation of gradations between and within institutions necessary for consumers to make decisions; as Readings puts it, "henceforth, the question of the University is only the question of relative value-for-money."[51]

Critically, excellence eliminates other, more substantive grounds for valuing what universities do or the quality of scholarly work, allowing any type of research to proliferate as long as it can be understood as excellent in the sense of its efficiency, cost–benefit analysis, or input–output ratios. Readings gives a concrete example of this in the enthusiasm for interdisciplinary programs. What makes this argument so trenchant is that interdisciplinary programs, including and especially cultural studies, have been institutional locations where critical or radical scholarship has thrived, and many critical scholars note the importance of interdisciplinarity for a critique of existing social relations. In contrast, Readings argues that the institutional commitment to interdisciplinarity is directly related to its lack of political orientation and the pressures it puts on existing disciplinary structures. Thus interdisciplinary programs offer "increased flexibility" that is "attractive to administrators as a way of overcoming entrenched practices of demarcation, ancient privileges, and fiefdoms in the university."[52] In this manner, interdisciplinarity makes existing units seem less than cutting edge. It also economizes research agendas, using the same resources as traditional disciplines but now speaking to multiple audiences. Readings worries that soon interdisciplinary departments "will be installed in order to replace clusters of disciplines," and indeed, others have made interdisciplinarity central to university reform.[53]

What, then, are the alternatives provided by critics of corporatization?

Given the scope of issues that fall under general discussions of the corporate university, responses are quite varied. Because so much of the corporatization argument is focused on U.S. institutions, some propose specific changes to U.S. law. For instance, Jennifer Washburn suggests a quartet of reforms by the U.S. federal government that include limiting the scope of the Bayh–Dole Act, strengthening federal oversight of technology transfer, and instituting more rigorous conflict of interest laws.[54] Other legal reforms reach further. For instance, Adolph Reed Jr. has argued for federally funded free higher education modeled on the GI Bill.[55] Jeffrey Williams has echoed this claim, while also proposing other measures, such as "income contingent loans," to address the growing problem of student debt.[56] Another set of recommendations focuses on the structure of universities themselves, along with changes to curriculum, administration, and governance. Aronowitz advocates for separating higher learning from vocational goals by replacing centralized, bureaucratic administration with active faculty and student governance and eliminating narrow specialization for an interdisciplinary curriculum focused on critical engagements with history, literature, science, and philosophy.[57] Much of the scholarship on the corporate university, however, emerged out of concrete struggles on campuses and looks to social movement activism—unionization efforts and workplace politics, on one side, and the tradition of student movements, on the other—to combat corporatization.[58] In some cases, these projects have been incorporated into broader autonomous political movements that seek to use the university as a location for proliferating new forms of social organization not captured by the corporate structure of the university.[59]

Antidisciplinarity in the Corporate University

The corporate university literature is vital to the struggles around the university as a place of work, research, teaching, and study and usefully demonstrates the university's centrality to the political and economic transformations of our age, primarily in the United States but increasingly globally as well. In addition to documenting important shifts in university policies and practices, there is much that is persuasive about the corporate university thesis itself, and personally, I am in solidarity with projects that seek to transform the conditions of work and politics on university campuses. That said, there is something strange about the ways in which corporations appear in these accounts as synonymous with business, and corporatization is presented as a radical change in the functioning of academic institutions. If, as Jeffrey Williams recently suggested in the *Chronicle of*

Higher Education, we are witnessing the emergence of a new interdisciplinary field of "critical university studies" that is not only scholarly but organically connected to the struggles over the precariousness of graduate student and adjunct labor, might it be useful to think carefully through the relations between corporations and universities that ostensibly constitute this new interdisciplinary domain's object of scholarly and political attention?[60] Moreover, because Williams suggests that it is corporateness ("the vast octopus of contemporary higher education"[61]) that distinguishes the university in the global present from its mom-and-pop predecessors, shouldn't we then clarify what it is about corporateness that leads us toward such an institutional monstrosity?

To do so, however, compels us to consider how disciplines form in relation to the objects they study. In the introduction, I discussed dominant approaches to corporations in fields such as economics, history, and political science. My purpose was to outline the ways these disciplines misrecognize corporate sovereignty precisely because of the way corporations appear as objects of disciplinary reflection. More specifically, I suggested that the problematics structuring these disciplines are constituted through a series of spatial and conceptual oppositions—between economics and politics, property and sovereignty, global capitalism and national states—that distort our understanding of the fundamental relationship between corporate capitalism and sovereign power, which I've termed *corporate sovereignty.* This misrecognition, however, is not the result of bad interpretation or inadequate social science; rather, it is symptomatic of the institutional conditions by which these disciplines come into being. Moreover, this is true not only of the relatively conservative fields of mainstream economics and political science but also of critical scholarship, including radical approaches to corporate power and, even, critical studies of the corporate university.

We can understand this relation by turning to John Mowitt's powerful analysis of the emergence of "text" as an object of disciplinary reflection across the humanities and the social sciences. Of course, Mowitt was not writing about corporations or corporate power but rather about the object—"the text"—that emerged through what has variously been called the postfoundationalist, postmodern, or poststructuralist critique of culture. Nevertheless, his account explains the processes by which disciplines encounter their objects of study in ways that are helpful for understanding the interdisciplinary critique of the corporate university. Central to his argument is Roland Barthes's 1971 agenda-setting essay "From Work to Text." In that essay, Barthes examined how changing conceptions of language had displaced traditional concerns with literary works and inaugurated "the text" as a new object of disciplinary reflection in literary studies but also in linguistics, anthropology, Marxism, and psychoanalysis. Outlining a series of "propositions" associated with the text, Barthes glossed many of the themes now associated with poststructuralism: (1) texts are not objects but methodological fields; (2) texts disrupt literary classification; (3) the symbolic meanings of texts are infinitely deferred; (4) texts, though composed of familiar codes, produce heterogeneous meanings; (5) texts shun authorial intent for networked exchanges; (6) texts connect writer, reader, and critic in a cycle, not of production and consumption, but of play; and (7) texts are "bound to *jouissance,* that is a pleasure without separation." As such, texts allow us to experience not the domination of one language over another but the circulation of languages in the infinite exchange of meaning.[62]

All of this, today, seems familiar. But Mowitt explains that Barthes came to focus on "the text" as a new object of study (with all of the complexity that poststructuralist considerations of textuality imply) not because of his own innate brilliance. Nor did scholars start writing about "the text" because of a simple transformation in the social relations of capitalism or in the mode of production of cultural objects. Rather, Mowitt argues that the emergence of the text was conditioned by and dependent on a crisis in the university and the academic disciplines. Barthes had already grasped this crisis, suggesting that the text

> comes not necessarily from the internal recasting of each of
> these disciplines, but rather from their encounter in relation to
> an object which traditionally is the province of none of them. It
> is indeed as though the interdisciplinarity which is today held
> up as a prime value in research cannot be accomplished by
> the simple confrontation of specialist branches of knowledge.
> Interdisciplinarity is not the calm of an easy security; it begins
> effectively (as opposed to the mere expression of a pious wish)
> when the solidarity of the old disciplines breaks down—perhaps
> even violently, via the jolts of fashion—in the interests of a new
> object and a new language neither of which has a place in the field
> of the sciences that were to be brought peacefully together.[63]

This focus on the crisis in the disciplines distinguished Barthes's and Mowitt's analyses from Marxist criticism of postmodernism, which treated the rise of textual approaches as symptomatic of the changing relations between the economic base and the cultural superstructure.[64] For Mowitt, however, the crisis in disciplinary knowledge represented by the text indexed broader transformations in disciplinary power and the particular ways those transformations were taken up in the academic disciplines.

How so? Mowitt turned to Foucault's notion that disciplines produce "docile bodies," human agents that are "empowered within a particular yet restricted mode of production."[65] Docile bodies were also objects of academic study, central to the rise of academic disciplines, as they served as the basic material from which objective knowledge about humans and their social relations could be produced. To ground objective knowledge, these agents had to achieve a type of normalized behavior predicated on the very techniques of disciplinary control Foucault attempted to chart. Thus the objective information gathered by the disciplines through practices such as "examination" presupposed "a certain saturation of society by disciplinary power."[66] The formation of academic disciplines and their ability to study discrete elements of social existence (such as economics, politics, history, law, or geography) required, as a precondition, disciplinary power to produce a society of individuals who understand themselves, their interrelations, their social order, and their power in specific and stable ways, corresponding to these divisions.

This leads Mowitt to two brilliant claims that are relevant to our discussion. First, to the extent that academic disciplines are predicated on disciplinary power, interdisciplinarity is already inherent in the objects we study. As a type of critique, interdisciplinarity, by itself, is insufficient as "rearranging disciplinary boundaries means little if this rearrangement is not understood to have consequences for the structure of disciplinary power within society at large."[67] In other words, the type of interdisciplinary scholarship that aims to get a better account of its objects by adding disciplines (in the sense that understanding the corporate university requires not only economics but also law, sociology, geography, and cultural studies or anthropology) simply reiterates that the objects of the world are inherently plural (that, say, "the economy" is also "political" and "cultural"). While important, Mowitt argues that critical scholarship must also grasp the manner in which this inherent plurality has been *re-pressed* by the very historical formations of knowledge and power that were designed to apprehend them. Mowitt calls for an antidisciplinary critique that exposes and disrupts the links between disciplinary power, academic disciplines, and their objects.

Mowitt's second radical proposition follows from the first. Disciplines, or more properly, adherents to disciplines (whom Mowitt calls "disciples") evince a defense mechanism around their objects of inquiry. Engaging René Girard's writing on the sacrificial logic of mimetic desire, Mowitt argues that though the object of disciplinary reflection originally brings disciples

together and mediates their exchanges, eventually the antagonisms between members of the group overtake the focus on the object. *Disciplines restore order and constitute themselves by regulating the scope of
these conflicts.* They do so, following Girard, by collectively designating a
"scapegoat" on which disciplinary antagonisms can be displaced. The *elimination or exile of the scapegoat establishes both the sacred nature of the
disciplinary object and the prohibition preventing future acts of violence
within the community.* Disciplinary identity comes into being through mis-
recognizing the interdisciplinary nature of its objects, which are displaced,
eliminated, and made sacred. For this reason, Mowitt claimed that "disciplines are structured by their immanent resistance to that which they claim
to know."[68] More strongly, "disciplines cannot know what they claim to
know, and what substitutes for this lack of knowledge is a bureaucrati-
cally articulated policing of fidelity."[69]

Universitas Magistrorum et Scholarium

If disciplines form around a denial of what they claim to know, what is
it about the corporate university that has been blocked but also spurs the
accumulation of disciplinary knowledge in critical university studies? How
does the failure to come to terms with this dynamic shape subsequent
research on corporatization as well as our engagements with corporate
power and the corporate university? My central claim is that the corporate
university thesis misrecognizes the corporateness that is at the core of what
is most important about the university, namely, the possibilities it fosters
for collective practices of critical thought and action. In this sense, we see
the doubling of corporate sovereignty once again. Critical university studies attempt to excise the corporation from the heart of the university. In
doing so, they challenge the exploitation of students and academic laborers by universities, along with the global labor markets with which they
conspire, while also saving and restoring the concept of higher learning as
a pure (one might even say sacred) object. Antidisciplinary critique reveals,
however, that the very thing we oppose and seek to destroy is the same
as our academic freedom and autonomy. Furthermore, antidisciplinarity
offers a different position, not one that is for or against the corporate university but one that reiterates the corporate foundations of the university
in terms that are unassimilable to the current politics of corporatization.

Such a critique involves radicalizing other elements in the history of
the corporate university. Whereas today's corporate university is founded
in the articulation between corporations and capitalist value, we might
mobilize different moments in the genealogy of the corporation as a

mechanism for countering this conjuncture. Ernst Kantorowicz provides another model of the corporate university directly at odds with contemporary corporatization in his 1950 pamphlet *The Fundamental Issue*.[70] Kantorowicz wrote the forty-page, self-published pamphlet as part of his opposition to the anticommunist loyalty oath issued by the University of California (UC) regents during the red scare of the 1940s and 1950s. UC president Robert G. Sproul first proposed the oath to the regents in March 1949, who unanimously adopted the proposal. By June of that year, Kantorowicz had emerged as a leading opposition figure to signing the oath.[71] During fall and winter 1949, the Academic Senate negotiated with the regents to support anticommunism while weakening any obligation with respect to the oath. By February 1950, the Board of Regents had adopted a more aggressive policy under the leadership of regent John Francis Neylan, in which any faculty member who had not signed the loyalty oath by June 30, 1950, would be fired.[72] Dismissals began in spring 1950, with first 6 and then 157 professors being terminated. By August, the remaining 31 faculty members who had refused to sign were fired.[73] Kantorowicz, who never signed the oath, took a visiting position at Harvard during the 1950–51 academic year, publishing *The Fundamental Issue* in October. Although the text was not widely available during the controversy, it circulated within the UC community, falling into the hands of both faculty and regents.[74] The pamphlet included a variety of university documents such as forms for appointment, salary, and tenure; two letters, from Kantorowicz and an art professor named Walter Horn, written to President Sproul; a proposed legislative bill on academic freedom; and a copy of the public statement that Kantorowicz made to the Northern Section of the UC Academic Senate in June 1949, at the beginning of the faculty mobilization. The crux of the text is a section of "marginal notes" that constitute a stinging critique of the content and logic of the loyalty oath, while also offering Kantorowicz's assessment of the essential aspects of the university.

It might seem odd that Kantorowicz was so vehemently opposed to the loyalty oath, much less that there would be something in the writings of an avowedly conservative, if not reactionary, historian that would be potentially useful for progressive reform. A German immigrant, Kantorowicz volunteered for military service in 1914 and fought for the kaiser in World War I. After the war, he joined the right-wing Freikorps and served in the bloody repression of the Sparticist Revolt in Berlin in January 1919. Later that year, Kantorowicz moved to Munich, where he also participated in the Freikorps's attack on and defeat of the Munich Republic of Councils. In the 1920s, as Kantorowicz was beginning his scholarly career, he became associated with the intellectual circle around the conservative romantic nationalist Stefan George. His scholarly work, at least initially, also partook of romantic German nationalism, with his first book being a lyrical biography lauding Frederick II, before turning to more critical examinations of the mystical foundations of the state and the sempiternal nature of political sovereignty later in his career.[75] But if Kantorowicz was, in his own words, "genuinely conservative and never have been taken for anything else,"[76] he was also an expert in the legal history and symbology of corporate institutions as well as a Jewish exile from the biopolitical totalitarianism of the Nazis. *The Fundamental Issue* weaved together these two personal and intellectual preoccupations of Kantorowicz—the history of corporate institutions and concerns over totalitarianism—as the basis of a critique of the loyalty oath.

In the somewhat scattershot format of the marginal notes, Kantorowicz attacks almost every argument of the regents for the oath. He contended that the oath did nothing to stem communism on UC campuses, was unconstitutional, and was politically motivated. Yet his central concern was establishing that the regents had no grounds to compel the faculty to sign the oath and that the oath constituted an attack on the traditional prerogatives of academic freedom, tenure, and faculty governance. Within the context of McCarthyism, many saw loyalty oaths as infringements on academic freedom, but Kantorowicz's defense of that concept was distinct in that he rooted academic freedom in the corporate structure of the university. Kantorowicz explained that universities are corporations of professors and students:

> According to the oldest definitions, which run back to the
> thirteenth century, "The University" is the *universitas magistrorum
> et scholarium,* "The Body Corporate of Masters and Students."
> Teachers and students together are the University regardless of the
> existence of gardens and buildings, or care-takers of gardens and
> buildings. One can envisage a university without a single gardener
> or janitor, without a single secretary, and even—a bewitching
> mirage—without a single Regent. The constant essence of a
> university is always the body of teachers and students.[77]

The corporate nature of the university established its autonomy, as professors were only responsible, at least in their capacity as professors, to "the body corporate which they served, the University."[78] This fact distinguished the corporate university from the business corporation, the professor from the employee, and the regent from the boss.

To be sure, Kantorowicz's defense of the university was a conservative and elitist defense of a medieval institution. The university was a gendered space of privilege. Repeatedly, throughout the text, he draws a sharp distinction between the professoriate—members of the autonomous and self-governing corporate body held in public trust—and janitors and gardeners as simple employees. Moreover, the distinction is directly linked to the nature of work: "the janitor is paid by the hour. He has his shift during which he is held to perform certain well described duties. His work is clearly defined and definable. Once he has performed his daily duties and has left off work he is a completely free man. Additional work is neither expected nor demanded, except by special agreement and with special pay."[79] But the professor has ill-defined and limited duties. Professorial work is independent of supervision, and—at least in Kantorowicz's idealized vision—professors are left to their own devices. "It is left to him how much time and energy he puts into his committee work, into his conferences with students, or into the aggrandizement of his university's library. In short, it is entirely up to him how much of his life, of his private life, he is wiling to dedicate to the University to which he belongs and which he, too, constitutes."[80] For these reasons, professors have tenure instead of employee unions. Whereas unions represent employees' interests against the countervailing interests of owners or management, tenure is a right of corporate self-government.

Kantorowicz framed the ends to which such self-government is directed in similarly conservative fashion, linking the prerogatives of the professoriate with those of other pillars of the social order, priests and judges, which constitute the "three professions ... entitled to wear a gown."[81] In his 1949 statement, he suggested, "The garment stands for the bearer's maturity of mind, his independence of judgment, and his direct responsibility to his conscience and to his God. It signifies the inner sovereignty of those three interrelated professions."[82] These, of course, are the individuals who serve the major corporate institutions of Western society: the professor and the universities, the priest and the church, the judge and the state. In each case, these individuals are entrusted with the responsibility of guiding these corporate bodies as the result of being disciples, well-disciplined subjects of the corporate sovereigns they serve. For the judge, this is training in the discipline of law; for the priest, it is the taking of vows and the submission to God as well as incorporation into religious orders. But what is it for the scholar?

Kantorowicz emphatically states, "It is purely a matter of Passion, of Love, and of Conscience."[83] He goes on to communicate the incommensurability between academic work, governed by these drives and desires, and the market for labor. "You can buy labor, but you cannot buy Passion and Love nor the scholarly Conscience. For once there is something that is not marketable, and the poorly informed Regents should know that by trying to make our conscience venal they kill our passion and love for our institutions because we cease to be one with it."[84] And this, we can assume, is why the CEO wears no gown. Precisely because the academic enterprise involves a corporate form of life that cannot be qualified in terms of a singular metric of capitalist value, the corporate university resists any specific determination. The university, by definition, is a corporate body that must remain open and free.

Thus, despite Kantorowicz's conservatism, he articulates a radical critique of the capitalist logics of the university and the attempt to govern life through labor and value, as well as outlining a form of being in common directed by the indefinable pursuit of passion, love, and scholarly conscience. "Through the sheer existence of this conscience, which is undefined and undefinable, the scholar ceases also to be an 'employee' of the Regents in any sense whatsoever of business language."[85] The university's categories are incomprehensible to the systems of capital accumulation. Serving a corporate body in this manner is not a function for which one can be paid a wage. It even resists the social ordering by "Time in general" that makes value and wages possible.[86] Kantorowicz could not be clearer that the regents' conflation of the corporate university with a business corporation "ruined, together with the academic profession, also the University!"[87] Finally, it was this attempt by the regents to "save the University" by destroying its essence—"to dismiss a scholar for the very conscience which makes him a scholar"—that linked, in Kantorowicz's mind, the institution of the oath with totalitarianism.[88] The loyalty oath represented a kind of immunitary disease in which the salvation of the corporate body of the university came at the expense of what made it distinct and important to begin with.

Kantorowicz's trenchant attack of the loyalty oath shows the complete noncorrespondence between a common enterprise driven by love, passion, and scholarly conscience and one driven by business, wages, and employee relations. Kantorowicz, however, was not the only scholar of corporate sovereignty to acknowledge the affective and collective undergirding of corporate power. Ernst Freund, whose book *The Legal Nature of Corporations* was responsible for bringing German ideas of corporate personhood into Anglo-American legal debates, also recognized the noncapitalist origins of corporate being in common. Recall that Freund's theory of corporate personhood was linked to the ability to accomplish some end. For Freund, the desire to undertake tasks that could only be done collectively constituted a corporate "will" independent of the individuals who composed the corporation. In chapter 3, I noted Freund's example of such ends to which the corporate will might be directed: science and art. Freund also presented "the cause of religion, charity, and education" as "abstract interests" that required collective effort.[89] In the same way that Kantorowicz linked the rights of tenure to the love of scholarship, Freund linked the "rights held by a museum or a library, by a hospital or by a college"[90] to the collective interests of "humanity and civilization."[91] Thus, for Freund, like Kantorowicz, it was the collective or corporate pursuit of such lofty goals as science, art, love, passion, conscience, humanity, and education that grounded the worldly rights of universities, among other institutions, and their denizens. More important, these abstract interests, which for Freund certainly represented the apex of human achievement, were unique in that they could not be achieved by individuals alone, working in isolation. They required corporate being in common.

Here we might find resources for wrenching this vision of the corporate university away from some of the conservatism subtending Kantorowicz's formulation. First, this corporate enterprise is inconceivable in terms of capitalist business, organizing life around the production and circulation of socially necessary value. It is also quite different from the corporate political body of the Hobbesian state, a political theological personification that stands outside of the order it constitutes, much less the totalitarian mutations that led to Nazi corporatism. As with all corporations, for Kantorowicz, the corporate body of the university depended on a certain economy or wise superintendence that it itself, as a corporate institution, was in charge of cultivating. This, of course, is always what universities, as police or disciplinary institutions, have done. Kantorowicz bristled at the imposition of rules and laws by regents who thought they were employers, but he surely did not see the university as a lawless place. Its rules, customs, and protocols were ancient, given by the traditions of scholarship and its customary rites. It was all of this regulation that enabled the well-disciplined scholar to lead a scholarly life, directed by affects of love, passion, and conscience and aimed at furthering scholarship, its institutional structure in the university, and its ennobling ideas of light and truth.[92]

We should ask, however, if it is only scholars who can cultivate love, passion, and conscience directed at promoting a distinct form of being in common. In what ways do janitors and secretaries, gardeners, and even regents hold potential for contributing to a collective project along these lines? And what about the miserable sectors? Are they similarly without love, passion, and conscience? What could constitute an affirmative biopolitics at the center of the university that could allow these dispositions to proliferate?

At the end of the last chapter, I examined the difference between legal liability and political responsibility in the work of Iris Marion Young and Hannah Arendt. Moreover, I noted that political responsibility was always directed to the world and must engage and address the paradox of what Arendt called the vicariously innocent. What would it mean to suggest the university as a physical space directed toward political responsibility to the world? What would it mean to offer this, what we might call a corporate love of the world (including a corporate love of and by the vicariously innocent), as the raison d'être of the university? What makes political responsibility to the world, in my estimation, a more useful organizing concept than Kantorowicz's scholarly love, passion, and conscience is that the world and our political responsibility to it are antidisciplinary objects par excellence. To think through how one not only *conceptualizes* but also *enacts* a political responsibility to the world is exactly the type of undefined and indefinable task that compels corporate organization on the basis of love, passion, and conscience, while simultaneously resisting our attempts to answer the question through narrow disciplinary frameworks. The persistence of this indefinable and inexhaustible undertaking distinguishes a progressive vision of the corporate university from the horrors of the business corporation and its biopolitical economy of value as well as the totalitarian state, with its biopolitical logics of race and nation. It is also this inexhaustibility that requires not a narrowly defined scholarly community but an open (and raucous) exchange between the university and the world.

One might justifiably argue that such a program for countering the contemporary corporatization of the university is utopian and idealist, as detached from the practical requirements of running actually existing universities as it is from the daily lives and concerns of the gardeners, janitors, and secretaries Kantorowicz excluded from the corporate body of scholars as well as the graduate students and contingent faculty that critics of the corporate university are attempting to organize. My response is twofold. On the utopian aspect of these claims, such ways of collective being are already internal to the institutions that we inhabit and that govern our lives. As this book has attempted to demonstrate, corporate institutions are complex, ambiguous, and multifaceted. As troubling as the corporate nature of the university is today, corporateness is also the very condition of possibility for the historical emergence of the university. If this genealogical and antidisciplinary critique of the corporation has any merit, it is precisely in allowing us to recognize this unrealized potentiality and to open space for intervening in the current political conjuncture by realizing not an anticorporate university but a different corporate university.

As for the argument that the proper approach to today's "knowledge factories" is to incorporate the language and politics of labor militancy into the workplace, I argue that such politics are *necessary but not sufficient* for radical transformation. It is certainly necessary to peel back the fetishism of higher education as a global commodity, as critics of corporatization have done, and reveal the conditions of production and exploitation in these institutions. If we are really headed toward a complete blurring in which business corporations become universities (think the Google or Microsoft campuses) and universities become businesses, organizing workers as workers and attempting to collectively transform the production process and the distribution of benefits garnered by these institutions is paramount. But we should also recognize that such politics implies accepting the language and identity given to us by our role in this production system. What do we ultimately achieve if we get what we want *as laborers* in the corporate university? We get not an open space of critical reflection or a new form of collectivity but rather capitalism's own unfulfilled and unfulfillable promise of the good life: a fair wage for a day's work. This falls far short of the possibilities present in the corporate university, asking us to abandon collective projects fostered through the love, passion, and consciousness of a community directed toward whatever ends for the solidarity derived from our position as exploited workers in a capitalist system.

An alternative would be to critique and challenge this system as a system of labor exploitation rooted in channeling life toward capitalist value that cannot deal with the inexhaustible collective projects of love, passion, conscience, and responsibility. Whereas the first set of struggles might possibly lead to redistribution of social goods or, even, an evolution from the capitalist to the socialist university, the second attempts to liberate the university as a space in which life could become otherwise in processes not determined by the logics of capitalist accumulation. Echoing Moishe Postone, we could say that the first politics is a critique of the corporate university from the standpoint of labor, whereas the second is a critique of labor in the corporate–capitalist university.[93] My point in this chapter is that the genealogy of the corporate university has resources toward that end. The corporate university emphasizes not the fact that, today, universities are factories but rather that, at their core, universities are collectivities completely and totally distinct from the logics of capitalist accumulation. It allows us to think about the ways capitalism has captured these institutions and transformed them in its own image.

Foucault's final lecture of his 1975–76 course at the Collège de France provides a trenchant formulation of our predicament. That year's course began with the proposition of inverting Clauswitz's famous statement that war is politics by other means. By focusing on politics as an extension of war, Foucault was able to lay bare the way the right of life and death has been constitutive of political order, leading from the sovereign power to kill to both disciplinary and biopolitical forms of control. As previously stated, once these two modes of governing are articulated to the norm, they take hold of life in general, reframing politics around techniques designed to *improve life*. The great problem Foucault posed is the reentry of death in the political order, or as he puts it, "given that this power's objective is essentially to make live, how can it let die? How can the power of death, the function of death, be exercised in a political system centered upon biopower?"[1]

It is an amazingly insightful question. I would argue that it continues to be vital to understanding the political problems of today. In fact, one could do much worse than this as a summation of the concerns that initiated this book and on which I touched in the introduction. Reframing Foucault, this book asks how a global order of corporate capitalism, created and repeatedly justified for its abilities "to improve life, to prolong its duration, to improve its chances, to avoid accidents, and to compensate for failings,"[2] results in a system that routinely denies housing, clothes, food, work, and essential medicines; that exposes populations to unsafe living conditions and environmental hazards; and that constantly attempts to push workers into depoliticized forms of bare life. If corporate power—by which I mean the ability of corporations to do all those things that Justice Field (and Berle and Means after him) indicated, from the construction of houses and the bringing of the products of earth and sea to market to the relief of the sick, the help of the needy, and the enrichment of humanity—has grown on its promise to provide for human welfare, how is it that so much death (in the sense of letting die and "indirect murder"[3]) appears as necessary to the corporate economy?

Although Foucault's formulation helps to clarify the question, his analysis scarcely resolves the problem. Linking the persistence of death with his peculiar reading of racism (where that term signifies "the break between what must live and what must die"[4]), Foucault was able to argue that totalitarian states, of both the Nazi and socialist varieties, used death to fortify the political body. In both cases, "racism justifies the death-function in the economy of biopower by appealing to the principle that the death of others makes one biologically stronger insofar as one is a member of a race or population, insofar as one is an element in a unitary living plurality."[5] The rub is that Foucault denied that a similar division was at play in liberal capitalist orders. Questioning whether capitalist states conjoined the sovereign right to kill with the biopower to improve life, Foucault answered circumspectly, "Perhaps not."[6] Even more curiously, he held up antagonisms that were *purely economic* as an alternative, less deadly formulation. As he argued, "when it is simply a matter of eliminating the adversary in economic terms, or of taking away his privileges, there is no need for racism," suggesting that economic relations are cleanly set off from the problems of life and death animating both sovereignty and biopolitics.

This book claims, to the contrary, that the death function is internal to the economic relations of capitalism. To the extent that capitalism has become the inescapable horizon for securing social welfare, it rearticulates the break between what must live and what must die. More specifically, it is the value-form of capitalism itself that becomes the mechanism for establishing this division. As such, we can think about capitalism as mode of governing life toward value that is bound up with sovereignty and biopolitics from its inception. If this is true, the precise significance of the corporation is the multiple ways it has articulated the *sovereign right to kill* and the *biopower to improve life* with the historical and geographic *circulation of capitalist value*. Because corporations were institutions inextricably linked to sovereignty—they were the very representation of the sovereign body in both its religious and secular forms—they served as a condensation point where different modes of disciplining and regulating life emerged. The transmutations discussed in this book explain the ways the value-form of capitalism came to occupy this point, structuring it, we might say following Althusser, in the last instance.

To argue that this articulation was socially constructed, an invention of legal scholars and practitioners, along with not being necessary or inevitable is, at this point, something of a platitude. After all, realizing the fact that people (pursuing purposeful ends as well as engaging in actions with unintended consequences) produced the sociospatial relations of the corporate economy does little to challenge or intervene in the current conjuncture. In this sense, the commitment of genealogy as an untimely meditation and a "history of the present" must go beyond highlighting the contingency of the past to identify its unacknowledged presuppositions and show the ways those presuppositions continue to structure politics today.[7] This, to my mind, is the specific role of theory, making it distinct from both history and direct political activism and, for that reason, all the more necessary.

On these terms, this book makes two direct contributions. The first concerns law, which, throughout the history of corporate sovereignty, has had an ambiguous position. As legal creations, law has been the primary mechanism for codifying corporate power in its various iterations. It was a set of politicolegal arguments and concepts that transformed the religious image of the corporate body into the sacralized secular sovereign. It was also law—through both its application and its *legally authorized exemption*—that made corporations into delocalized machines for the police of society. Much later, the law rearticulated these exceptional powers in ways consonant with liberal rights. Nevertheless, in our contemporary political struggles over corporate power, *legality itself* continues to function as a primary object of struggle. As chapter 5 demonstrated, a range of debates have focused on getting laws on the books, almost irrespective of their particular content, as if legal regulation was an end in itself for progressive politics. This is also (and more depressingly) true of radical critiques focused on neoliberalism, in which justifiable concerns about privatization, deregulation, and the hollowing out of the state obscure the long traditions by which law and state power promoted the uneven development of capitalism and imperialism as well as their racial and gendered exclusions.

How, then, do we think about the law? At the end of his magisterial *Whigs and Hunters*, E. P. Thompson articulated one of the strangest defenses of the liberal rule of law to date. After some 250 odd pages explaining how the law was used to consolidate the class power and property of the Whig elite in eighteenth-century England, Thompson presented his own position on law as "on a very narrow ledge, watching the tides come up."[8] The tide was the Marxist critique of law as a superstructural element of class domination, of which the account in *Whigs and Hunters* (at least up until that final section) could only be understood as the leading edge. Arguing against the trajectory of his own analysis, Thompson claimed that law codified customary assumptions about social relations and that elites therefore need law for legitimacy. More interestingly, Thompson stressed the ways class relations inhabited the *"forms of law,"* endowing legal debate with "its own characteristics, its own independent history and logic of evolution."[9] The poor foresters whose disenfranchisement and exploitation Thompson chronicled had their own "strong sense of justice" that could use legal reasoning to assert claims.[10] In this way, "law mediated these class relations through legal forms, which imposed, again and again, inhibitions upon the actions of the rulers."[11] As such, this allowed, "in certain limited areas, the law itself to be a genuine forum within which certain kinds of class conflict were fought out."[12]

For all its incongruousness, Thompson's defense clarifies the stakes of abandoning liberal law as a political tactic. As he notes, law's commitment to "standards of universality and equity"[13] obviously can create openings for strategic assertions of power by the oppressed and marginalized. Where this study suggests more cautious enthusiasm, however, is in recognizing that even the strong sense of justice that makes the legal form more than an expression of class power is conditioned by the problematic structuring legality as such. As the genealogy of the corporation demonstrates, there is never some pure origin of the concepts of personhood, property rights, sovereign territory, or responsibility that is free from the social relations structuring the emergence of these legal forms themselves. There is, in other words, a gap between law and justice that cannot be traversed.[14] One might justifiably respond to this criticism by noting that this book has focused primarily on the legal realm and the public sphere to the exclusion of the social mobilizations and daily political struggles by which groups contest corporate power over life in nonlegal ways. That criticism is valid and suggests an opening for further study; however, it also reiterates my central contention with respect to the law. To engage the legal realm as a domain where arguments for justice can be put forward and even, in rare occasions, win the day means also recognizing the ways the problematic shapes law in content *as well as form,* enabling and limiting the types of claims that are made.

Today, capitalism structures the problematic of corporate law, if not the rule of law in general.[15] Thus the second contribution of this genealogy concerns how we think about the articulation of corporations and capitalism. Although corporate power is often presented as a problem of the size of corporations, their legal status as persons, or their lack of democratic accountability, this book suggests that these issues are symptoms of the problematic structuring corporate power and corporate sovereignty. Making corporations smaller, accountable to their owners or society, or rescinding their status as legal persons is quite different from (and far short of) altering the social relations of capitalism that animate these institutions.

Instead, this book would have us focus on the articulation itself, the joint connecting the corporation's powers to capitalist accumulation. As such, it suggests a need to maintain the corporation's power to collectively improve life, while setting it out from the capitalist regulation of life in terms of value and the sovereign right to kill. It would amount to nothing less than an affirmative biopolitics.

That this book ended up on a hopeful note was something of a surprise to me. Less surprising was that I found political possibilities within the university, as this book would not have come to fruition without the extreme generosity, support, and care of an expansive community of scholars. Funding and support of this project were provided by a Jacob K. Javits Fellowship from the U.S. Department of Education, by the University of Minnesota Graduate School and Department of American Studies, by the Committee on Institutional Cooperation Traveling Scholar Program, by a Copeland Postdoctoral Fellowship at Amherst College, and by the University of Georgia. Thanks go to the University of Minnesota Press and Jason Weidemann, my editor, for the patience and continued encouragement they gave this work. Thanks are also due to the reviewers, for their insightful comments, to Danielle Kasprzak, Alicia Gomez, and David Fideler, who provided assistance in bringing the details together and readying the manuscript for publication, and to Holly Monteith, for many improvements in style and clarity. Thanks also go to Matt Wuerker for allowing me to use his fantastic cartoon.

This project owes an incalculable debt to Vinay Gidwani, whose careful, rigorous thought; political engagement; and openness to new or unexpected ideas has been an inspiration to me. Vinay was an extraordinary doctoral advisor. His excitement about the project fortified my own. The same could be said for Adam Sitze, who generously read many pieces of this manuscript over many years. Conversations with Adam forced me to clarify my understanding of the relations between politics and critical thought. Having the time in Amherst to talk with him on a daily basis was a great privilege, and I'm grateful to him for facilitating my participation in the Copeland Fellowship. Eric Sheppard gave unstintingly of his time, energy, and intellect. That Eric found enough interest in me to sign on as a co-advisor was reassuring beyond measure. His reading of my work forced me to sharpen ideas in a number of ways. Working with Vinay, Eric, Barbara Welke, Bruce Braun, and Lisa Disch was a singular experience.

Barbara, Bruce, and Lisa made lasting marks on the shape of this book as well as on my entire approach to scholarship. The major concepts that orient my thinking are simply unintelligible without their influences. The first germ of the idea for this book was a direct outgrowth of Bill Novak's seminar on the modern American state at the University of Chicago. As the notes to this book demonstrate, I still find myself learning from and arguing with Bill many years later. His influence on this project is much greater than he could ever imagine.

A number of teachers, friends, and colleagues over many years have read and commented on parts of this book and have provided all-around support. Riv-Ellen Prell made American studies a welcoming department for the disciplinarily restless. I'm beyond indebted to Libby Lunstrum and Megan Casey, who read early drafts of many of these chapters, and to Kate Kane and Joyce Mariano, for years of friendship, discussion, and support. Thanks also go to Hoku Aikau, Rich Byrne, Mike Carrier, Mat Coleman, John Conely, Billy Davies, David Delaney, Maria Fannin, Jim Glassman, Darryl Harper, Leila Harris, Rich Heyman, Molly Hudgens, Najeeb Jan, Michael Lansing, Paola Loreto, Dave Monteyne, Richa Nagar, Mae Ngai, David Noble, Tom Pepper, Gautham Rao, Sayres Rudy, Michael Stamm, Mary Strunk, Mary Thomas, and Amy Tyson. My short time hanging around the Department of Law, Jurisprudence, and Social Thought at Amherst was a true privilege, and I thank that department's faculty for engaging my ideas. Before I had figured out that it was the final chapter of the book, Trevor Barnes gave an initial version of chapter 6 a typically devastating reading, which, of course, improved the chapter's arguments greatly. Marion Werner has been a constant intellectual companion, a trenchant critic, and a dear friend whose conversations have always pushed my thinking in new ways. Thanks to her for showing enthusiasm when my own was starting to flag. Joel Wainwright gave the entire manuscript a final read and me an important pep talk as the book was nearing completion. His solidarity and encouragement were vital.

This book never would have been completed without the support of my colleagues in the Department of Geography at the University of Georgia. Thanks to all of them, but in particular, to George Brook, Andy Herod, Steve Holloway, Hilda Kurtz, Tom Mote, Dave Porinchu, Jenn Rice, and Amy Trauger for ongoing conversations about my work and so much more. I am truly lucky to work among an amazing group of faculty, staff, and students, who nevertheless manage to be warm and welcoming folks. The students in my political geography class on legal emergencies and my graduate seminars on biopolitics, law, and space, often co-taught with Amy Ross, forced me to rethink many of these arguments, both in substance and in presentation. I am fortunate to have worked with fantastic graduate students. Matt Mitchelson was a rock during my first years at the University of Georgia and continues to be a cherished friend and colleague. Conversations with Jason Rhodes have been important to my thinking about race and value. Thanks also go to Peter Hossler, Seth Gustafson, Graham Pickren, Levi Van Sant, Richard Milligan, and Stan Underwood. My life in Georgia would be totally different without Nik Heynen and Amy Ross, who have gone far beyond the duties of collegiality again and again to support my work. I cannot thank enough Nik and the entire crazy and wonderful Heynen clan for all their friendship, smarts, good humor, and uncommon decency. I thank them for all the long conversations that improved this book as well as life in general. Amy read just about every word of this book and argued with me about many of them. As one of the sharpest critics I know, I'm ever appreciative to have her in my corner.

Many old friends from my hometown of Tucson, Arizona, have sustained me over the years, often by providing needed distraction from this very project. Benj and Kelly were a home away from home in Minneapolis, as were Talia and Evan in Los Angeles. Robb, Sarah, Marc, and Noaa were always a welcome sight during a tough couple of years in Washington, D.C. Fred Finan has been a stalwart friend and sounding board about ideas and life in the academy. He has tolerated more rants about mainstream economics than any individual justifiably deserves to hear. For all of that, he still puts up with me and continues to embody much of what is best about the life of the mind (even if he disagrees with all the arguments presented here).

This book is dedicated to the memory of Frieda Koren Barkan, whose approach to the world indelibly shaped my thinking about politics and ethics. There are no words to express my gratitude to my family: Jerry and Kathy; Shawnie and Steve; Gil and Nano; Sam, Laura, Jonathan, and Lila; Leah, Max, Adam, and Alex; and of course, Simon. I hope this at least begins to answer what it is I've been thinking about for all these years. None of it would have happened without all of you. Special thanks also go to my mother and father, who continue to give a kind of unflagging love, faith, and support (only slightly tinged with my mother's worry) that I scarcely understood before having a child of my own. And to Susan, my love, and Sasha Felix, the center of my world, for everything, always.

Introduction

1. Peter Dicken, *Global Shift: Mapping the Changing Contours of the World Economy,* 5th ed. (New York: Guilford Press, 2007), 106.

2. Ronald Coase, "The Nature of the Firm," *Economica* 4, no. 16 (1937): 386–405; Oliver Williamson, "The Modern Corporation: Origins, Evolution, Attributes," *Journal of Economic Literature* 19, no. 4 (1981): 1537–68. This approach is echoed in Alfred Chandler, *The Visible Hand: The Managerial Revolution in American Business* (Cambridge, Mass.: Harvard University Press, 1977).

3. Frank Easterbrook and Daniel Fischel, *The Economic Structure of Corporate Law* (Cambridge, Mass.: Harvard University Press, 1996). The dominance of methodological individualism, microeconomic foundations, and model building in economics has not always been the case. See the essays by Robert Solow, David Kreps, and William Barber in Thomas Bender and Carl Schorske, eds., *American Academic Culture in Transformation: Fifty Years, Four Disciplines* (Princeton, N.J.: Princeton University Press, 1997).

4. Adam Smith, *An Inquiry into the Nature and Causes of the Wealth of Nations* (Oxford: Liberty Classics, 1978), 135, 141.

5. Naomi R. Lamoreaux, *The Great Merger Movement in American Business, 1895–1904* (Cambridge: Cambridge University Press, 1988); Colleen Dunlavy, *Politics and Industrialization: Early Railroads in the United States and Prussia* (Princeton, N.J.: Princeton University Press, 1994); Dunlavy, "From Partners to Plutocrats: Nineteenth-Century Shareholder Voting Rights and Theories of the Corporation," in *Constructing Corporate America: History, Politics, Culture,* ed. Kenneth Lipartito and David Sicilia, 63–93 (Oxford: Oxford University Press, 2004).

6. Dunlavy, *Politics and Industrialization;* Gerald Berk, *Alternative Tracks: The Constitution of American Industrial Order, 1865–1917* (Baltimore: Johns Hopkins University Press, 1997); Martin Sklar, *The Corporate Reconstruction of American Capitalism, 1890–1916: The Market, the Law, and Politics* (Cambridge: Cambridge University Press, 1988).

7. Peter Gourevitch and James Shinn, *Political Power and Corporate Control: The New Global Politics of Corporate Governance* (Princeton, N.J.: Princeton University Press, 2007); Mark Roe, *Political Determinants of Corporate Governance: Political Context, Corporate Impact* (Oxford: Oxford University Press, 2003).

8. Corporate interests can thus stand in for the class domination of the state, while at other times, they are presented as a hegemonic cross-class coalition. See Gabriel Kolko, *The Triumph of Conservatism: A Reinterpretation of American History, 1900–1916* (New York: Free Press, 1963); Kolko, *Railroads and Regulation, 1877–1916* (Princeton, N.J.: Princeton University Press, 1965); Sklar, *Corporate Reconstruction*; James Weinstein, *The Corporate Ideal in the Liberal State* (Boston: Beacon, 1962).

9. I discuss these aspects of the globalization of U.S. business law in "Law and the Geographic Analysis of Economic Globalization," *Progress in Human Geography* 35, no. 5 (2011): 589–607.

10. Louis Althusser, "Ideology and Ideological State Apparatuses: Notes towards an Investigation," in *Lenin and Philosophy and Other Essays*, trans. Ben Brewster (1971; repr., New York: Monthly Review Press, 2001), 109. This is the standard Marxist analysis of the corporation that it is an ideological cover for the real relations of class exploitation and shields the property of capitalists from having to undertake the full risk and liability of investment. Clearly we do not fully recognize the social relations present in the corporation. But there are political reasons, discussed later, for asking not only how this misrecognition relates to capitalism but how it articulates capitalism to sovereign power.

11. Edward Bellamy, *Looking Backward: 2000–1887* (1888; repr., New York: Signet Classic, 2000). For a literary rendering of corporate power in a dystopian present, see the corporate ownership of time ("Year of Glad"; "Year of the Depend Adult Undergarment") in David Foster Wallace's *Infinite Jest: A Novel* (Boston: Little, Brown, 1996). Other classics of the corporate-state genre include Aldous Huxley, *Brave New World* (1932; repr., New York: HarperCollins, 2005); William Gibson, *Neuromancer* (New York: Ace, 1984); and Neal Stephenson, *Snow Crash* (New York: Bantam, 1992).

12. See Medard Gabel and Henry Bruner, *Global, Inc.: An Atlas of the Multinational Corporation* (New York: New Press, 2003), and Sarah Anderson and John Cavanagh, *Top 200: The Rise of Global Corporate Power* (Washington, D.C.: Institute for Policy Studies, 2000).

13. Frederic Maitland, *State, Trust, and Corporation*, ed. David Runciman and Magnus Ryan (Cambridge: Cambridge University Press, 2003).

14. Morris Cohen, "Property and Sovereignty," *Cornell Law Quarterly* 13, no. 1 (1927): 8–30; Robert Lee Hale, "Coercion and Distribution in a Supposedly Non-coercive State," *Political Science Quarterly* 38, no. 3 (1923): 470–94.

15. Adolf Berle and Gardiner Means, *The Modern Corporation and Private Property* (New York: Macmillan, 1932); Sigmund Timberg, "Corporate Fictions:

Logical, Social, and International Implications," *Columbia Law Review* 46, no. 4 (1946): 533–80; Timberg, "International Combines and National Sovereigns: A Study in Conflict Laws and Mechanisms," *University of Pennsylvania Law Review* 95, no. 5 (1947): 575–620; Arthur S. Miller, *The Modern Corporate State: Private Governments and the American Constitution* (Westport, Conn.: Greenwood Press, 1976).

16. During the 1940s and 1950s, the Committee on Research in Economic History, working under the auspices of the Social Science Research Council, funded a number of monographs on nineteenth-century economic policy in the United States. Countering the received accounts of nineteenth-century U.S. history as a period of laissez-faire capitalism, the monographs focused on the ways individual states promoted economic growth. As these accounts made clear, chartering corporations was fundamental to these development strategies. For an overview of the project, see Arthur Cole, "Committee on Research in Economic History: A Description of Its Purposes, Activities, and Organization," *Journal of Economic History* 13, no. 1 (1953): 79–87. Two important monographs out of that series were Oscar Handlin and Mary Frug Handlin, *Commonwealth: A Study of the Role of Government in the American Economy, Massachusetts 1774–1861* (Cambridge, Mass.: Harvard University Press, 1947), and Louis Hartz, *Economic Policy and Democratic Thought, Pennsylvania 1776–1860* (Cambridge, Mass.: Harvard University Press, 1948).

17. J. Willard Hurst, *Law and the Conditions of Freedom in the Nineteenth Century United States* (Madison: University of Wisconsin Press, 1956); Hurst, *The Legitimacy of the Business Corporation in the Law of the United States, 1780–1970* (Charlottesville: University Press of Virginia, 1970); Morton Horwitz, "*Santa Clara* Revisited: The Development of Corporate Theory," *West Virginia Law Review* 88, no. 2 (1985): 173–224; Hendrik Hartog, *Public Property and Private Power: The Corporation of the City of New York in American Law, 1730–1870* (Chapel Hill: University of North Carolina Press, 1983); Pauline Maier, "The Revolutionary Origins of the American Corporation," *William and Mary Quarterly* 50, no. 1 (1993): 51–84; William Novak, "The American Law of Association: The Legal-Political Construction of Civil Society," *Studies in American Political Development* 15, no. 2 (2001): 163–88; Novak, "Public–Private Governance: A Historical Introduction," in *Government by Contract: Outsourcing and American Democracy,* ed. J. Freeman and M. Minow, 23–40 (Cambridge, Mass.: Harvard University Press, 2009).

18. T. M. Knox, trans., *Hegel's Philosophy of Right* (London: Oxford University Press, 1967), 152–55.

19. Derrida articulated the notion of the supplement in his reading of Rousseau, showing that the presence of something taken as natural and self-sufficient (in Derrida's case, speech; in ours, the State) actually depends on a substitution. With the inability of what is taken as natural to come fully to presence, the supplement marks an excess or surplus that adds to and fills while also taking the place of the original object. Moreover, the relation of supplementarity is *primary* as the supplement comes

to condition any access we have to the object in itself. See part II of *Of Grammatology*, trans. Gayatri Spivak (Baltimore: Johns Hopkins University Press, 1974).

20. Giorgio Agamben, *Homo Sacer: Sovereign Power and Bare Life*, trans. Daniel Heller-Roazen (Stanford, Calif.: Stanford University Press, 1998); Jean-Luc Nancy, *Being Singular Plural*, trans. Robert Richardson and Anne O'Byrne (Stanford, Calif.: Stanford University Press, 2000).

21. This is *homo sacer*, the archaic figure from Roman law who can be killed but not sacrificed. But Agamben also points out the close relation between the sovereign body of the king that, following the work of Ernst Kantorowicz, never dies and the sacred body of *homo sacer*. The ban is better understood as not only the sacred body that is "at the mercy of" sovereign power but also simultaneously the insignia of the sovereign (the *bandon*) and that which is done "out of free will, freely." See Agamben, *Homo Sacer*, 91–103, 110; Kantorowicz, *The King's Two Bodies: A Study in Medieval Political Theology* (Princeton, N.J.: Princeton University Press, 1957).

22. Carl Schmitt, *Political Theology: Four Chapters on the Concept of Sovereignty*, trans. George Schwab (1922; repr., Chicago: University of Chicago Press, 2005), 5.

23. Agamben, *Homo Sacer*, 19.

24. This is the ontological dimension of the ban. Agamben transposes legal and political concepts into ontological terms. To think about what sovereignty or the constituted power of the state *is* (ontologically) is to think about the modes of being of power. Treated as such, sovereignty becomes intertwined with the ontological problem of "the 'constitution of potentiality'" (ibid., 44). Potentiality, however, is a complicated concept. On one hand, potentiality has the radical openness and undetermined quality, as something that exists prior to its determination, that scholars like Antonio Negri valorize as a force against the constituted power of the state. But unlike Negri, Agamben reads potentiality through Aristotle, and thus potentiality's openness is always situated in relation to its actualization. Rather than an excess that sovereignty cannot capture, Agamben treats potentiality as the effect of sovereign power inasmuch as potentiality is always subordinate to its actualization. The task, then, for Agamben is freeing politics from sovereign power, or, put in ontological terms, freeing potentiality from its actualization. This requires a paradox not dissimilar to the sovereign exception, namely, the maintenance of potentiality in a state of suspension in which it is both something to be actualized and something not to be. As Agamben argues, for "potential to have its own consistency and not always disappear immediately into actuality, it is necessary that potentiality be able *not* to pass over into actuality, that potentiality constitutively be the *potentiality not to* (do or be), or, as Aristotle says, that potentiality be also im-potentiality" (ibid., 45). The dominance of the category of actuality over being (including being-in-potential) leaves us in the paradox of sovereign abandonment. But Agamben also notes the possibility within this formulation, as the modes of

being of politics already rely on nonbeing and the impossible. See ibid., 42–48; Antonio Negri, *Insurgencies: Constituent Power and the Modern State*, trans. Maurizia Boscagli (Minneapolis: University of Minnesota Press, 1999). For a lucid discussion of the debate between Agamben and Negri, see Brett Neilson, "*Potenza Nuda?* Sovereignty, Biopolitics, Capitalism," *Contretemps* 5 (2004): 63–78. On the ontological dimensions of Agamben's argument, see Adam Sitze "At the Mercy of...," in *The Limits of Law*, ed. Austin Sarat, Lawrence Douglas, and Martha Umphrey, 246–308 (Stanford, Calif.: Stanford University Press, 2005).

25. On deductive power, see Michel Foucault, *History of Sexuality*, vol. I, *An Introduction*, trans. Robert Hurley (1978; repr., New York: Vintage Books, 1990), 135–45. On the government of "men and things," see Foucault, *Security, Territory, Population: Lectures at the Collège de France, 1977–1978*, trans. Graham Burchell (New York: Palgrave Macmillan, 2007), 96.

26. Foucault, *History of Sexuality*, I.144.

27. Giorgio Agamben, *State of Exception*, trans. Kevin Attell (Chicago: University of Chicago Press, 2005); Derek Gregory, *The Colonial Present: Afghanistan, Palestine, Iraq* (Malden, Mass.: Blackwell, 2004).

28. I detail this argument in "Use beyond Value: Giorgio Agamben and a Critique of Capitalism," *Rethinking Marxism* 21, no. 2 (2009): 243–59.

29. Oliver Belcher, Lauren Martin, Anna Secor, Stephanie Simon, and Tommy Wilson, "Everywhere and Nowhere: The Exception and the Topological Challenge to Geography," *Antipode* 40, no. 4 (2008): 499–503.

30. Jamie Peck and Adam Tickell, "Neoliberalizing Space," *Antipode* 34, no. 3 (2002): 381.

31. Paolo Virno, *A Grammar of the Multitude*, trans. Isabella Bertoletti, James Cascaito, and Andrea Casson (Los Angeles, Calif.: Semiotext(e), 2004).

32. Karl Marx, *Capital*, vol. 1, trans. Ben Fowkes (New York: Penguin), 283. See also Virno, *Grammar of the Multitude*, 82–83.

33. Although the gendered language in the preceding quotation suggests that this is the work of "men," Marx also wrote of it in species-specific terms: "We presuppose labour in a form in which it is an exclusively human characteristic. A spider conducts operations which resemble those of the weaver, and a bee would put many a human architect to shame by the construction of its honeycomb cells. But what distinguishes the worst architect from the best of bees is that the architect builds the cell in his mind before he constructs it in wax. At the end of every labour process, a result emerges which had already been conceived by the worker at the beginning, hence already existed ideally." Marx, *Capital*, 1:283–84.

34. Ibid., 289.

35. Virno, *Grammar of the Multitude*, 83.

36. Ibid., 84.

37. Marx, *Capital*, 1:302. The quotation is from Goethe's *Faust*.

38. Ibid., 280.

39. Much of the most interesting critical work on sovereignty considers it in relation to questions about constituting and constituted power that are inherently temporal. See, e.g., Walter Benjamin, "Critique of Violence," in *Reflections: Essays, Aphorisms, Autobiographical Writing*, trans. E. Jephcott, 277–300 (New York: Harcourt Brace, 1978); Negri, *Insurgencies*; and Antonio Negri, *Time for Revolution*, trans. M. Mandarini (New York: Continuum, 2003).

40. David Harvey, of course, has taught us about the absolute centrality of space to the process of value creation, circulation, realization, and destruction in his pivotal *Limits to Capital* (London: Verso, 1999).

41. This has been an overriding question in the development of radical geography. See ibid.; Neil Smith, *Uneven Development: Nature, Capital, and the Production of Space* (Athens: University of Georgia Press, 2008); Edward Soja, *Postmodern Geographies: The Reassertion of Space in Critical Social Theory* (London: Verso, 1989); and, with a special emphasis on the law, Nicholas Blomley, *Law, Space, and the Geographies of Power* (New York: Guilford Press, 1994). Within the corpus of radical geography, my understanding of spatial history shares philosophical precepts with Stuart Elden's careful reading of Heidegger and Foucault in *Mapping the Present: Heidegger, Foucault, and the Project of a Spatial History* (London: Continuum, 2001).

42. On implicit spatiality and the spatiality of thinking, see Adam Sitze, introduction to Carlo Galli, *Political Spaces and Global War*, trans. Elisabeth Fay (Minneapolis: University of Minnesota Press, 2010).

43. For an outline of contemporary geographic engagements with corporations, see Michael Taylor and Päivi Oinas, eds., *Understanding the Firm* (Oxford: Oxford University Press, 2006). See also Phillip O'Neill, "Financial Narratives of the Modern Corporation," *Journal of Economic Geography* 1, no. 2 (2001): 181–99; O'Neill, "Where Is the Corporation in the Geographical World?" *Progress in Human Geography* 27, no. 6 (2003): 677–80; and O'Neill and J. K. Gibson-Graham, "Enterprise Discourse and Executive Talk: Stories that Destabilize the Company," *Transactions of the Institute of British Geographers* 24, no. 1 (1999): 11–22.

44. A massive literature, but for useful introductions stressing the spatial complexity of globalizing processes, see Neil Brenner, *New State Spaces: Urban Governance and the Rescaling of Statehood* (Oxford: Oxford University Press, 2004), and Doreen Massey, *For Space* (London: Sage, 2005).

45. See, e.g., Dicken, *Global Shift*; Leslie Sklair, *Globalization: Capitalism and Its Alternatives* (Oxford: Oxford University Press, 2002).

46. Louis Althusser, *For Marx*, trans. Ben Brewster (New York: Pantheon, 1969), 67n30.

47. Although there are differences between Foucault's and Nietzsche's genealogies and Althusser's symptomatic reading, there is enough correspondence between their arguments that I run them together here. After all, Althusser repeatedly emphasizes his debt to Foucault's work on madness and the clinic in his discussion of

the problematic in *Reading "Capital,"* trans. Ben Brewster (1970; repr., New York: Verso, 1997), 26, 45. See also Friedrich Nietzsche, *On the Genealogy of Morals*, trans. Walter Kaufmann and R. J. Hollingdale (1967; repr., New York: Vintage, 1989); Michel Foucault, *The Archaeology of Knowledge* (New York: Pantheon Books, 1972); Foucault, "Nietzsche, Genealogy, History," in *Language, Counter-memory, Practice*, ed. D. Bouchard (Ithaca, N.Y.: Cornell University Press, 1977); and chapters 1 and 2 of Foucault, *"Society Must Be Defended": Lectures at the Collège de France, 1975–1976*, trans. D. Macey (New York: Picador, 2003).

48. On Spinoza's concept of retrospective inversions, see William Connolly, *Pluralism* (Durham, N.C.: Duke University Press, 2005), 19–25.

49. Thomas Hobbes, *Leviathan* (1651; repr., Cambridge: Cambridge University Press, 1991), 200.

50. John P. Davis, *Corporations: A Study of the Origins and Development of Great Business Combinations and of the Relation to the Authority of the State*, 2 vols. (New York: Knickerbocker Press, 1905).

51. "The law is the quintessential form of 'active' discourse, able by its own operation to produce its effects. It would not be excessive to say that it *creates* the social world, but only if we remember that it is this world which first creates the law." Pierre Bourdieu, "The Force of Law: Toward a Sociology of the Juridical Field," *Hastings Law Journal* 38, no. 5 (1987): 839. See also William Novak, "The Legal Origins of the Modern American State, in *Looking Back at Law's Century*, ed. A. Sarat, B. Garth, and R. Kagan, 272–73 (Ithaca, N.Y.: Cornell University Press, 2002) and Alexandre Lefebvre, *The Image of Law: Deleuze, Bergson, Spinoza* (Stanford, Calif.: Stanford University Press, 2008).

1. The Sovereign Gift

1. Nick Robbins, "The World's First Multinational," *New Statesman* 133, no. 4718/9 (2004): 31–33. Other examples of the genre include John Micklethwait and Adrian Wooldridge, *The Company: A Short History of a Revolutionary Idea* (New York: Random House, 2005); Alfred Chandler Jr. and Bruce Mazlish, *Leviathans: Multinational Corporations and the New Global History* (New York: Cambridge University Press, 2005); Saskia Sassen, *Territory, Authority, Rights: From Medieval to Global Assemblages* (Princeton, N.J.: Princeton University Press, 2006); Paul Hirst and Grahame Thompson, *Globalization in Question: The International Economy and the Possibilities of Governance* (Malden, Mass.: Blackwell, 1996); and John Stopford, "Multinational Corporations," *Foreign Policy*, no. 113 (1998–99): 12–24.

2. This explains why both corporations and states shared the designation "bodies politic" in legal and political discourses.

3. For important readings of Hobbes that place him in historical context, while emphasizing very different aspects of that history, see C. B. Macpherson, *The Political Theory of Possessive Individualism* (London: Oxford University Press,

1962), and Quentin Skinner, *Reason and Rhetoric in the Philosophy of Hobbes* (Cambridge: Cambridge University Press, 1997).

4. Thomas Hobbes, *Leviathan* (1651; repr., Cambridge: Cambridge University Press, 1991), 120.

5. On the function of the corporate body in Hobbes, see Mark Neocleous, *Imagining the State* (Berkshire, U.K.: Open University Press, 2003), 72–78; Foucault, "*Society Must Be Defended*," 89–99.

6. "A Multitude of men, are made *One* Person, when they are by one man, or one Person, Represented; so that it be done with the consent of everyone of that Multitude in particular. For it is the *Unity* of the Representer, not the *Unity* of the Represented, that maketh the Person *One*. And it is the Representer that beareth the Person, and but one Person: And *Unity*, cannot otherwise be understood in Multitude." Hobbes, *Leviathan*, 114. See also Neocleous, *Imagining the State*, 77.

7. This discussion focuses on the law's relation to the bodies of corporations and states, yet it does not exhaust the ways law shapes bodies or the political bodies produced by law. See, e.g., Mary Poovey's insightful account of social difference and the social body in *Making a Social Body: British Cultural Formation, 1830–1864* (Chicago: University of Chicago Press, 1995) as well as Pheng Cheah, David Fraser, and Judith Grbich, eds., *Thinking through the Body of the Law* (New York: New York University Press, 1996).

8. On Hobbes's fear of associations within civil society, see Richard Boyd, "Thomas Hobbes and the Perils of Pluralism," *Journal of Politics* 63 (2001): 392–413. On the religious context of his concept of corporations, see Patricia Springborg, "*Leviathan*, the Christian Commonwealth Incorporated," *Political Studies* 24, no. 2 (1976): 171–83.

9. On the corporation in ancient Greece and Rome, see Max Radin, *The Legislation of the Greeks and Romans on Corporations* (New York: Tuttle, Moorehouse, and Taylor, 1909). On the revival of the corporation in the Middle Ages, see Otto von Gierke, *Political Theories of the Middle Ages*, trans. F. W. Maitland (Boston: Beacon Press, 1959). For the English context, see Frederick Pollock and Frederic W. Maitland, *History of English Law before the Time of Edward I*, 2 vols. (Cambridge: Cambridge University Press, 1923), 486.

10. Kantorowicz, *King's Two Bodies*, 198.

11. Ibid.

12. Ibid., 197.

13. Ibid., 172. Gaines Post described the importance of the phrase *quod omnes tangit*, or "that which touches all," for conceptualizing state power in "A Roman–Canonical Maxim, *Quod Omnes Tangit*, in Bracton and in Early Parliaments," in *Studies in Medieval Legal Thought: Public Law and the State*, 163–238 (Princeton, N.J.: Princeton University Press, 1964).

14. On the fisc, see ibid., 361; Kantorowicz, *King's Two Bodies*, 164–92.

15. *Oxford English Dictionary*, 2nd ed. (Oxford: Oxford University Press, 1989).

16. Foucault outlined "deductive" sovereignty as an extension of the *patria potestas*, which ordered the Roman family. *Patria potestas* represented the power of the patriarch to take away the life—to "dispose"—of children or slaves. Secular states did not maintain an absolute right to dispose of life, but they could do so in defense of state sovereignty. Foucault quoted the natural law theorist Samuel Pufendorf: "If he [the sovereign] were threatened by external enemies who sought to overthrow him or contest his rights, he could then legitimately wage war, and require his subjects to take part in the defense of the state; without 'directly proposing their death,' he was empowered to 'expose their life': in this sense, he wielded an 'indirect' power over them of life and death." Foucault, *History of Sexuality*, I:135.

17. Ernst Kantorowicz, "*Pro Patria Mori* in Medieval Political Thought," in *Selected Studies*, 308–24 (New York: J. J. Augustin, 1965).

18. Ibid., 491.

19. Gaines Post, "The Two Laws and the Statute of York," *Speculum* 29, no. 2 (1954): 422. See also Carl Schmitt, *Political Theology: Four Chapters on the Concept of Sovereignty*, trans. George Schwab (1922; repr., Chicago: University of Chicago Press, 2005). Schmitt connected this legal maxim to the sovereign exception. For Schmitt, it captured the very essence of the way the sovereign places itself outside of the law to save the law. If necessity knows no law, then there can be no law or procedural norm that can determine when a given set of actions is necessary for the state's own security.

20. This is the argument in Foucault's famous governmentality lecture of February 1, 1978. See Foucault, *Security, Territory, Population*, 87–114, and Graham Burchell, "Peculiar Interests: Civil Society and Governing the System of Natural Liberty," in *The Foucault Effect: Studies in Governmentality*, ed. Graham Burchell, Colin Gordon, and Peter Miller, 119–50 (Chicago: University of Chicago Press, 1991). On the unpredictability of fortune, see J. G. A. Pocock, *The Machiavellian Moment: Florentine Political Thought and the Atlantic Republican Tradition* (Princeton, N.J.: Princeton University Press, 1975).

21. Foucault, *Security, Territory, Population*, 99.

22. Ibid., 93.

23. Ibid., 94.

24. In *The Cameralists* (Chicago: University of Chicago Press, 1909), Albion Small chronicles police ordinances going back to 1555. Pasquale Pasquino's account of the police focuses on Georg Obrecht, the Strasburg official whose writings from the early seventeenth century "speak no longer in the political language of prince and people, but instead in that of population and *Obrigkeit*, a term which means authority but also public power or government." Pasquino, "Theatrum Politicum: The Genealogy of Capital—Police and the State of Prosperity," in Burchell et al., *The Foucault Effect*, 112. Marc Raeff argues that "we encounter the first significant examples of the interventionist and regulatory *Polizeistaat* in the Protestant states of Germany, such as Saxony and Hessen, in the second half of the sixteenth

century" in "The Well Ordered Police State and the Development of Modernity in Seventeenth and Eighteenth-Century Europe: An Attempt at a Comparative Approach," *American Historical Review* 80, no. 5 (1975): 1223. See also Keith Tribe, "Cameralism and the Science of Government," *Journal of Modern History* 56 (1984): 263–84.

25. Franz-Ludwig Knemeyer, "Polizei," *Economy and Society* 9, no. 2 (1980): 172. Knemeyer links the concept to the Greek polis and the Latin *politia*. Like these terms, "'Polizei' signified not only the satisfactory regulation of the community but the community itself—in an exact analogy with the twin meaning the word possessed in Aristotelian ethics and politics" (179). For this reason, Tribe describes police as an "ethico-political" as opposed to legal discourse in his introduction to Knemeyer's article.

26. Raeff, "Well Ordered Police State."

27. The presence or absence of police in England has been a point of controversy. Mitchell Dean and Mark Neocleous have argued that Britain was similar to the continent in the use of police regulation. See Dean, *The Constitution of Poverty: Toward a Genealogy of Liberal Governance* (London: Routledge, 1991), and Neocleous, *The Fabrication of Social Order: A Critical Theory of Police Power* (London: Pluto Press, 2000). Mary Poovey challenges the claim in *A History of the Modern Fact* (Chicago: University of Chicago Press, 1998), arguing that "the relatively weak constitutional basis for central government in Britain, combined with a persistent resistance to such centralization, which was advanced in the name of 'liberty' and cultivated in the periodical publications that circulated information in the newly emergent public sphere, meant that developing anything like a science of police in Britain in the eighteenth century would have been very difficult" (366n3). Poovey argues that an emergent concept of publicness prevented the centralization of knowledge and administration into a strong state form. Although British regulation may not have been centralized to the degree it was in German states, it does seem clear that concepts of public health, welfare, and order were central to eighteenth-century British notions of government and were pursued, as I hope to make clear, through a practice of chartered grants of incorporation.

28. On the police in England, see St. George Tucker, ed., *Blackstone's Commentaries: With Notes of Reference to the Constitution and Laws of the Federal Government of the United States and of the Commonwealth of Virginia*, 5 vols. (Philadelphia: Birch and Small, 1803); Adam Smith, *Lectures on Jurisprudence*, ed. R. Meek, D. Raphael, and P. Stein (Oxford: Liberty Classics, 1978); and Smith, *An Inquiry into the Nature and Causes of the Wealth of Nations* (Oxford: Liberty Classics, 1978). Relevant discussions on the relation between liberalism and the police also include William Novak, *The People's Welfare: Law and Regulation in Nineteenth Century America* (Chapel Hill: University of North Carolina Press, 1996); Christopher Tomlins, *Law, Labor, and Ideology in the Early American Republic* (Cambridge: Cambridge University Press, 1993); Markus Dubber and

Mariana Valverde, eds., *The New Police Science: The Police Power in Domestic and International Governance* (Stanford, Calif.: Stanford University Press, 2006); and Dubber and Valverde, eds., *Police and the Liberal State* (Stanford, Calif.: Stanford University Press, 2008).

29. The problem of government—of which the police is one mode—has been unhelpfully obscured by the now exhausted debate on the differences between republicanism and liberalism in seventeenth- and eighteenth-century political thought. In truth, the problematic of government is not wholly consistent with either side of the republican–liberalism divide. This is only in part because, as James Kloppenberg demonstrated, Christian doctrine, republican virtue, and liberal individualism were overlapping discourses, or as Steven Pincus contends, republican and liberal theories both considered problems of trade, revenue, and finance relevant to public welfare in seventeenth-century debates about the English Commonwealth. By displacing entirely the republicanism–liberalism debate for a focus on the shifting forms of political rationality, we can see both civic virtue and liberal economics as techniques for ordering society that produced new social objects, new forms of knowledge, and new social subjectivities. See Burchell, "Peculiar Interests," 122; Kloppenberg, "The Virtues of Liberalism: Christianity, Republicanism, and Ethics in Early American Political Discourse," *Journal of American History* 74, no. 1 (1987): 9–33; Pincus, "Neither Machiavellian Moment nor Possessive Individualism: Commercial Society and the Defenders of the English Commonwealth," *American Historical Review* 103, no. 3 (1998): 705–36.

30. Burchell, "Peculiar Interests," 122.

31. Tucker, *Blackstone's Commentaries*, 5:162.

32. Ibid., 5:161–75 passim.

33. Tribe, "Camerialism," 266.

34. Ibid., 267.

35. Mitchell Dean, *Governmentality: Power and Rule in Modern Society* (London: Sage, 1999), 105.

36. Raeff, "Well Ordered Police State," 1227.

37. Jacques Donzelot, *The Policing of Families* (New York: Pantheon, 1979); Nikolas Rose, "Beyond the Public/Private Division: Law, Power and the Family," in *Critical Legal Studies*, ed. P. Fitzpatrick and A. Hunt, 61–76 (Oxford: Blackwell, 1986).

38. Davis, *Corporations*, 2:50–51.

39. Stewart Kyd, *A Treatise on the Laws of Corporations* (London: J. Butterworth, 1794), 1.

40. On this development, see Pollock and Maitland, *History of English Law*, 488–508.

41. Cecil Carr argues that this form was established under Queen Elizabeth I by 1564. He also notes that these chartered organizations were defined "partly upon inevitable self-government partly upon royal condescension." Carr, ed.,

Select Charters for Trading Companies, 1530–1707 (London: Quaritch, 1913).

42. Sir Edward Coke, *Case of Sutton's Hospital,* 10 Rep. 30-1. Coke has at times been presented as a forerunner of eighteenth-century liberalism. See, e.g., Eli Heckscher, *Mercantilism,* 2 vols. (London: Allen and Unwin, 1935). For a view that situates him as a theorist of the public order, see Barbara Malament, "The 'Economic Liberalism' of Sir Edward Coke," *Yale Law Journal* 76 (1967): 1321–58. See also Samuel Williston, "History of the Law of Business Corporations before 1800," in *Select Essays in Anglo-American Legal History,* ed. Ernst Freund (Boston: Little, Brown, 1907–9), 2:204–9.

43. Tucker, *Blackstone's Commentaries,* 2:475–76.

44. Carr, *Select Charters,* xiii–xix. At times, the grant of perpetual succession was replaced with clauses that established time limits on the grant. Time limits were more often found in charters that established monopoly privileges, as opposed to municipal grants. See, e.g., the charter for the Levant Company. Ibid., 42.

45. Tucker, *Blackstone's Commentaries,* 2:346.

46. Carr, *Select Charters,* xv; and Tucker, *Blackstone's Commentaries,* vol. 2, chapter 18. See also Williston, "History of the Law of Business Corporations," 207–9.

47. Carr, *Select Charters,* 4.

48. Albert O. Hirschman, *The Passions and the Interests: Arguments for Capitalism before Its Time* (Princeton, N.J.: Princeton University Press, 1977).

49. Carr, *Select Charters,* 70; Poovey, *History of the Modern Fact.*

50. Carr, *Select Charters,* 8.

51. Williston, "History of the Law of Business Corporations."

52. Maud Sellers, *Acts and Ordinances of the Eastland Company* (London: Royal Historical Society, 1906), 27.

53. Ibid., 7–10.

54. Carr, *Select Charters,* 12.

55. Ibid., 53.

56. John Wheeler, *A Treatise of Commerce Wherein are shewed the Commodities arising by a well ordered and ruled Trade, such as that of the Societie of Merchants Aduenturers is proued to be* (London: John Harrison, 1601), 95.

57. Ibid., 6.

58. Ibid., 54, 56. In this respect, Wheeler can be assimilated into a growing seventeenth-century discourse on the interrelation between manners (as ethical mores) and commerce. J. G. A. Pocock describes this discourse as a part of the natural law tradition "carried out with the weapons of humanism"—in other words, a nascent liberal humanism. "The effect was to construct a liberalism which made the state's authority guarantee the liberty of the individual's social behavior, but had no intention whatever of impoverishing that behavior by confining it to rigorous assertion of ego-centered individual right.... Now, at last, a right to things became a way to the practice of virtue, so long as virtue could be defined as the practice and refinement of manners. A commercial humanism had been not unsuccessfully constructed." Pocock, "Virtues, Rights, and Manners: A

Model for Historians of Political Thought," *Political Theory* 9 (1981): 353–68.

59. That the logic of the police and the charter are fully realized in colonization supports my argument that the corporation and the charter were created as a legally authorized exemption from law. Although the space most closely connected with the exemption of law has been the camp, the colony is more appropriate as the originary gap produced through the legal exception, in which the division between qualified and abandoned life is established. Before Agamben's writing on the camp, Hannah Arendt had already argued that the Nazi death machine required the bloody mix of nineteenth-century imperialism, race, and bureaucracy. See Arendt, *Origins of Totalitarianism* (New York: Harcourt, 1968); Nasser Hussain, *The Jurisprudence of Emergency: Colonialism and the Rule of Law* (Ann Arbor: University of Michigan Press, 2003); Achille Mbembe, *On the Postcolony* (Berkeley: University of California Press, 2001); and Adam Sitze, "Capital Punishment as a Problem for the Philosophy of Law," *CR: The New Centennial Review* 9, no. 2 (2009): 221–70. On the relation between police and colonialism in other historical moments, see Mariana Valverde, "'Peace, Order, and Good Government': Policelike Powers in Postcolonial Perspective," in Dubber and Valverde, *New Police Science*, 73–106, and Christopher Tomlins, "The Supreme Sovereignty of the State: A Genealogy of Police in American Constitutional Law, from the Founding Era to *Lochner*," in Dubber and Valverde, *Police and the Liberal State*, 33–53.

60. Carr, *Select Charters*, 191.

61. Jean Bodin, *The Six Bookes of a Common-Weale*, trans. Richard Knolles (London: Bishop, 1606), 364. See also Preston King, *The Ideology of Order: A Comparative Analysis of Jean Bodin and Thomas Hobbes* (London: Allen and Unwin, 1974), 106–25.

62. Bodin, *Six Bookes*, 363.

63. Ibid., 361, 365.

64. Hobbes, *Leviathan*, 155.

65. Ibid., 163, 155–65 passim.

66. For Hobbes, representation goes beyond the sense of either a proxy or a picture. Hobbes's theory of undivided sovereignty required a form of representation that was absolute. The notion that individuals could come together and express a collective will was the grounds for sovereign power—the idea that they could do so and make a fictional person was a threat to sovereignty. See Hanna Pitkin, *The Concept of Representation* (Berkeley: University of California Press, 1967).

67. Hobbes, *Leviathan*, 230. Hobbes also refers to monopolies as "a Disease, which resembleth the Pleurisie; and that is when the Treasure of the Commonwealth, flowing out of its due course, is gathered together in too much abundance in one, or a few private men, by Monopolies, or by Farmes of the Publique Revenues; in the same manner as the Blood in a Pleurisie, getting into the Membrane of the breast, breedeth there an Inflammation, accompanied with a Fever, and painfull stitches" (229). See also Boyd, "Thomas Hobbes and the Perils of Pluralism."

68. Hobbes, *Leviathan*, 200.

2. Property

1. Sklar, *Corporate Reconstruction*; Alan Trachtenberg, *The Incorporation of America: Culture and Society in the Gilded Age* (New York: Hill and Wang, 1982).

2. See Martin Shapiro, "The Globalization of Law," *Indiana Journal of Global Legal Studies* 1, no. 1 (1993): 37–64; R. Daniel Keleman and Eric C. Sibbitt, "The Globalization of American Law," *International Organization* 58, no. 1 (2004): 103–36; and, more generally, Yves Dezalay and Bryant Garth, eds., *Global Prescriptions: The Production, Exportation, and Importation of a New Legal Orthodoxy* (Ann Arbor: University of Michigan Press, 2002).

3. Foucault, *Security, Territory, Population*, 95.

4. Michel Foucault, "History of Systems of Thought, 1979," *Philosophy and Social Criticism* 8 (1981): 357, as quoted in Colin Gordon, "Governmental Rationality: An Introduction," in Burchell et al., *Foucault Effect*, 19.

5. Standard economic texts on the corporation, including Chandler, Coase, and Williamson, agree that the corporation's primary strength is its ability to internalize competitive pressures. Marxists and regulation theorists, such as Michel Aglietta, have also suggested that the corporation, by concentrating and consolidating various fragments of capital, was important for the maintenance of the process of valorization in the early-twentieth-century United States. My argument is that the law had a role in producing corporations with such abilities (or to use Aglietta's language, the law produced the "structural form" that enabled consolidation). Furthermore, these legal changes were conceptualized in terms of questions about the best ways to serve the public welfare. The corporation gives us a way to consider how "economy," as both the science and practices designed to optimally organize society under conditions of scarcity, developed in response to problems of government and sovereignty. See Aglietta, *A Theory of Capitalist Regulation: The US Experience* (London: Verso, 1979).

6. The bank was once a major topic for U.S. historians and central to studies of Jacksonian America. For an introduction, see Bray Hammond, "Jackson, Biddle, and the Bank of the United States," *Journal of Economic History* 7 (1947): 1–23; Marvin Meyers, *The Jacksonian Persuasion: Politics and Belief* (New York: Vintage, 1960).

7. Hammond, "Jackson, Biddle, and the Bank," 12.

8. Theodore Sedgwick, *What Is a Monopoly?, or, Some Considerations upon the Subject of Corporations and Currency* (New York: George Scott, 1835), 8.

9. Ibid., 13.

10. Ibid., 7, 13.

11. Ibid., 23. I have left the emphases of the original documents in all of the quotations in this chapter, unless otherwise noted.

12. Ibid., 35.

13. Ibid.

14. Meyers, *Jacksonian Persuasion*, chapter 8; Steve Fraser, *Every Man a Speculator: A History of Wall Street in American Life* (New York: HarperCollins, 2005), chapter 2. Meyers presents Sedgwick as an interesting variation on Jacksonian themes, resulting from his unique background as a Democrat from a patrician Massachusetts Federalist family. In Meyers's reading of Sedgwick's *Public and Private Economy* (1836), the writer appears to be nostalgic for a mythical agrarian past being swept up by the tide of capitalism.

15. Interestingly, Henshaw, the Democrat, was also a banker. His attempts to charter a new bank in 1832, as an alternative to Biddle's BUS, gave further impetus to the movement to veto the BUS. See U.S. Senate, *Memorial of David Henshaw, and Others*, 22nd Cong., 1st Session, No. 37; Bray Hammond, "The Second Bank of the United States," *Transactions of the American Philosophical Society* 43 (1953): 80–85; A. B. Darling, "Jacksonian Democracy in Massachusetts, 1824–1848," *American Historical Review* 29 (1924): 271–87.

16. David Henshaw, *Remarks upon the Rights and Powers of Corporations, and of the Rights, Powers, and Duties of the Legislature toward Them* (Boston: Beals and Greene, 1837), 9.

17. Ibid.

18. Ibid.

19. Ibid., 10.

20. Ibid., 11.

21. Smith, *Lectures on Jurisprudence*, 398.

22. Ibid., 486.

23. Ibid., 489.

24. For Smith, the division of labor was the sign of civilization's progress and, coincidentally, unique to Europe. Against the division of labor, Smith presented the poverty of "an Indian sovereign" compared to "a common day labourer in Britain," suggesting "An European prince, however, does not so far exceed a commoner as the latter does the chief of a savage nation." Ibid.

25. Ibid., 496, 356.

26. Ibid., 497.

27. Ibid., 498.

28. Mary Poovey has provided a useful investigation of Smith's epistemology and notes the central role of "the system" in constituting "the market" as an object which follows its own natural laws. Smith devalued observed particulars in favor of formal coherence. "The trope of system helped produce the entity it claimed simply to describe (the market)." Poovey, *History of the Modern Fact*, 237, 236–49 passim.

29. Smith, *An Inquiry into the Nature and Causes of the Wealth of Nations*, 135, 141.

30. Istvan Hont and Michael Ignatieff, "Needs and Justice in the *Wealth of Nations*: An Introductory Essay," in *Wealth and Virtue: The Shaping of Political*

Economy in the Scottish Enlightenment, 1–45 (Cambridge: Cambridge University Press, 1983). Smith's notion of property derived from a tradition of natural law, which Hont and Ignatieff trace back to Grotius's, Pufendorf's, and Locke's reformulation of Aquinas. For Aquinas, private property was derived from the common grant of earth that God made to humanity. Aquinas argued that private property rights could be suspended by the sovereign in cases of extreme need. Later natural law theorists abandoned this precept, arguing that scarcity was critical for the working of the market to serve the public good. Only for the most severe emergencies, such as devastating famines, could the sovereign suspend property rights. Property was primary—a "perfect right"—because it entailed a series of exchanges between formally equal individuals. Need, conversely, was subjective and constituted only an "imperfect right" that did not entail reciprocal obligations. As Hont and Ignatieff explain, for natural law theorists from Grotius to Smith, needs "were theorized as exceptions, rather than as rules, as they had been in Thomist jurisprudence. A man had a right only to what was his own. He had no right to what was his due. His imperfect right to be treated with humanity only hardened into a perfect right under conditions of gravest necessity" (29–30). Given that property preceded the creation of the state in natural law theories, the sovereign was precluded from exercising distributive justice that would entail benefits to some without demanding obligations in return. Natural law instead demanded a more limited protection of "perfect rights" that were the result of exchange, consent, and compact. Hont and Ignatieff argue that the discourse of the market and the division of labor allowed Smith to "transpose the question [of justice] from the terrain of jurisprudence and political theory to the terrain of political economy, using natural modeling to demonstrate that by raising the productivity of agriculture, commercial society could provide adequately for the needs of the wage-earner without having to resort to any form of redistributive meddling in the property rights of individuals" (25).

31. Police "gave voice to a concept of governance expressing the community's right of response to communal necessity recast in the language of inherent popular rights of control and direction of government." Tomlins, *Law, Labor, and Ideology,* 56–57.

32. Ibid., 58–59.

33. Novak, *People's Welfare,* 9.

34. On *sic utere,* ibid., 42–50. *Sic utere* was also the aspect of the police powers emphasized by legal writers like Christopher Tiedeman, who were considered to be advocates of "laissez-faire constitutionalism." See Tiedeman, *Treatise on the Limitations of Police Power* (St. Louis: H. F. Thomas Law Books, 1886); Clyde Jacobs, *Law Writers and the Courts: The Influence of Thomas M. Cooley, Christopher G. Tiedeman, and John F. Dillon upon American Constitutional Law* (Berkeley: University of California Press, 1954). Laissez-faire ideology thus included a role for state action but limited that action to only those moments in which private property was threatened.

35. On the power of vested rights in U.S. history, see Morton Horwitz, *The Transformation of American Law, 1780–1880,* vol. 1 (Cambridge, Mass.: Harvard University Press, 1977). On the strength of public regulation, see Novak, *People's Welfare.* In short, I am suggesting that we abandon the debate between public power and vested rights for one focused on the diverse and contradictory tactics used to solve problems of government. Moreover, these tactics of government were already bound up with the legally authorized suspension of law and led to the sacrifice of some for the salvation of others. As Adam Sitze has noted, this concept is internal to the concept of *salus,* which combines notions of health and salvation. See Sitze, "Denialism," *South Atlantic Quarterly* 103, no. 4 (2004): 768–811. Many commentators on the nineteenth-century United States have noted the ways doctrines of public rights and vested rights have intermingled and reinforced one another. See Harry Scheiber, "Public Rights and the Rule of Law in American Legal History," *California Law Review* 72, no. 2 (1984): 217–51. My argument is not only that public power could be used to promote certain forms of private property—a statement, I believe, that both Horwitz and Novak would accept—but that both have to be thought in terms of the problematic of government, which remained inextricably structured by the paradox of the sovereign ban.

36. This complexity is reflected in the case law on police power. Take, e.g., *Commonwealth v. Alger,* 7 Cush. 53 (1851), which is commonly cited as evidence of the supremacy of state police power over individual property rights. The case, decided by the Massachusetts Supreme Court in 1851, concerned the ability of commissioners to establish a line in the Boston Harbor beyond which any construction of wharfs or piers was prohibited. Chief Justice Lemuel Shaw used the opportunity to outline the commonwealth's police powers over property, even in cases in which it infringed on individual rights, because the commonwealth was the ultimate owner of the land. While Shaw's decision in *Alger* clearly stated the primacy of public rights, the critical element was less whether the legislature could act against the rights of private individuals to preserve public rights of fishing or navigation and more who would decide and under what protocols these actions were appropriate. The police power had to adjudicate between competing rights of the community and the individual. Shaw elaborated, "It is subject for them, [the legislature] under a high sense of duty to the public and to individuals, with a sacred regard to the rights of property and all other private rights, to make such reasonable regulations as they may judge necessary to protect public and private rights, and to impose no larger restraints upon the use and enjoyment of private property, than are in their judgment strictly necessary to preserve and protect the rights of others" (102).

37. As Shaw noted in *Commonwealth v. Alger,* the grant made by the King to establish the property rights of the colony over the harbor spoke in terms of propriety. Shaw clarified the meaning: "The word 'propriety' is nearly, if not precisely, equivalent to 'property,'" and later, "Here it [the term *propriety*] obviously

means his real estate, his farm, including its most valuable part, his tillage and mowing lands. The word 'propriety' is used in the same sense by Lord Hale, and many other writers of that period, and is obviously a translation of the Latin word *'proprietas,'* Latin being the language then chiefly used in legal writings and proceedings. Yet it is the term 'propriety,' in the enacting clause, which is called 'this liberty' in the proviso" (71–72).

38. *License Cases (Thurlow v. Massachusetts),* 5 How. 583 (1847). This reference was also highlighted by Chief Justice Waite in his important decision in *Munn v. Illinois,* 94 U.S. 125 (1877).

39. Foucault, *Security, Territory, Population,* 96.

40. Maier, "Revolutionary Origins of the American Corporation," 53.

41. On variations in state corporate laws, compare the commonwealth studies such as Handlin and Handlin, *Commonwealth: A Study of the Role of Government in the American Economy;* Hartz, *Economic Policy and Democratic Thought;* John Cadman Jr., *The Corporation in New Jersey: Business and Politics, 1791–1875* (Cambridge, Mass.: Harvard University Press, 1949); and G. Herberton Evans Jr., *Business Incorporation in the United States, 1800–1943* (New York: National Bureau of Economic Research, 1948). William Roy has an interesting study comparing the strategies of state legislatures in New Jersey, Ohio, and Pennsylvania, each of which adopted contrasting regulatory stances. See Roy, *Socializing Capital: The Rise of the Large Industrial Corporation in America* (Princeton, N.J.: Princeton University Press, 1997).

42. Hartog's *Public Property and Private Power* explains how a corporation— the city of New York—gave up its chartered rights to the state legislature and made itself subject to government regulation.

43. *Dartmouth College v. Woodward,* 17 U.S. 518 (1819).

44. Ibid., 636.

45. Ibid., 637.

46. Ibid., 636.

47. *Bank of Augusta v. Earle,* 38 U.S. 587 (1839).

48. Ibid., 588.

49. Tiedeman, *Treatise on the Limitations of Police Power,* 578, and quoted in Novak, *People's Welfare,* 110. Novak also notes the central importance of *Thorpe v. Rutland,* 27 Vt. 140 (1855), as a key case in establishing the limits of corporate rights in relation to the police power. Indeed, Tiedeman opens his *Treatise on the Limitations of Police Power* by quoting Justice Redfield's decision in the case—even before referencing the more familiar statement of Blackstone: "The power of the government to impose this restraint [*sic utere*] is called POLICE POWER. By this general police power of the State, persons and property are subjected to all kinds of restraints and burdens, in order to secure the general comfort, health and prosperity of the State; of the perfect right in the legislature to do which no question ever was or upon acknowledged general principles ever can be made, so far as natural

persons are concerned" (2). *Thorpe v. Rutland* was an 1855 Vermont case that held a railroad company liable for injuries to animals caused by not fixing fencing and cattle guards along the line. Novak also cites the cases of *Brick Presbyterian Church v. Mayor of New York,* 5 Cow. 538 (NY, 1826), and *Coates v. Mayor of New York,* 7 Cow. 585 (NY, 1827), as two cases that invalidated granted rights to corporations as to the locations of burials.

50. On this generally, see Joseph Davis, *Essays on the Earlier History of American Corporations* (Cambridge, Mass.: Harvard University Press, 1917).

51. Sedgwick, *What Is a Monopoly?,* 35.

52. In the nineteenth century, one strategy states used to promote economic development was the "mixed corporation," which was backed by public funds. The best accounts of the use of mixed corporations are Hartz, *Economic Policy and Democratic Thought,* and Handlin and Handlin, *Commonwealth.* One of the BUS's most controversial aspects was its funding by the federal government, though it was chartered in individual states. See Hammond, "Jackson, Biddle, and the Bank."

53. E.g., in Massachusetts, general incorporation laws were passed for banking in 1829, for insurance in 1818, and for manufacturing in 1809. See Edwin Merrick Dodd, "The First Half Century of Statutory Regulation of Business Corporations in Massachusetts," in *Harvard Legal Essays,* 65–132 (Cambridge, Mass.: Harvard University Press, 1934). Bray Hammond discusses the development of general incorporation laws for banks in New York and Michigan in the 1830s in "Free Banks and Corporations: The New York Free Banking Act of 1839," *Journal of Political Economy* 44, no. 2 (1936): 184–209. He notes the profound change in the understanding of corporations, as New York's free banking law "presented a conflict of economic evolution and law from which the characteristic nineteenth century conception of the corporation as an instrumentality of individualism and laissez faire emerged. . . . Before the transition from the old conception to the new, the corporation was identical with monopoly and antithetical to democracy; following the transition it lost its hateful connotations and became the guileless handmaid of free enterprise. Later, after a prolific marriage with laissez faire, the corporation was again to be identified with monopoly; but this modern identification is the product of economic forces, whereas the old was a matter of law" (185).

54. On the development of general incorporation laws, see Davis, *Essays;* Andrew Creighton, "The Emergence of Incorporation as a Legal Form for Organizations," PhD diss., Stanford University, 1990; "Note—Incorporating the Republic: The Corporation in Antebellum Political Culture," *Harvard Law Review* 102, no. 8 (1998): 1883–1903; and Evans, *Business Incorporation in the United States.* A number of historians have approached the development of general incorporation laws by asking why these laws were passed. Henry Butler provides a useful overview of the debates in "Nineteenth Century Jurisdictional Competition in the Granting of Corporate Privileges," *Journal of Legal Studies* 14, no. 1 (1985): 129–66. Answers include pragmatic, functionalist, market-based, and ideological reasons. For

instance, Edwin Merrick Dodd and Joseph Blandi argue that general incorporation laws were designed to ease the burden on overtaxed legislatures of having to pass special acts of incorporation for every group that sought a charter. Louis Hartz claims that general incorporation laws responded to Jacksonian attacks on corporate privilege by democratizing the granting of charters. William Roy suggests that general incorporation laws were part of an organizational transformation to socialize capital. John Cadman suggests a more technical rationale, that general incorporation laws limited abuse of the special charter system and standardized corporate regulation. Butler suggests that states stopped issuing special charters when they could no longer receive monopoly rents in return for their services. Ronald Seavoy and Bray Hammond suggest that it was a response to the economic crash of 1837. See Blandi, *Maryland Business Corporations, 1783–1852* (Baltimore: Johns Hopkins University Press, 1934); Dodd, *American Business Corporations until 1860* (Cambridge, Mass.: Harvard University Press, 1934); Hartz, *Economic Policy and Democratic Thought*; Roy, *Socializing Capital*; Cadman, *Corporation in New Jersey*; Seavoy, *The Origins of the American Business Corporation, 1784–1855* (Westport, Conn.: Greenwood Press, 1982); and Hammond, "Free Banks and Corporations."

While I recognize that determining the cause of general incorporation laws is an important historical undertaking, my interest in general incorporation laws is primarily in their effects. I take it as axiomatic that general incorporation laws were the result of politics and power struggles, determined on the basis of a number of causal factors that were specific to place and time. I also understand that individuals advocate for a policy for various reasons and that the policy might produce unintended consequences. Yet, by the 1870s, general incorporation was a fact, for whatever reason. My question, however, is what did the fact of general incorporation laws mean in terms of the exercise of corporate power and the problematic of sovereignty and government?

55. Creighton, "Emergence of Incorporation," 133.

56. Ibid., 40.

57. Ibid., 39–40; Dodd, *American Business Corporations*; Roy, *Socializing Capital*.

58. Horwitz, "*Santa Clara* Revisited," 187.

59. Ibid., 186–90. On the development of limited liability, see Edwin Merrick Dodd, "The Evolution of Limited Liability in American Industry: Massachusetts," *Harvard Law Review* 61, no. 8 (1948): 1351–79. Dodd shows how Massachusetts experimented with a variety of systems for assessing liability before settling on limited liability in the 1850s. See also Roy, *Socializing Capital*, 158–75, who stresses the contingent ways that states developed provisions for assessing liability. Interestingly, he notes that early in the nineteenth century, limited liability was viewed as a threat to businesses, as investors would be less scrupulous in monitoring the activities of companies if they did not bear the burden of full liability.

60. Roy, *Socializing Capital*, 159.

61. Or as Foucault, *Security, Territory, Population,* 96, framed it, "the complex of men and things."

62. On railroads, see Chandler, *Visible Hand;* Berk, *Alternative Tracks;* Kolko, *Railroads and Regulation;* and Dunlavy, *Politics and Industrialization.* On financial markets, see Richard Bensel, *Yankee Leviathan: The Origins of Central State Authority in America, 1859–1877* (Cambridge, Mass.: Cambridge University Press, 1990); Roy, *Socializing Capital.*

63. Charles F. Adams, "The Granger Movement," *North American Review* April (1875): 394–424; Salon Buck, *The Granger Movement* (Cambridge, Mass.: Harvard University Press, 1933).

64. *Munn v. Illinois,* 94 U.S. 126. The quote is taken from Sir Matthew Hale's *De Portibus Maris.* See Harry Scheiber, "The Road to *Munn:* Eminent Domain and the Concept of Public Purpose in the State Courts," *Perspectives in American History* 5 (1971): 327–402.

65. Charles McCurdy, "Justice Field and the Jurisprudence of Government–Business Relations: Some Parameters of Laissez-Faire Constitutionalism, 1863–1897," *Journal of American History* 61, no. 4 (1975): 970–1005.

66. Berk, *Alternative Tracks,* 85.

67. Stephen Skowronek, *Building a New American State: The Expansion of National Administrative Capacities, 1877–1920* (Cambridge: Cambridge University Press, 1982), esp. chapter 5; I. L. Sharfman, *The Interstate Commerce Commission: A Study in Administrative Law and Procedure,* 4 vols. (New York: Commonwealth Fund, 1931).

68. 24 Stat. 379; Sharfman, *The ICC,* vol. I, chapter 1.

69. Skowronek, *Building a New American State,* 151. Skowronek also provides a nice summary of the cases that limited the powers of the ICC. The *Import Rate Case,* 162 U.S. 197 (1896), concerned the different rates between goods that came from abroad into the United States and those that were shipped from the same entry point as the imported goods and ended at the same destination. The Court overturned the ICC's ruling against the importers, limiting the commission's decisions to the U.S. market. In *ICC v. Alabama Midland Ry. Co. et al.,* 168 U.S. 144 (1897), the Court ruled against the ICC's powers to declare rates unreasonable and discriminatory between short and long hauls. In the *Social Circle Case,* 162 U.S. 184 (1896), and the *Maximum Freight Rate Case,* 167 U.S. 479 (1897), the Court invalidated the ICC's power to set rates.

70. Sherman Antitrust Act, 26 Stat. 209. Sklar gives a thorough account of the act and its aftermath, complete with treatment of the intellectual currents that structured thinking in the courts and in administrative agencies, including the Industrial Commission, the Bureau of Corporations, and the Federal Trade Commission. See *Corporate Reconstruction,* esp. part I, chapter 3 and part II, chapter 4.

71. Ibid., 127.

72. Ibid., 127–39.

73. *United States v. Trans-Missouri Freight Association,* 166 U.S. 290 (1897); *United States v. American Tobacco Co.,* 221 U.S. 106 (1911); *Standard Oil Co. of New Jersey v. United States,* 221 U.S. 1 (1911).

74. U.S. Industrial Commission, *Annual Reports of the Industrial Commission,* 19 vols. (Washington, D.C.: Government Printing Office, 1900–3).

75. U.S. Bureau of Corporations, *Report of the Commissioner of Corporations on the Beef Industry* (Washington, D.C.: Government Printing Office, 1905); U.S. Bureau of Corporations, *Report of the Commissioner of Corporations on the Petroleum Industry* (Washington, D.C.: Government Printing Office, 1907); U.S. Bureau of Corporations, *Preliminary Report of the Inland Waterways Commission* (Washington, D.C.: Government Printing Office, 1908); U.S. Bureau of Corporations, *Report of the Commissioner of Corporations on the Cotton Exchange* (Washington, D.C.: Government Printing Office, 1909); U.S. Bureau of Corporations, *Report of the Commissioner of Corporations on the Tobacco Industry* (Washington, D.C.: Government Printing Office, 1909); U.S. Bureau of Corporations, *Report of the Commissioner of Corporations on the Steel Industry* (Washington, D.C.: Government Printing Office, 1911–13); U.S. Bureau of Corporations, *The Lumber Industry* (Washington, D.C.: Government Printing Office, 1913–14).

76. U.S. Bureau of Corporations, *Taxation of Corporations* (Washington, D.C.: Government Printing Office, 1909–15); U.S. Bureau of Corporations, *Trust Laws and Unfair Competition* (Washington, D.C.: Government Printing Office, 1916); U.S. Bureau of Corporations, *Report of the Commissioner of Corporations on State Laws Concerning Foreign Corporations* (Washington, D.C.: Government Printing Office, 1915).

77. Skowronek, *Building a New American State.* In addition to the now classic accounts of Richard Hofstadter, *The Age of Reform* (New York: A. A. Knopf, 1955), and Robert Wiebe, *The Search for Order, 1877–1920* (New York: Hill and Wang, 1967), New Left historians, such as Gabriel Kolko, have considered the development of these administrations as emblematic of the ways state regulation promoted the interests of capitalists. More recently, this argument has been extended, qualified, and challenged as more pluralistic theories suggest the creation of a "new American state," a "modern liberal state," or "corporate liberalism." See Kolko, *Triumph of Conservatism*; Novak, "The Legal Origins of the Modern American State"; Sklar, *Corporate Reconstruction*; Berk, *Alternative Tracks.*

78. As Sklar put it, "the trust question was the corporation question.... The great question of the day, as Woodrow Wilson defined the issue on more than one occasion, 'we sum up under the general term of the corporation question, the trust question.' Accordingly, 'We state our problem for the statesman by saying that it is the problem of the corporation.'" Sklar, *Corporate Reconstruction,* 179. See also Jeremiah Jenks, *The Trust Problem* (New York: McClure, Phillips, 1900), and William W. Cook, *The Corporation Problem* (New York: G. P. Putnam's, 1891).

79. Cook, *Corporation Problem.*

80. U.S. Industrial Commission, *Preliminary Report on Trusts and Industrial Combinations* (Washington, D.C.: Government Printing Office, 1900), 9; capitalization in original.

81. See Roy, *Socializing Capital.*

82. Walter Noyes, *A Treatise on the Law of Intercorporate Relations* (Boston: Little, Brown, 1902), 3.

83. William Ripley, "The Work of Trained Economists in the Industrial Commission," *Quarterly Journal of Economics* 16, no. 1 (1901): 121–22.

84. "It should be kept clearly in mind through all the discussions that great capital or a great combination of capital has no necessary relation to monopoly, though it seems to be established that a virtual monopoly may at times be secured through the influence that comes merely from great capital." U.S. Industrical Commission, *Preliminary Report on Trusts and Industrial Combinations,* 9.

85. Ibid., 5.

86. Ibid., 6.

87. Jeremiah Jenks, "Capitalist Monopolies and Their Relation to the State," *Political Science Quarterly* 9, no. 3 (1894): 486–87.

88. Jenks, *Trust Problem,* 10.

89. Dean, *Governmentality,* 115.

90. Marx was highly ambivalent about corporations, terming them "the abolition of the capitalist mode of production within the capitalist mode of production itself, and hence a self-abolishing contradiction, which presents itself *prima facie* as a mere point of transition to a new form of production." Marx, *Capital,* 3:569; Thorstein Veblen, *The Theory of the Business Enterprise* (New York: Scribner, 1904).

3. Personhood

1. Ernst Kantorowicz traces the original phrase of "The king is dead! Long live the king!" back to sixteenth-century succession ceremonies, as a demonstration of the "perpetuity of kingship." Kantorowicz, *King's Two Bodies,* 409–12.

2. The favorable stance of the Court to corporate and business interests has been documented by Jeffrey Rosen, "Supreme Court Inc," *New York Times Magazine,* March 16, 2008; Adam Liptak, "Justices Offer Receptive Ear to Business Interests," *New York Times,* December 19, 2010, A1; *Citizen's United v. Federal Election Commission,* 558 U.S. 50 (2010).

3. Quoted in Jess Bravin, "Sotomayor Issues Challenge to a Century of Corporate Law," *Wall Street Journal,* September 17, 2009.

4. Horwitz, "*Santa Clara* Revisited," 176.

5. Ralph Nader, "Time for Impeachment? The Corporate Supreme Court," *Counterpunch,* http://counterpunch.org/nader07192011.html; International Forum on Globalization, *Alternatives to Economic Globalization: A Better World Is*

Possible (San Francisco: Berrett-Koehler, 2002); Barry Yeoman, "When Is a Corporation Like a Freed Slave?," *Mother Jones* 31, no. 6 (2006): 63–66.

6. Nader, "Time for Impeachment?"

7. *Santa Clara v. Southern Pacific Railroad,* 18 U.S. 394 (1886).

8. John Dewey, "The Historic Background of Corporate Legal Personality," *Yale Law Journal* 35, no. 6 (1926): 655.

9. Foucault, *Security, Territory, Population,* 96.

10. Berle and Means, *Modern Corporation,* famously emphasized corporate property as a new form of property distinct from the private property relations of classical liberalism. Horwitz, "*Santa Clara* Revisited," also reiterates the relation between personhood and the separation of ownership and control.

11. Paddy Ireland's excellent work on company law in the British context has demonstrated the way the property right of shareholding became a form of finance capital. See Ireland, Ian Grigg-Spall, and Dave Kelly, "The Conceptual Foundations of Modern Company Law," in *Critical Legal Studies,* ed. Alan Hunt and Peter Fitzpatrick (Oxford: Blackwell, 1987), and Ireland, "Capitalism without the Capitalist: The Joint Stock Company Share and the Emergence of the Modern Doctrine of Separate Corporate Personality," *Legal History* 17, no. 1 (1996): 40–72.

12. David Millon, "Theories of the Corporation," *Duke Law Journal* 1990, no. 2 (1990): 201–62; Lawrence Mitchell, "The Relevance of Corporate Theory to Corporate Economic Development: Comment on *The Transplantation of the Discourse on Corporate Personality Theories,*" *Washington and Lee Law Review* 63, no. 4 (2006): 1491–92.

13. My reading of the case law here follows Gerard Henderson, *The Position of Foreign Corporations in American Constitutional Law* (Cambridge, Mass.: Harvard University Press, 1918); see also William Overton Harris, "A Corporation as a Citizen in Connection with the Jurisdiction of United States Courts," *Virginia Law Review* 1, no. 7 (1914): 507–19.

14. *Bank of United States v. Deveaux,* 9 U.S. 61 (1809), 86.

15. *Strawbridge v. Curtis,* 7 U.S. (3 Cranch) 267 (1806); *Bank of Augusta v. Earle,* 38 U.S. 519 (1839); *Commercial & Ry Bank of Vicksburg v. Slocumb,* 39 U.S. (14 Peters) 60 (1840).

16. *Louisville Railroad Co. v. Letson,* 43 U.S. 497 (1844), 558.

17. *Rundle v. Delaware and Raritan Canal Co.,* 55 U.S. (14 How.) 80 (1852).

18. *Marshall v. Baltimore and Ohio Ry.,* 57 U.S. (16 How.) 314 (1854); Henderson, *Position of Foreign Corporations,* 61.

19. *Dred Scott v. Sandford,* 60 U.S. 393 (1856).

20. U.S. Constitution, Amend. 14, sec. 1, reads as follows: "All persons born or naturalized in the United States and subject to the jurisdiction thereof, are citizens of the United States and of the State wherein they reside. No State shall make or enforce any law which shall abridge the privileges or immunities of citizens of the United States; nor shall any State deprive any person of life, liberty, or property,

without due process of law; nor deny to any person within its jurisdiction the equal protection of the laws."

21. On the contingency of constitutional amendments as a strategy for ending the war, see Michael Vorenberg, *Final Freedom: The Civil War, the Abolition of Slavery, and the Thirteenth Amendment* (Cambridge: Cambridge University Press, 2001). For general background on the amendment, see Eric Foner, *A Short History of Reconstruction* (New York: Harper and Row, 1990); Ronald Labbe and Jonathan Lurie, *The Slaughterhouse Cases: Regulation, Reconstruction, and the Fourteenth Amendment* (Lawrence: University Press of Kansas, 2003).

22. Horwitz, "*Santa Clara* Revisited."

23. *Slaughterhouse Cases,* 83 U.S. 36 (1873), 88–89, 90.

24. Thomas Wuil Joo, "New 'Conspiracy Theory' of the Fourteenth Amendment: Nineteenth Century Chinese Civil Rights Cases and the Development of Substantive Due Process Jurisprudence," *University of San Francisco Law Review* 29, no. 2 (1994–95): 353–88.

25. Ibid., 384–85; *Ho Ah Kow v. Nunan,* 12 F. Cas. 252 (C.C.D. Cal. 1879); *In re Ah Fong,* 1 F. Cas. 213 (C.C.D. Cal. 1874); *In re Quong Woo,* 13 F. 229 (C.C.D. Cal. 1882); *The Stockton Laundry Case, In re Tie Loy,* 26 F. 611 (C.C.D. Cal. 1886); *In re Parrott,* 1 F. 481 (C.C.D. Cal 1880); *Yick Wo v. Hopkins,* 118 U.S. 356 (1886).

26. *Railroad Tax Cases; County of San Mateo v. Southern Pacific R. Co.,* 13 F. 722 (C.C.D. Cal. 1882).

27. Ibid., 757.

28. *Santa Clara County v. Southern Pacific,* 118 U.S. 394 (1886), 396.

29. Charles Beard and Mary Beard, *The Rise of American Civilization* (New York: Macmillan, 1927).

30. These essays have been collected in Howard Jay Graham, *Everyman's Constitution: Historical Essays on the Fourteenth Amendment, the "Conspiracy Theory," and American Constitutionalism* (Madison: State Historical Society of Wisconsin, 1968).

31. In refuting the Beards, Graham focused on Representative John Bingham of Ohio, one of the drafters of the amendment. Graham's point was that the framers of the amendment did not *intend* that the word *person* within the amendment should apply to corporations before they drafted it; however, Graham agreed with the Beards that the amendment benefited corporate interests.

32. Horwitz, "*Santa Clara* Revisited."

33. See Ernst Freund, *The Legal Nature of Corporations* (Chicago: University of Chicago Press, 1897); Otto von Gierke, *Political Theories of the Middle Ages,* trans. F. W. Maitland (Boston: Beacon Press, 1959).

34. *Hale v. Henkel,* 201 U.S. 43 (1906); Horwitz, "*Santa Clara* Revisited," 182.

35. Horwitz, "*Santa Clara* Revisited."

36. Charles McCurdy, "Justice Field and the Jurisprudence of Government-

Business Relations: Some Parameters of Laissez-Faire Constitutionalism, 1863–1897," *Journal of American History* 61, no. 4 (1975): 970–1005.

37. Novak, "Legal Origins of the Modern American State," 265. Harry Scheiber has pursued a similar line of reasoning in "Public Rights and the Rule of Law," 217–51; Harry Scheiber and Charles McCurdy, "Eminent Domain Law and Western Agriculture, 1849–1900," *Agricultural History* 49, no. 1 (1975): 112–30.

38. See esp. the very useful table summarizing this position in Novak, *People's Welfare*, 238.

39. Novak, "Legal Origins," 267.

40. Ibid.

41. Foucault, *History of Sexuality*, I:138, I:141.

42. Ibid., I:144.

43. Ibid.

44. Ibid.

45. Ibid., I:145.

46. Of which Novak's *People's Welfare* is an exhaustive and exemplary account.

47. Paraphrasing Foucault, *History of Sexuality*, I:138.

48. Agamben, *Homo Sacer*, 125, 128.

49. These two opposed meanings are both ascribed to "the ban" in romance languages, as the person who is banned or exiled but also the sovereign *bandon* that issues the command. Ibid., 110.

50. Roberto Esposito, "The *Dispositif* of the Person," *Law, Culture, and the Humanities* 8, no. 1 (2012): 17–30. See also Esposito, *Bios: Biopolitics and Philosophy*, trans. Timothy Campbell (Minneapolis: University of Minnesota Press, 2008); Esposito, *Tercera Persona: Política de la Vida y Filosofía de lo Impersonal* (Buenos Aires: Amorrortu, 2009); Esposito, "For a Philosophy of the Impersonal," trans. Timothy Campbell, *CR: New Centennial Review* 10, no. 2 (2010): 121–34; Esposito, "Totalitarianism or Biopolitics? A Philosophical Interpretation of the Twentieth Century," trans. Timothy Campbell, *Critical Inquiry* 34, no. 4 (2008): 633–44.

51. Esposito, *Bios*, 63–77.

52. Personhood also creates new divisions, which Esposito clarifies through an engagement with Simone Weil's critique of rights: "Weil sets out with remarkable clarity the dehumanizing function of the mask of the person; once the mask is made safe, it doesn't matter what happens to the face on which it rests and even less to the faces that do not own masks; to those who still aren't persons, or who no longer are persons, or to those who were never declared to be persons." See Esposito, "*Dispositif* of the Person," 30.

53. Some representative writing includes Freund, *Legal Nature of Corporations*; Dewey, "Historic Background"; Harris, "A Corporation as a Citizen"; Dwight Jones, "A Corporation as 'a Distinct Entity,'" *Counsellor* 2, no. 3 (1892–93): 79–81; John Davis, "The Nature of Corporations," *Political Science Quarterly* 12, no. 2 (1897): 273–94; George Wharton Pepper, "A Brief Introduction to the Study of the

Law of Associations," *American Law Register* 49, no. 5 (1901): 255–69; W. Jethro Brown, "The Personality of the Corporation and the State," *Law Quarterly Review* 21, no. 4 (1905): 365–79; Robert Raymond, "The Genesis of the Corporation," *Harvard Law Review* 19, no. 5 (1906): 350–65; George Deiser, "Juristic Persons, I–III," *University of Pennsylvania Law Review* 57, nos. 3–5 (1908–9): 131–42, 216–35, 300–14; Arthur Machen Jr., "Corporate Personality, I–II," *Harvard Law Review* 24, nos. 4–5 (1911): 253–67, 347–65; W. M. Geldart, "Legal Personality," *Law Quarterly Review* 27, no. 1 (1911): 90–108; Ernest Schuster, "The Nationality and Domicil of Trading Corporations," *Transactions of the Grotius Society* 2 (1916): 57–85; Harold Laski, "The Personality of Associations," *Harvard Law Review* 29, no. 4 (1916): 404–26; E. D. Dickinson, "The Analogy between Natural Persons and International Persons in the Law of Nations," *Yale Law Journal* 26, no. 7 (1916–17): 564–91; T. Baty, "The Rights of Ideas: And of Corporations," *Harvard Law Review* 33, no. 3 (1920): 358–75; Arnold McNair, "The National Character and Status of Corporations," *British Yearbook of International Law* 4, no. 1 (1923): 44–59; Paul Vinogradoff, "Juridical Persons," *Columbia Law Review* 24, no. 6 (1924): 594–604; P. W. Duff, "The Personality of an Idol," *Cambridge Law Journal* 3, no. 1 (1927): 42–48; Bryant Smith, "Legal Personality," *Yale Law Journal* 37, no. 3 (1928): 283–99; Joseph Francis, "Domicil of a Corporation," *Yale Law Journal* 38, no. 3 (1929): 335–58; Max Radin, "The Endless Problem of Corporate Personality," *Columbia Law Review* 32, no. 4 (1932): 643–67; Frederick Green, "Corporations as Persons, Citizens, and Possessors of Liberty," *University of Pennsylvania Law Review* 94, no. 2 (1946): 202–37. Many of these titles deal not only with personality but also with citizenship and therefore with domicile, as all three concepts are interrelated.

54. Gierke, *Political Theories of the Middle Ages*; Ernst Freund, *Legal Nature of Corporations*. See also Gierke, *Natural Law and the Theory of Society,* trans. Ernst Barker (Cambridge: Cambridge University Press, 1934); Gierke, *Associations and the Law: the Classical and Early Christian Stages,* trans. George Heiman (Toronto: University of Toronto Press, 1977); Gierke, *Community in Historical Perspective,* trans. M. Fischer, ed. Anthony Black (Cambridge: Cambridge University Press, 1990).

55. Ron Harris, "The Transplantation of the Legal Discourse on Corporate Personality Theories: From German Codification to British Political Pluralism and American Big Business," *Washington and Lee Law Review* 63, no. 4 (2007): 1421–78.

56. On the German historical context, see Frederic Maitland's introduction to von Gierke, *Political Theories of the Middle Ages*, and Harris, "Transplantation of the Legal Discourse." On the relation between Gierke and Hegel, see George Heiman's essay "State and Law" in Gierke, *Associations and the Law.*

57. Knox, *Hegel's Philosophy of Right,* 154. In addition to the corporation and the family, Hegel gives this role of mediating between individuals and the ethical life of the state to the police (in the form of public authority). Giving further evidence for the argument advanced in chapter 1, Hegel situates police and corporation together.

58. Anthony Black, introduction to Gierke, *Community in Historical Perspective*, xxxii.

59. For Gierke's relation to Savigny, see Frederic Maitland, introduction to Gierke, *Political Theories of the Middle Ages*, xvi.

60. Gierke, *Community in Historical Perspective*, 9–10.

61. Ibid., chapters 12–14.

62. See Foucault's lecture of "11 February 1976" in *"Society Must Be Defended,"* 115–40.

63. Harold Laski, "Morris Cohen's Approach to Legal Philosophy," *University of Chicago Law Review* 15, no. 3 (1948): 578.

64. Ibid., 579.

65. See Frederic Maitland, *Selected Essays* (Cambridge: Cambridge University Press, 1936).

66. Freund, *Legal Nature of Corporations*, 13.

67. Ibid.

68. Ibid., 15.

69. Ibid., 16.

70. Ibid., 17–18.

71. Ibid., 47–48.

72. Jones, "A Corporation as 'a Distinct Entity,'" 80–81.

73. See Dewey, "Historic Background"; Radin, "Endless Problem of Corporate Personality."

74. Smith, "Legal Personality," 292–93.

75. Radin, "Endless Problem of Corporate Personality," 653.

76. Ibid., 658.

77. *Railroad Tax Cases; County of San Mateo v. Southern Pacific R. Co.*, 13 F. 743–44.

78. Foucault emphasized this aspect of Sieyès's famous pamphlet "What Is the Third Estate?" in his lecture from March 10, 1976, in *"Society Must Be Defended."*

79. Agamben discusses the people as both "the constitutive political subject" and "the poor, the disinterested, and the excluded" in *Homo Sacer,* 176–77. See also Esposito, *"Dispositif* of the Person"; Agamben, "What Is a People?," in *Means without End: Notes on Politics,* trans. Vincenzo Binetti and Cesare Casarino, 29–35 (Minneapolis: University of Minnesota Press, 2000).

4. Territory

1. On territory and territoriality, see Robert Sack, *Human Territoriality: Its Theory and History* (Cambridge: Cambridge University Press, 1986); David Delaney, *Territory: A Short Introduction* (Malden, Mass.: Blackwell, 2005). On territory and the historical emergence of state sovereignty (along with critiques of dominant narratives on territorial sovereignty), see John Agnew and Stuart Corbridge, *Mastering Space: Hegemony, Territory, and International Political Economy*

(London: Routledge, 1995); Stephen Krasner, *Sovereignty: Organized Hypocrisy* (Princeton, N.J.: Princeton University Press, 1999).

2. Max Weber, "Politics as a Vocation," in *From Max Weber: Essays in Sociology*, ed. H. Gerth and C. W. Mills (New York: Oxford University Press, 1946), 78.

3. On capital flight, see Jefferson Cowie, *Capital Moves: RCA's Seventy Year Quest for Cheap Labor* (Ithaca, N.Y.: Cornell University Press, 1999). On the transnational dimensions of tax policy, see Reuven S. Avi-Yonah, *International Tax as International Law*, Cambridge Tax Law Series (Cambridge: Cambridge University Press, 2007). On financialization and the geography of finance, see Nigel Thrift, Stuart Corbridge, and Ron Martin, eds., *Money, Power, and Space* (Oxford: Basil Blackwell, 1994); Andrew Leyshon and Nigel Thrift, *Money/Space: Geographies of Monetary Transformation* (London: Routledge, 1997); Gordon Clark and Dariusz Wójcik, *The Geography of Finance: Corporate Governance in a Global Marketplace* (Oxford: Oxford University Press, 2007).

4. E. Hilton Young, *Foreign Corporations and Other Corporations* (Cambridge: Cambridge University Press, 1912); Young, "The Status of Foreign Corporations and the Legislature—I and II," *Law Quarterly Review* 23, nos. 2–3 (1907): 151–64, 290–303; Henderson, *Position of Foreign Corporations*.

5. Committee of Experts for the Progressive Codification of International Law, Report to the Council of the League of Nations, "Recognition of the Legal Personality of Foreign Commercial Corporations" and "Nationality of Commercial Corporations and Their Diplomatic Protection," *American Journal of International Law, Special Supplement* 22 (1928): 157–70, 171–214.

6. On the development of the Bretton Woods institutions, see Robert Gilpin, *The Political Economy of International Relations* (Princeton, N.J.: Princeton University Press, 1987). See also Louis Pauly, "The League of Nations and the Foreshadowing of the International Monetary Fund," *Essays in International Finance*, Department of Economics, Princeton University, 1996.

7. For introductions to the comity doctrine, see Kurt Nadelmann, "The Comity Doctrine: Introduction," *Michigan Law Review* 65, no. 1 (1966): 1–8; Hessel E. Yntema, "Basic Issues in the Conflict of Laws," *American Journal of Comparative Law* 12, no. 3 (1963): 474–82; Herbert Barry, "Comity," *Virginia Law Review* 12, no. 5 (1926): 353–75.

8. Yntema, "Basic Issues"; Alan Watson, *Joseph Story and the Comity of Errors: A Case Study in Conflict of Laws* (Athens: University of Georgia Press, 1991), esp. chapters 1 and 2.

9. Hugo Grotius, *The Freedom of the Seas, or the Right Which Belongs to the Dutch to take part in the East Indian Trade*, trans. R. V. D. Magoffin, Carnegie Endowment for International Peace (New York: Oxford University Press, 1916), chapter 2, "The Portuguese have no right by title of discovery to sovereignty over the East Indies to which the Dutch make voyages."

10. See the discussion of Grotius's views on trade in Richard Tuck, *The Rights*

of War and Peace: Political Thought and the International Order from Grotius to Kant (Oxford: Oxford University Press, 1999), chapter 3.

11. On the Voets, see Watson, *Joseph Story and the Comity of Errors,* chapter 1; Yntema, "Basic Issues"; Friedrich Carl von Savigny, *A Treatise on the Conflict of Laws* (Edinburgh: T. and T. Clark, 1880).

12. Yntema, "Basic Issues," 480.

13. Alan Watson has suggested that U.S. commentators on the Dutch theory of comity, from Joseph Story forward, have misread Huber's notion of comity in such a way as to make it an extension of the theory advanced by the Voets, namely, that comity is a custom and thus lacks the force of law. Watson argues that Huber followed Grotius in asserting a stronger notion of comity as having force internationally. Unlike the theory of comity ultimately adopted in the nineteenth-century United States through Story's writings, Huber argued that in cases involving conflict of law, courts are bound to consider the laws of other sovereigns. See Watson, *Joseph Story and the Comity of Errors*; Joseph Story, *Commentaries on the Conflict of Laws* (Boston: Little, Brown, 1865).

14. *Emory v. Grenough,* 3 U.S. 369 (1797).

15. Ibid. The translation went on to outline examples of conflicts and to discuss a series of exceptions to the rules, or ways of dealing with contradictions between the first and second rules and the third.

16. Samuel Livermore, *Dissertations on the Questions Which Arise from the Contrariety of the Positive Laws of Different States and Nations* (New Orleans, 1828).

17. Ibid., 21–22.

18. Ibid., 31–32. See also Paul Finkleman, *An Imperfect Union: Slavery, Federalism, and Comity* (Chapel Hill: University of North Carolina Press, 1981).

19. Livermore, *Dissertations,* 43.

20. Watson, *Joseph Story and the Comity of Errors.*

21. Ibid., 22.

22. Savigny, *A Treatise on the Conflict of Laws,* 68; Watson, *Joseph Story and the Comity of Errors.*

23. *Bank of Augusta v. Earle,* 38 U.S. 519 (1839).

24. Ibid., 588.

25. Ibid., 589.

26. Ibid.

27. Horwitz, *Transformation of American Law*; Novak, *People's Welfare.*

28. Thomas Reed Powell, "The Changing Law of Foreign Corporations," *Political Science Quarterly* 33, no. 4 (1918): 549–69.

29. The claim that these legal ideas were too abstract for normal business relations reflected the broader response to theories of corporate personhood in Anglo-American law. Opponents claimed that these ideas were too "metaphysical," "philosophical," or simply "German." For examples, see Radin, "Endless Problem of Corporate Personhood"; Freund, *Legal Nature of Corporations.* A review of Henderson's *Position of Foreign Corporations* penned by E. H. Y. (almost certainly

E. Hilton Young) attributed the problems in corporate law to "the almost metaphysical speculations of the French and Italian schools." See *Journal of Comparative Legislation and International Law* 1 (1919): 154–55.

30. E. H. Y., "Position of Foreign Corporations," 155.

31. A. V. Dicey, "The Positions of Foreign Corporations in American Constitutional Law," *Harvard Law Review* 32, no. 7 (1919): 864.

32. E.g., see Young, *Foreign Corporations*; Henderson, *Position of Foreign Corporations*.

33. Henderson discussed state restrictions on foreign-owned banking and insurance corporations in New Jersey, New York, and Virginia before the Civil War but suggested that these restrictions were designed "to put foreign insurance companies on a parity with domestic corporations." Moreover, the states had wide latitude to exclude foreign corporations or assess special fees and taxes through their police powers. See Henderson, *Position of Foreign Corporations*, 102–4.

34. *Paul v. Virginia*, 75 U.S. 168 (1868). On the privileges and immunities of citizenship, see the U.S. Constitution, Article 4, section 2: "The Citizens of each State shall be entitled to all Privileges and Immunities of Citizens in the several States."

35. U.S. Constitution, Article 1, section 8, paragraph 3: "The Congress shall have Power . . . To regulate Commerce with foreign Nations, and among the several States, and with the Indian Tribes."

36. Young, *Foreign Corporations*; Young, "Status of Foreign Corporations."

37. Young, "Status of Foreign Corporations," 154.

38. Ibid., 160.

39. Ibid., 158.

40. Ibid., 162.

41. Ibid., 163.

42. Henderson, *Position of Foreign Corporations*; Walter W. Cook, *The Logical and Legal Basis of the Conflict of Laws* (Cambridge, Mass.: Harvard University Press, 1949); Wesley Hohfeld, "Nature of Stockholders' Liability for Corporation Debts," *Columbia Law Review* 9, no. 4 (1909): 285–320; Hohfeld, "The Individual Liability of Stockholders and the Conflicts of Laws," *Columbia Law Review* 9, no. 6; 10, nos. 4, 6 (1909–10): 492–522, 283–326, 520–49; Ernst Lorenzen, *Selected Articles on the Conflict of Laws* (New Haven, Conn.: Yale University Press, 1947).

43. Walter W. Cook, "The Logical and Legal Basis of the Conflict of Laws," *Yale Law Journal* 33, no. 5 (1924): 458.

44. Henderson, *Position of Foreign Corporations*, 7–8.

45. The only states that did not require foreign corporations to file evidence of incorporation were Kentucky, Louisiana, New Hampshire, Pennsylvania, and Rhode Island, in addition to the District of Columbia. See U.S. Department of Commerce, Bureau of Corporations, *Report of the Commissioner of Corporations on State Laws Concerning Foreign Corporations* (Washington, D.C.: Government Printing Office, 1915), 29.

46. See also Joseph Beale, *Law of Foreign Corporations* (Boston: William

Nagel, 1904) for full text of the state statues concerning foreign corporations.

47. U.S. Department of Commerce, Bureau of Corporations, *Report of the Commissioner of Corporations*, 10.

48. Ibid.

49. *Paul v. Virginia*, 75 U.S. 168 (1868). Justice Field made the distinction clear: "the defect of the argument lies in the character of their business. Issuing a policy of insurance is not a transaction of commerce. The policies are simple contracts of indemnity against loss by fire, entered into between the corporations and the assured" (183). See also U.S. Constitution, Article 1, section 8, paragraph 3.

50. Horwitz, "*Santa Clara* Revisited," discusses *Western Union Telegraph Co. v. Kansas*, 216 U.S. 1 (1910); *Pullman Co. v. Kansas*, 216 U.S. 56 (1910); as well as *Ludwig v. Western Union Tel. Co.*, 216 U.S. 146 (1910) and *Southern Ry. v. Greene*, 216 U.S. 400 (1910). See also Henderson, *Position of Foreign Corporations*, 128–31.

51. *Western Union v. Kansas*, 216 U.S. 18, 52 (1910).

52. *United States v. E.C. Knight Co.*, 156 U.S. 1 (1895). Though for some time, historians interpreted the *Knight* decision as an example of laissez-faire constitutionalism (see Edward Corwin, "The Anti-Trust Acts and the Constitution," *Virginia Law Review* 18, no. 4 [1932]: 355–78), more recent interpretations have stressed the way the ruling was grounded in an older notion of state, rather than federal, governmental authority over corporations. See Charles McCurdy, "The Knight Sugar Decision of 1895 and the Modernization of American Corporate Law, 1869–1903," *Business History Review* 53, no. 3 (1979): 304–42; Sklar, *Corporate Reconstruction*, 123–27.

53. *Standard Oil Co. v. U.S.*, 221 U.S. 1 (1911); *American Tobacco v. U.S.*, 221 U.S. 106 (1911); Sklar, *Corporate Reconstruction*, chapter 3.

54. That this transformation related to the spatial context of the economy should be clear, as the new regulatory structure changed the terms by which corporations engaged in transactions in different jurisdictions, essentially creating a standardized legal–economic space that was linked to national territory. A vital question that I have not pursued is how this more abstract economic space was linked to particular places, structuring, for instance, the locational geography of investment or production. One point to note is that the establishment of a new system of regulation specified what constituted "doing business" in a state. For a state-by-state listing of these stipulations, see Beale, *Law of Foreign Corporations*; U.S. Department of Commerce, Bureau of Corporations, *Report of the Commissioner of Corporations*. Many states required some indication of real presence in a jurisdiction, such as the establishment of a corporate office or the maintenance of a real person as a representative of the business, to do business. In a broader sense, the question of the physical location of corporate business has contemporary resonance with questions about the assessment of taxes. Should a corporation that has a post office box in Bermuda or Luxembourg be considered a "resident" of

that state for the purpose of taxation? What sort of taxes could be levied against a foreign corporation chartered in a tax haven but doing business abroad?

55. On these problems, see Committee of Experts for the Progressive Codification of International Law, "Recognition of the Legal Personality of Foreign Commercial Corporations" and "Nationality of Commercial Corporations and Their Diplomatic Protection."

56. Other examples of the effort to regulate international commerce through comity and sovereignty include *Rose v. Himley*, 8 U.S. 241 (1807) and *Mason v. Ship Blaireau*, 6 U.S. (2 Cranch) 240 (1804), in which the question of prizes was raised when a British ship, the *Firm*, salvaged a sinking French vessel, *Le Blaireau*, and carried it into the Chesapeake Bay. All parties involved submitted to U.S. jurisdiction, and thus the U.S. courts did not violate comity. In *The Schooner Exchange v. M'Faddon*, 11 U.S. 116 (1812), the Court decided a case concerning the title of an American ship impressed by the French military while the two nations were at peace. The court ruled that the question of ownership of a French public vessel could not be tried in an American court without violating the principle of comity by bringing the French military under the jurisdiction of an American court. In *United States v. Furlong*, 18 U.S. (5 Wheat) 184 (1820), the Court asserted jurisdiction over criminal actions (murder and piracy) in foreign vessels on the high seas. See also *The Santissima Trinidad*, U.S. (7 Wheat) 129 (1822), on the limits to comity and the right of U.S. courts to decide on the legality of acts between U.S. citizens. A useful review of these cases is provided by Jonathan Turley, "Legal Theory: 'When in Rome': Multinational Misconduct and the Presumption against Extraterritoriality," *Northwestern University Law Review* 84, no. 2 (1990): 598–664.

57. *Vasse v. Ball*, 2 U.S. 270 (1797).

58. Ibid., 275.

59. *Murray v. The Schooner Charming Betsy*, 6 U.S. (2 Cranch) 64 (1802).

60. Ibid., 118. See also Turley, "Legal Theory," 606.

61. *Mason v. Intercolonial RR of Canada*, 197 Mass. 349 (1908); *Schooner Exchange v. M'Faddon*, 11 U.S. 116 (1812).

62. *Bank of United States v. Deveaux*, 5 Cranch 61 (1809).

63. *Bank of Augusta v. Earle*, 38 U.S. 519 (1839).

64. Nathan Wolfman, "Sovereigns as Defendants," *American Journal of International Law* 4, no. 2 (1910): 373.

65. Ibid., 374. Wolfman based his arguments against strict comity on two exceptions to the rule: "First, where the sovereign or state goes into the municipal courts of another country for the purpose of obtaining a remedy, then by way of defense to that proceeding, by way of counterclaim if necessary, to the extent of defeating that claim, the person sued may file a crossbill or take other proceedings against that sovereign or state for the purpose of enabling complete justice to be done between them. The other exception is the case in which a foreign sovereign may be named as defendant for the purpose of giving him notice of the claim which

the plaintiff makes to funds in the hands of a third person or trustee over whom the court has jurisdiction in which the cause of action arises from a transaction by the sovereign private or commercial in its character" (374–75).

66. *American Banana Company v. United Fruit Company*, 213 U.S. 347 (1909); for additional background information on the case, see John Noonan Jr., "The Overlord of American Law and the Sovereign of Costa Rica," in *Persons and Masks of the Law*, 65–110 (New York: Farrar, Straus, and Giroux, 1976).

67. *American Banana Company v. United Fruit Company*, 213 U.S. 347 (1909), 357–58.

68. On the blurring of fact and law in relation to the ban, see Agamben, *State of Exception*.

69. Noonan, *Persons and Masks of the Law*, 93.

70. Gordon Ireland, "Observations upon the Status of Corporations in Cuba since 1898," *University of Pennsylvania Law Review and American Law Register* 76, no. 1 (1927): 43–73.

71. Ibid., 61.

72. Schuster, "Nationality and Domicil of Trading Corporations," 73.

73. "U.S. Treaty with Japan—Commerce and Navigation," *Treaties Series* 558 (July 17, 1911); George S. Knight, *Treatment of Foreign Corporations in International Law with Particular Reference to Protection of American Interests* (Washington, D.C.: Georgetown University School of Law, 1938), 18.

74. "Treaty of Amity and Commerce with the Unites States of American and Siam," *Treaty Series* 665 (September 1, 1921); "Treaty of Friendship, Commerce and Consular Rights between the United States of American and Germany," *Treaty Series* 725 (October 14, 1925).

75. "Treaty of Friendship, Commerce and Consular Rights between the United States of America and the Republic of Austria," *Treaty Series* 838 (May 27, 1931); "Treaty of Friendship, Commerce and Consular Rights between the United States of American and Salvador," *Treaty Series* 827 (September 5, 1930); "U.S.–Estonia: Protocol Accompanying Treaty of Friendship, Commerce and Consular Rights," *Treaty Series* 736 (May 22, 1926); "U.S. Treaty with Finland—Friendship, Commerce and Consular Rights," *Treaty Series* 868 (February 13, 1934); "U.S. Treaty with Hungary—Friendship, Commerce and Consular Rights," *Treaty Series* 748 (October 4, 1926); "U.S. Treaty with Honduras—Friendship, Commerce and Consular Rights," *Treaty Series* 764 (July 19, 1928); "U.S. Treaty with Latvia—Friendship, Commerce and Consular Rights," *Treaty Series* 765 (July 25, 1928); "U.S. Treaty with Liberia—Friendship, Commerce and Navigation," *Treaty Series* 956 (November 21, 1939); "U.S. Treaty with Norway—Friendship, Commerce and Consular Rights," *Treaty Series* 852 (September 13, 1932); "U.S. Treaty with Poland—Friendship, Commerce and Consular Rights," *Treaty Series* 862 (July 9, 1933); "Treaty of Establishment between the United States of America and the Kingdom of Greece," *Treaty Series* 930 (October 22, 1937);

"U.S.–Turkey; Establishment and Sojourn," *Treaty Series* 859 (February 15, 1933).
   76. Knight, *Treatment of Foreign Corporations in International Law*, 21–26.
   77. *Continental Tyre and Rubber Co. v. Daimler Co.*, 2 A.C. 344 (1916).
   78. See also Schuster, "Nationality and Domicil of Trading Corporations"; McNair, "National Character and Status of Corporations"; Ralph Norem, "Determination of Enemy Character of Corporations," *American Journal of International Law* 24, no. 2 (1930): 310–36.
   79. As Lord Parker noted in the ruling, the corporation was an enemy "if its agents or the persons in *de facto* control of its affairs, whether authorized or not, are resident in an enemy country, or, wherever resident, are adhering to the enemy or taking instructions from or acting under the control of enemies. A person knowingly dealing with the company in such a case is trading with the enemy."
   80. These cases were difficult because the United States did not recognize the new Soviet government. In *Sokoloff v. National City Bank*, 239 N.Y. 158 (1924), the New York Court of Appeals ruled that courts could acknowledge the decrees of an unrecognized government "if violence to fundamental principles of justice or to our own public policy might otherwise be done." In *Salimoff and Co. v. Standard Oil Co. of N.Y.*, 262 N.Y. 693 (1933), the court recognized the Soviet Union as de facto sovereigns. See Edwin Dickinson, "The Case of Salimoff & Co.," *American Journal of International Law* 27, no. 4 (1933): 743–47.
   81. For detailed discussion of cases involving the nationalization of corporations and assets in Russia during and after the revolution, including case law from European countries, see "Confiscation and Corporations in Conflict of Laws," *University of Chicago Law Review* 5, no. 2 (1938): 280–95.
   82. Ernst Feilchenfeld, "Foreign Corporations in International Public Law, I and II," *Journal of Comparative Legislation and International Law* 8 (1926): 81–106, 260–74.
   83. Ibid., 88.
   84. Ibid.
   85. Ibid., 260.
   86. Committee of Experts for the Progressive Codification of International Law, "Recognition of the Legal Personality of Foreign Commercial Corporations" and "Nationality of Commercial Corporations and Their Diplomatic Protection."
   87. Committee of Experts for the Progressive Codification of International Law, "Nationality of Commercial Corporations and Their Diplomatic Protection," 175.
   88. Timberg, "International Combines and National Sovereigns," 575–77.
   89. Gilpin, *Political Economy of International Relations*.
   90. Turley, "Legal Theory."
   91. Michael Hardt and Antonio Negri, *Empire* (Cambridge, Mass.: Harvard University Press, 2000), esp. chapter 2.6, "Imperial Sovereignty," and the discussion on pp. 84–87 and 323–29.
   92. Schmitt made the argument etymologically, suggesting that the active form

of the Greek verb *nemein* combines three meanings: "to appropriate," "to divide, measure, or distribute," and "pasturage," which Schmitt linked to the German verbs *nehmen, teilen,* and *weiden,* respectively. Though he gave priority to the first meaning of *nomos* as "appropriation," he suggested that division and pastoral power were equally presupposed in every legal order. Schmitt, "Appropriation/Distribution/Production: An Attempt to Determine from *Nomos* the Basic Question of Every Social and Economic Order," in *The Nomos of the Earth in the International Law of the Jus Publicum Europaeum,* trans. Gary Ulmen (New York: Telos Press, 2003), 326–27.

    93. Agamben, *Homo Sacer,* 175; italics original.

5. Responsibility

    1. David Sadler and Stuart Lloyd, "Neo-liberalizing Corporate Social Responsibility: A Political Economy of Corporate Citizenship," *Geoforum* 40, no. 4 (2009): 613.

    2. Other accounts of the relation between CSR as neoliberalism include Ronen Shamir, "The Age of Responsibilization: On Market-Embedded Morality," *Economy and Society* 37, no. 1 (2008): 1–19; Shamir, "Capitalism, Governance, and Authority: The Case of Corporate Social Responsibility," *Annual Review of Law and Social Science* 6 (2010): 531–53; Shamir, "Socially Responsible Private Regulation: World-Culture or World-Capitalism?," *Law and Society Review* 45, no. 2 (2011): 313–36; Susanne Soederberg, "Taming Corporations or Buttressing Market-Led Development? A Critical Assessment of the Global Compact," *Globalizations* 4, no. 4 (2007): 500–13; Leslie Sklair, *The Transnational Capitalist Class* (Oxford: Blackwell, 2001); and Gerard Hanlon, "Rethinking Corporate Social Responsibility and the Role of the Firm—On the Denial of Politics," in *The Oxford Handbook of Corporate Social Responsibility,* ed. A. Crane, A. McWilliams, D. Matten, J. Moon, and D. Siegel, 156–72 (Oxford: Oxford University Press, 2008).

    3. Sadler and Lloyd, "Neo-Liberalising Corporate Social Responsibility," 618.

    4. Clive Barnett, "The Consolations of 'Neoliberalism,'" *Geoforum* 36, no. 1 (2005): 7–12; Barnett, "Publics and Markets: What's Wrong with Neoliberalism?," in *The Sage Handbook of Social Geography,* ed. S. Smith, S. Marston, R. Pain, and J. P. Jones III, 269–96 (London: Sage, 2010); Barnett, Paul Cloke, Nick Clarke, and Alice Malpass, *Globalizing Responsibility: The Political Rationalities of Ethical Consumption* (Malden, Mass.: Wiley-Blackwell, 2011).

    5. Barnett, "Consolations," 9.

    6. Barnett et al., *Globalizing Responsibility.*

    7. Barnett, "Consolations," 9.

    8. In this sense, my argument with Barnett et al. is not with their conceptualization of responsibility as a form of political rationality but with their assessment of "*who* is doing the problematization and *how* this process works by circulating

various 'moral dilemmas' through the public sphere." Barnett et al., *Globalizing Responsibility,* 83. Barnett et al. focus on contemporary fair trade and ethical consumption campaigns in Britain. As this chapter demonstrates, conceptions of responsibility look different when the genealogical sources include the arguments of jurists, diplomats, administrators, legal theorists, and activists engage in legal struggles. Like the research subjects Barnett et al. study, these articulations of responsibility were plural and heterogeneous. They were also institutionalized in particular forms that stabilized and limited the inherent plurality of these concepts.

9. Milton Friedman, "A Friedman Doctrine—The Social Responsibility of Business Is to Increase Its Profits," *New York Times Magazine,* September 13, 1970.

10. Henry Hansmann and Reiner Kraakman, "The End of History for Corporate Law," *Georgetown Law Journal* 89, no. 2 (2001): 439–68. An interesting ethnographic account of the promotion of shareholder primacy within financial firms is provided in Karen Ho, *Liquidated: An Ethnography of Wall Street* (Durham, N.C.: Duke University Press, 2009).

11. Friedman, "A Friedman Doctrine."

12. Ibid.

13. Douglas Schwartz, "The Public-Interest Proxy Contest: Reflections on Campaign GM," *Michigan Law Review* 69, no. 3 (1971): 419–538.

14. Friedman, "A Friedman Doctrine."

15. Schwartz, "Public-Interest Proxy Contest," 422.

16. Schwartz also referenced Berle to support his argument that corporate law "has been fashioned as the constitutional law of our economic state based on the traditional economic model." Schwartz, "Public-Interest Proxy Contest," 422, 463.

17. From both his individual work and his study with Means.

18. Milton Friedman, *Capitalism and Freedom* (Chicago: University of Chicago Press, 1962), 135–36.

19. Adolf Berle, "Corporate Powers as Powers in Trust," *Harvard Law Review* 44, no. 7 (1931): 1049–74; Edwin Merrick Dodd, "For Whom Are Corporate Managers Trustees?," *Harvard Law Review* 45, no. 7 (1932): 1145–63; Berle, "For Whom Corporate Managers Are Trustees: A Note," *Harvard Law Review* 45, no. 8 (1932): 1365–72; Berle and Means, *Modern Corporation.*

20. William Bratton, "Never Trust a Corporation," *George Washington Law Review* 70, nos. 5/6 (2002): 876. Similarly, Douglas Branson began his account of the "New Corporate Social Responsibility" by stating "the history of corporate 'reform' begins with Adolf Berle and Gardiner Mean's 'The Modern Corporation and Private Property.'" Branson, "Corporate Governance 'Reform' and the New Corporate Social Responsibility," *University of Pittsburgh Law Review* 62, no. 4 (2001): 605. Moreover, legal scholars committed to radically different political visions of the corporation also give the Berle–Dodd debate pride of place in the story of competing visions of corporate regulation and governance. See, e.g., the treatment of the debate in such disparate accounts as Hansmann and Kraakman,

"End of History for Corporate Law," and Paddy Ireland, "Limited Liability, Shareholder Rights, and the Problem of Corporate Irresponsibility," *Cambridge Journal of Economics* 34, no. 5 (2010): 837–56. Of course, prior to the Berle–Dodd debate, there was a long history of corporations with a variety of systems for voting and internal governance. Economic and business historians, such as Colleen Dunlavy and Naomi Lamoreaux, have exposed the complex processes by which actual firms organized themselves, including in terms of the representation of competing interests within corporations. See in particular Dunlavy, "*Citizens to Plutocrats*: Nineteenth-century Shareholder Voting Rights and Theories of the Corporation," in Lipartito and Sicilia, *Constructing Corporate America,* 66–93, as well as Lamoreaux, "Partnerships, Corporations, and the Limits on Contractual Freedom in U.S. History: An Essay in Economics, Law, and Culture," in ibid., 29–65.

21. Berle, "Corporate Powers as Powers in Trust," 1049.

22. See, e.g., book 1, chapter 4, "The Dispersion of Stock Ownership," in Berle and Means, *Modern Corporation.* One of the problems with turning to Berle's vision of CSR today is the concentration of shareholding by institutional investors and financial firms. On the development of a shareholding class in England, see Paddy Ireland, "Shareholder Primacy and the Distribution of Wealth," *Modern Law Review* 68, no. 1 (2005): 49–81. On problems with Berle and Means in the U.S. context, see Doug Henwood, *Wall Street: How It Works and for Whom* (New York: Verso, 1998), 252–55.

23. Dodd, "For Whom Are Corporate Managers Trustees?," 1148.

24. Ibid.

25. Ibid., 1149.

26. Ibid., 1152.

27. William Bratton and Michael Wachter, "Shareholder Primacy's Corporatist Origins: Adolf Berle and *The Modern Corporation,*" *Journal of Corporation Law* 34, no. 1 (2008): 125.

28. Berle and Means, *Modern Corporation,* 312–13.

29. Bratton and Wachter argue, "Although the battle lines wax and wane, shareholder primacy prevails today as the dominant view, with management discretion advocates in the minority, and with advocates of corporate social responsibility as a rearguard.... The generally accepted historical picture puts Berle in the position of being the grandfather of shareholder primacy. Dodd, on the other hand, is cast as the original ancestor of CSR. But this categorization of Berle and Dodd is mistaken." As already indicated, Bratton and Wachter treat contemporary shareholder primacy as a radical departure from Berle and instead present Berle as the advocate of CSR and Dodd as the promoter of managerial discretion. Bratton and Wachter, "Shareholder Primacy's Corporatist Origins," 100–1, 125.

30. Ibid., 152.

31. See Frederick Winslow Taylor's conversation with the "mentally sluggish" pig-iron handler, Schmidt, in *Principles of Scientific Management* (Minneola, N.Y.: Dover, 1998), 20–21.

32. Cohen, "Property and Sovereignty," 29.

33. Berle and Means, *Modern Corporation*, 19.

34. Ibid., 27.

35. Ibid., 27–28.

36. On this read, the problem with progressive corporate law is not merely, as Dalia Tsuk has argued, that it failed to consider class and thus "helped to remove the interests of workers (as differentiated from shareholders, officers, and directors) from the core concerns of corporate law and theory." See Tsuk, "Corporations without Labor: The Politics of Progressive Corporate Law," *University of Pennsylvania Law Review* 151, no. 6 (2003): 1864. To argue as much suggests that workers have a coherent set of "interests" given by the mode of production and that including them in corporate law would transform the structure of the legal institution. Though Tsuk is certainly correct that even the progressive vision of CSR articulated in U.S. legal theory has ignored workers, class, and Marxian analysis, the vision for progressive corporate law implicit in her argument suggests that there is a kind of redistributive answer in which the workers of corporations under capitalism could, indeed, get their fair share. The problem with the progressive attempt to institutionalize responsibility is that it is predicated on the corporate government of life toward capitalist value embedded in the concept of corporate property.

37. See Tagi Sagafi-nejad with John Dunning, *The UN and Transnational Corporations: From Code of Conduct to Global Compact* (Bloomington: Indiana University Press, 2008); Jennifer Bair, "From the Politics of Development to the Challenges of Globalization," *Globalizations* 4, no. 4 (2007): 486–99.

38. Agnew and Corbridge, *Mastering Space*, 38–39.

39. John Dunning, "Changes in the Level and Structure of International Production: The Last One Hundred Years," in *The Growth of International Business,* ed. Mark Casson (London: George Allen and Unwin, 1983), 93. Dunning presents the numbers on FDI in Table 5.1 on p. 87.

40. Agnew and Corbridge, *Mastering Space*, 39.

41. Dunning, "Changes in the Level and Structure of International Production," 94.

42. The involvement of ITT in Chile was the primary focus of the Church Hearings that Idaho senator Frank Church organized in the U.S. Senate in 1973. See U.S. Senate, "The International Telephone and Telegraph Company and Chile, 1970–1971," vols. 1 and 2 of *Hearings before the Subcommittee on Multinational Corporations of the Committee on Foreign Relations*, 93rd Cong. (Washington, D.C.: Government Printing Office, 1973).

43. Sagafi-nejad, *UN and Transnational Corporations*, chapter 3, situates the turn toward the UN in the context of these national hearings.

44. UN Department of Economic and Social Affairs, *The Impact of Multinational Corporations on Development and on International Relations* (New York: United Nations, 1974), 5.

45. UN Department of Economic and Social Affairs, *Multinational Corporations in World Development* (New York: United Nations, 1973), vi.

46. UN Department of Economic and Social Affairs, *Impact of Multinational Corporations*, 21–22.

47. On the Code of Conduct, see ibid., 54–55. The nine statements drafted by individual members of the GEP and included at the end of the publication indicated the unresolved nature of the recommendations in their entirety, including any potential code of conduct.

48. Peter Muchlinski, *Multinational Enterprise and the Law*, 2nd ed. (Oxford: Oxford University Press, 2007); Sagafi-nejad, *UN and Transnational Corporations*; Bair, "From the Politics of Development."

49. Bair, "From the Politics of Development," 489.

50. "A large number of representatives expressed the view that the starting point for the work of the Commission—in particular, the elaboration of a code of conduct—should be the Charter of Economic Rights and Duties of States, the Declaration and the Programme of Action on the Establishment of a New International Economic Order and other relevant resolutions of the General Assembly and the Economic and Social Council. Other representatives stated that that would not be appropriate, as certain provisions of those documents were not accepted by a number of State Members." UNCTC, Economic and Social Council, Official Records, 1975, 59th Session, Supplement 12, *Report on the First Session* (E/5655 E/C.10/6), 1, 7. The *Report on the First Session* also included three separate annexes listing contrasting areas of concern for G-77 countries, advanced industrial countries (including France, the Federal Republic of Germany, Italy, the United Kingdom, and the United States), and the Soviet bloc.

51. UN Department of Economic and Social Affairs, *Multinational Corporations in World Development*, 77. See also Bair, "From the Politics of Development," 491–92.

52. UN Department of Economic and Social Affairs, *Summary of the Hearings before the Group of Eminent Persons to Study the Impact of Multinational Corporations on Development and International Relations* (New York: United Nations, 1974), 27.

53. Published as Annex IV in UNCTC, Economic and Social Council, Official Records, 1976, 61st Session, Supplement 5, *Report on the Second Session* (E/5782 E/C.10/16), 27–34.

54. UN Department of Economic and Social Affairs, *Summary of the Hearings before the Group of Eminent Persons*, 68–69.

55. Ibid., 122.

56. Ibid., 83.

57. Ibid., 296.

58. In addition to the annual reports submitted to ECOSOC, see UN Centre on Transnational Corporations, *Transnational Corporations: Issues Involved in the*

Formulation of a Code of Conduct (New York: United Nations, 1976); Patrick Robinson, *The Question of a Reference to International Law in the United Nations Code of Conduct on Transnational Corporations*, UNCTC Current Studies, series A, no. 1 (New York: United Nations, 1986); UN Centre on Transnational Corporations, *The New Code Environment*, UNCTC Current Studies, series A, no. 16 (New York: United Nations, 1990).

59. See UNCTC, Economic and Social Council, Official Records, 1978, Supplement 12, *Report on the Fourth Session* (E/1978/52 E/C.10/43), 7–8.

60. UNCTC, *Report on the Second Session*, 3.

61. UNCTC, Economic and Social Council, Official Records, 1979, Supplement 8, *Report of the Fifth Session* (E/1979/38/Rev.1 E/C.10/59), 8–9; UNCTC, Economic and Social Council, Official Records, 1980, Supplement 10, *Report of the Sixth Session* (E/1980/40/Rev.1 E/C.10/75), 13–15.

62. UNCTC, Economic and Social Council, Official Records, 1982, Supplement 8, *Report of the Eighth Session* (E/1982/18 E/C.10/1982/19), 16.

63. See "Annex II—Draft United Nations Code of Conduct on Transnational Corporations," UNCTC, Economic and Social Council, Official Records, 1983, Supplement 7, *Report of the Special Session* (E/1983/17.Rev.1 E/C.10/1983/S/5/Rev.1).

64. UNCTC, *New Code Environment*, 3.

65. Ibid., 4.

66. Report by the president of the 46th Session of the General Assembly, as quoted in Sagafi-nejad, *UN and Transnational Corporations*, 122–23.

67. Sagafi-nejad, *UN and Transnational Corporations*, 120–23. Discussing UNCTC executive director Peter Hansen's attempts to maintain negotiations on the code and his ultimate dismissal by Secretary-General Boutros Ghali in 1992, Sagafi-nejad writes, "Hansen's efforts were not sufficient to soothe the new secretary-general or the U.S. administration that had initially supported his appointment. The issue for the U.S. administration was fairly simple: it felt that the UNCTC was hostile to TNCs and its residence in New York was not viable" (121).

68. UNCTC, *New Code Environment*, 1.

69. UNCTC, Economic and Social Council, Official Records, 1991, Supplement 10, *Report of the Seventeenth Session* (E/1991/31 E/C.10/1991/17), 41.

70. A point noted at length in UNCTC, *New Code Environment*.

71. http://www.unglobalcompact.org/AboutTheGC/TheTenPrinciples/index.html.

72. "Secretary-General Proposes Global Compact on Human Rights, Labour, Environment, in Address to World Economic Forum in Davos," UN Press Release SG/Sm/6881, 4.

73. Ibid.

74. Ibid.

75. UNCHR, Subcommission on the Promotion and Protection of Human Rights, 55th Session, *Economic, Social, and Cultural Rights: Norms on the Responsibilities*

of Transnational Corporations and Other Business Enterprises with Regard to Human Rights (E/CN.4/Sub.2/2003/12/Rev.2), August 2003. This history is provided by David Weissbrodt and Muria Kruger, "Norms on the Responsibilities of Transnational Corporations and Other Business Enterprises with Regards to Human Rights," *American Journal of International Law* 97, no. 4 (2003): 901–22. Weissbrodt was one of the original members of the working group involved with drafting the Norms. Additional information on the history of the draft Norms is available in John Ruggie, "Business and Human Rights: The Evolving International Agenda," *American Journal of International Law* 101, no. 4 (2007): 819–40.

76. Weissbrodt and Kruger, "Norms on the Responsibilities of Transnational Corporations," 901.

77. Ibid., 902–3.

78. Ruggie, "Business and Human Rights," 821.

79. UNCHR, "Human Rights and Transnational Corporations and Other Business Enterprises," Human Rights Resolution 2005/69.

80. See, e.g., Georg Kell and John G. Ruggie, "Global Markets and Social Legitimacy: The Case for the 'Global Compact,'" *Transnational Corporations* 8, no. 3 (1999): 101–20.

81. Ruggie, "Business and Human Rights," 822. That article lays out Ruggie's rationale for abandoning the UN Norms.

82. Ibid., 821.

83. Ibid., 826.

84. Ibid., 838.

85. Ibid., 839.

86. Ibid.

87. David Weissbrodt, "International Standard-Setting on the Human Rights Responsibilities of Business," *Berkeley Journal of International Law* 26, no 2 (2008): 390.

88. Soederberg, "Taming Corporations or Buttressing Market-Led Development?," 503.

89. Bair, "From the Politics of Development," 497.

90. Vinay Gidwani, "The Unbearable Modernity of 'Development'? Canal Irrigation and Development Planning in Western India," *Progress in Planning* 58, no. 1 (2002): 5.

91. Joel Wainwright highlights the problem of capitalism qua development as follows: "A truly global consensus emerged concerning political-economic management—a form of hegemony in Gramsci's sense—that the world's poor should enjoy the fruits of development. The fact that global capitalism has increased inequality without substantially reducing poverty raises stark questions. . . . How is it that capitalism reproduces inequality in the name of *development*? Indeed, how is it that the deepening of capitalist social relations comes to be taken *as* development?"

Wainwright, *Decolonizing Development: Colonial Power and the Maya* (Malden, Mass.: Blackwell, 2008), 2.

92. S. K. Chatterjee, "The Charter of Economic Rights and Duties of States: An Evaluation after 15 Years," *International and Comparative Law Quarterly* 40, no. 3 (1991): 669–84.

93. Much less is there room within this framework to address larger questions concerning the utility of the current human rights regime, which not only fails to eliminate state violence but has increasingly been used to justify imperial wars under the banner of "humanitarism."

94. Iris Marion Young advances this argument in slightly different forms in "From Guilt to Solidarity," *Dissent* 50, no. 2 (2003): 39–45; "Responsibility and Global Labor Justice," *Journal of Political Philosophy* 12, no. 4 (2004): 365–88; "Responsibility and Global Justice: A Social Connection Model," *Social Philosophy and Policy* 23, no. 1 (2006): 102–30; and the posthumously published *Responsibility for Justice* (Oxford: Oxford University Press, 2011).

95. Young, "Responsibility and Global Labor Justice," 116–18.

96. Ibid., 118.

97. Young, *Responsibility for Justice*, 105.

98. Ibid.

99. Hannah Arendt, "Collective Responsibility," in *Amor Mundi: Explorations in the Faith and Thought of Hannah Arendt*, ed. J. Bernauer (Boston: Martinus Nijhoff, 1987), 45.

100. A powerful theme at the center of her account of the Eichmann trial in *Eichmann in Jerusalem: A Report on the Banality of Evil* (1963; repr., New York: Penguin Classics, 2006).

101. Arendt, "Collective Responsibility," 46.

102. Ibid., 47.

103. Ibid.

104. Ibid., 45.

105. Ibid.

106. UN Department of Economic and Social Affairs, *Summary of the Hearings before the Group of Eminent Persons*, 229.

107. Ibid., 215–16.

108. Ibid., 216.

109. Ibid., 223.

110. Ibid.

111. Ibid., 224.

112. Ibid., 223.

113. For a summary of that later work in corporate geography, see my "Corporations as Disciplinary Institutions," in *The Wiley-Blackwell Companion to Economic Geography*, ed. T. Barnes, J. Peck, and E. Sheppard, 472–85 (Oxford: Wiley-Blackwell, 2012).

114. UN Department of Economic and Social Affairs, *Summary of the Hearings before the Group of Eminent Persons*, 236–37.

115. Ibid., 237.

116. Ibid., 238.

6. The Corporate University

1. On the tragic qualities of political thought and the nonnecessity of political domination, see Adam Sitze, editor's introduction to Galli, *Political Spaces and Global War.*

2. See Rich Heyman's destruction of the idea that politics only occurs outside of institutions of higher education in "'Who's Going to Man the Factories and Be the Sexual Slaves If We All Get PhDs?' Democratizing Knowledge Production, Pedagogy, and the Detroit Geographical Expedition and Institute," *Antipode* 39, no. 1 (2007): 99–120.

3. Ann Markusen, Peter Hall, and Amy Glasmeier, *High Tech America: The What, How, Where, and Why of the Sunrise Industries* (Boston: Allen and Unwin, 1986); Anna Lee Saxenian, *Regional Advantage: Culture and Competition in Silicon Valley and Route 128* (Cambridge, Mass.: Harvard University Press, 1994); Henry Etzkowitz and Loet Leydesdorff, eds., *Universities and the Global Knowledge Economy: A Triple Helix of University–Industry–Government Relations* (London: Pinter, 1997); John Dunning, ed., *Regions, Globalization, and the Knowledge-Based Economy* (Oxford: Oxford University Press, 2000).

4. Susan Robertson, "'Europe/Asia' Regionalism, Higher Education, and the Production of World Order," *Policy Futures in Education* 6, no. 6 (2008): 718–28.

5. Kris Olds, "Global Assemblage: Singapore, Foreign Universities, and the Construction of a 'Global Education Hub,'" *World Development* 35, no. 6 (2007): 959–75; Kris Olds and Nigel Thrift, "Cultures on the Brink: Reengineering the Soul of Capitalism—on a Global Scale," in *Global Assemblages: Technology, Politics, and Ethics as Anthropological Problems*, ed. A. Ong and S. Collier, 270–90 (Malden, Mass.: Blackwell, 2005); Etzkowitz and Leydesdorff, *Universities and the Global Knowledge Economy.*

6. See Sheila Slaughter and Gary Rhoades, *Academic Capitalism and the New Economy: Markets, State, and Higher Education* (Baltimore: Johns Hopkins University Press, 2004).

7. Jeffery Williams reported in 2006 that over half of the students attending college in the United States take out student loans and has documented the staggering and ever-growing levels of indebtedness for U.S. students. See "Debt Education: Bad for the Young, Bad for America," *Dissent* 53, no. 3 (2006): 53–59.

8. Robin Wilson, "For-Profit Colleges Change Higher Education's Landscape," *Chronicle of Higher Education*, February 7, 2010; Sandy Baum, "Drowning in Debt: Financial Outcomes of Students at For-Profit Colleges," testimony to

the U.S. Senate Health, Education, Labor, and Pensions Committee, June 7, 2011, http://www.help.senate.gov/imo/media/doc/Baum.pdf.

9. Although it is not a comprehensive account of a singular global movement (and does not purport to be), one can get some sense of the scope of the diverse and heterogeneous contemporary struggles around the university in Edu-factory Collective, ed., *Toward a Global Autonomous University: Cognitive Labor, the Production of Knowledge, and Exodus from the Education Factory* (New York: Autonomedia, 2009).

10. This is a large literature, but see Bill Readings, *The University in Ruins* (Cambridge, Mass.: Harvard University Press, 1996); Sheila Slaughter and Larry Leslie, *Academic Capitalism: Politics, Policies, and the Entrepreneurial University* (Baltimore: Johns Hopkins University Press, 1997); Wesley Shumar, *College for Sale: A Critique of the Commodification of Higher Education* (London: Falmer Press, 1997); Stanley Aronowitz, *The Knowledge Factory: Dismantling the Corporate University and Creating True Higher Learning* (Boston: Beacon Press, 2000); David F. Noble, *Digital Diploma Mills: The Automation of Higher Education* (New York: Monthly Review Press, 2001); Derek Bok, *Universities in the Marketplace: The Commercialization of Higher Education* (Princeton, N.J.: Princeton University Press, 2003); Slaughter and Rhoades, *Academic Capitalism and the New Economy*; Jennifer Washburn, *University, Inc.: The Corporate Corruption of Higher Education* (New York: Basic Books, 2005); Henry Giroux, *The University in Chains: Confronting the Military–Industrial–Academic Complex* (Boulder, Colo.: Paradigm, 2007); Frank Donoghue, *The Last Professors: The Corporate University and the Fate of the Humanities* (New York: Fordham University Press, 2008); Marc Bousquet, *How the University Works: Higher Education and the Low-Wage Nation* (New York: New York University Press, 2008); Christopher Newfield, *Unmaking the Public University: The Forty-Year Assault on the Middle Class* (Cambridge, Mass.: Harvard University Press, 2008); and Ellen Schrecker, *The Lost Soul of Higher Education: Corporatization, the Assault on Academic Freedom, and the End of the American University* (New York: New Press, 2010). Among geographers, see Katharyne Mitchell, "Scholarship Means Dollarship, or, Money in the Bank Is the Best Tenure," *Environment and Planning A* 31, no. 3 (1999): 381–88, and Mitchell, "The Value of Academic Labor: What the Market Has Wrought," *Environment and Planning A* 32, no. 10 (2000): 1713–18, as well as the special edition of *Antipode* 32, no. 3 (2000) on the corporatization of the university.

11. Aronowitz, *Knowledge Factory*.

12. Jeffrey Williams, "Deconstructing Academe: The Birth of Critical University Studies," *Chronicle of Higher Education: The Chronicle Review*, February 19, 2012.

13. On reification, see Fredric Jameson, "Reification and Utopia in Mass Culture," *Social Text* 1 (1979): 130–48. I thank Adam Sitze for suggesting this formulation.

14. Mitchell, "Scholarship Means Dollarship," 384.

15. Washburn, *University, Inc.*, ix; Noel Castree and Matthew Sparke, "Professional Geography and the Corporatization of the University: Experiences, Evaluations, and Engagements," *Antipode* 32, no. 3 (2000): 222.

16. Thomas Bender, "Politics, Intellect, and the American University, 1945–1995," in Bender and Schorske, *American Academic Culture in Transformation*, 23, 17.

17. Roger Geiger, *Research and Relevant Knowledge: American Research Universities since World War Two* (New York: Oxford University Press, 1993). Of course, big science in the United States in the 1940s and 1950s also had ties with the research and development arms of large corporations. Places like Bell Laboratories attracted top scientists, while many of the national scientific laboratories were run on contracts sponsored by corporations. DuPont and Monsanto both ran contracts at the Clinton Laboratories in Tennessee during the 1940s, and Union Carbide held contracts for running its successor institution, the Oak Ridge National Laboratory, during the 1950s and 1960s. A chronology of these contracts is available at http://www.ornl.gov/ornlhome/contractors.shtml.

18. For general summaries of the political and economic contexts of academic research in relation to the Cold War, see Noam Chomsky, Ira Katznelson, R. C. Lewontin, David Montgomery, Laura Nader, Richard Ohmann, Ray Siever, Immanuel Wallerstein, and Howard Zinn, *The Cold War and the Universities* (New York: New Press, 1997).

19. Trevor Barnes, "Geography's Underworld: The Military–Industrial Complex, Mathematical Modeling, and the Quantitative Revolution," *Geoforum* 39, no. 1 (2008): 3–16; Trevor Barnes and Matthew Farish, "Between Regions: Science, Militarism, and American Geography from World War to Cold War," *Annals of the Association of American Geographers* 96, no. 4 (2006): 807–26; Neil Smith, *American Empire: Roosevelt's Geographer and the Prelude to Globalization* (Berkeley: University of California Press, 2003).

20. Readings, *University in Ruins*, as well as David W. Noble, *Death of a Nation: American Culture and the End of Exceptionalism* (Minneapolis: University of Minnesota Press, 2002).

21. Although, to be clear, what constituted that "cultural authority" was different in different national educational systems. On this point generally, see Reading, "The Time of Study: 1968," in *University in Ruins*, 135–49.

22. Sheila Slaughter and Gary Rhoades, *Academic Capitalism and the New Economy*, 35; Roger Geiger, *Knowledge and Money: Research Universities and the Paradox of the Marketplace* (Stanford, Calif.: Stanford University Press, 2004), 22.

23. Here, too, these arguments focus on both structural and ideological causes. For instance, Mitchell, Slaughter and Leslie, and Slaughter and Rhoades emphasized the transformation of institutional capacities flowing from technological change and global political economy as shaping the corporatization of the university but also processes in which universities play an important role. Readings, however, presents the corporation of the university in much more politico-ideological terms:

"since the nation-state is no longer the primary instance of the reproduction of global capitals, 'culture'—as the symbolic and political counterpart to the project of integration pursued by the nation-state—has lost its purchase. The nation-state and the modern notion of culture arose together, and they are, I argue, ceasing to be essential to an increasingly transnational global economy." Readings, *University in Ruins*, 12.

24. See Geiger, *Knowledge and Money*, esp. chapters 4 and 5, and Geiger, "Organized Research Units—Their Role in the Development of University Research," *Journal of Higher Education* 61, no. 1 (1990): 1–19.

25. Noble, *Digital Diploma Mills*.

26. On the scope of industry influence in medical research and education, see Bernard Lo and Marilyn Field, eds., *Conflict of Interest in Medical Research, Education, and Practice* (Washington, D.C.: National Academies Press, 2009). On notable controversies, see Eyal Press and Jennifer Washburn, "The Kept University," *Atlantic Monthly* 285, no. 3 (2000): 39–54, and Alan Rudy et al., *Universities in the Age of Corporate Science: The UC Berkeley–Novartis Controversy* (Philadelphia: Temple University Press, 2007).

27. Materials chronicling the conflict over Middlesex's philosophy department are available at http://savemdxphil.com/. See also David Glenn, "Notre Dame Plans to Dissolve the 'Heterodox' Side of Its Split Economics Department," *Chronicle of Higher Education*, September 16, 2009, http://chronicle.com/article/Notre-Dame-to-Dissolve/48460; Scott Jaschik, "Disappearing Languages at Albany," *Inside Higher Ed*, October 4, 2010, http://www.insidehighered.com/news/2010/10/04/albany.

28. Jay Greene, "Administrative Bloat at American Universities: The Real Reason for High Costs in Higher Education," *Goldwater Institute Policy Report, no. 239, August 17, 2010.*

29. John Curtis and Monica Jacobe, *AAUP Contingent Faculty Index, 2006* (Washington, D.C.: AAUP Press, 2006).

30. Jack Schuster and Martin Finkelstein, *The American Faculty: The Restructuring of Academic Work and Careers* (Baltimore: Johns Hopkins University Press, 2006), 197–99.

31. Bousquet, *How the University Works*, 24.

32. Ibid., 40.

33. On the structure of these sectors of the higher education labor force, see ibid., 94–98; Sheila Slaughter and Gary Rhoades, "The Neo-Liberal University," *New Labor Forum* 6 (Spring/Summer 2000): 73–79. On the attempts to organize both university-employed and subcontracted service and clerical staff on campuses through living wage campaigns and unionization efforts, see Jess Walsh, "Living Wage Campaigns Storm the Ivory Tower: Low Wage Workers on Campus," *New Labor Forum* 6 (Spring/Summer 2000): 80–89.

34. *Constructing Knowledge Societies: New Challenges for Tertiary Education* (Washington, D.C.: World Bank, 2002).

35. Ibid., xix. For the bank, the problems associated with higher education in developing countries are "generated by the process of shifting from elite to expanded, mass tertiary education under severe resource constraints and with the burden of a legacy of persistent inequalities in access and outcomes, inadequate educational quality, low relevance to economic needs, and rigid governance and management structures" (46). Many of the responses the bank advocates and funds, including its emphasis on assessment, distance learning, and linkages with local industry, are the same processes that critics link with corporatization in the Anglo-American academic context.

36. Bousquet, *How the University Works*, 27, 125–56.

37. Ross Perlin, "Unpaid Interns, Complicit Colleges," *New York Times*, April 2, 2011.

38. Bok, *Universities in the Marketplace*, chapters 3 and 7.

39. Samantha King and Sheila Slaughter, "Sports 'R' Us: Contracts, Trademarks, and Logos," in Slaughter and Rhoades, *Academic Capitalism and the New Economy*, 256.

40. Ibid., 267.

41. Harvey Araton, "Athletes Toe the Nike Line, but Students Apply Pressure," *New York Times*, November 22, 1997; Marion Traub-Werner and Altha Cravey, "Spatiality, Sweatshops, and Solidarity in Guatemala," *Social and Cultural Geography* 3, no. 4 (2002): 383–401; Kitty Krupat, "Rethinking the Sweatshop: A Conversation about United Students against Sweatshops (USAS) with Charles Eaton, Marion Traub-Werner, and Evelyn Zepeda," *International Labor and Working Class History*, no. 61 (2002): 112–27.

42. Andrew Ross, "Global U," in *The University against Itself: The NYU Strike and the Future of the Academic Workplace*, ed. M. Krause, M. Nolan, M. Palm, and A. Ross, 211–23 (Philadelphia: Temple University Press, 2008); Roberta Malee Bassett, *The WTO and the University: Globalization, GATS, and American Higher Education* (New York: Routledge, 2006).

43. In 2001, the Association of Universities and Colleges of Canada, the American Council on Education, the European University Association, and the Council for Higher Education Accreditation signed a Joint Declaration opposing the inclusion of higher education in GATS. Links to this statement, along with those issued by many other academic associations from around the world, are available at UNESCO's website on Higher Education and GATS, http://portal.unesco.org/education/en/ev.php-URL_ID=21767&URL_DO=DO_TOPIC&URL_SECTION=201.html. See also Ross, "Global U."

44. Ross, "Global U"; Tamar Lewin, "U.S. Universities Rush to Set Up Outposts Abroad," *New York Times*, February 10, 2008.

45. Olds, "Global Assemblage."

46. See the special issue edited by Kanishka Jayasuriya and Susan Robertson, "Regulatory Regionalism and the Governance of Higher Education," *Globalization, Societies, and Education* 8, no. 1 (2010).

47. See Carter Daniel, *MBA: The First Century* (London: Associated University Presses, 1998).

48. Hyeyoung Moon and Christine Min Wotipka, "The Worldwide Diffusion of Business Education, 1881–1999: Historical Trajectory and Mechanisms of Expansion," in *Globalization and Organization: World Society and Organizational Change*, ed. G. Drori, J. Meyer, and H. Hwang (Oxford: Oxford University Press, 2006), 122–23.

49. Readings, *University in Ruins*, 24.

50. Ibid., 27.

51. Ibid.

52. Ibid., 39.

53. Ibid. For the argument to restructure the university on interdisciplinary lines, see Mark Taylor, "End the University as We Know It," *New York Times*, April 26, 2009. Taylor fundamentally mischaracterizes the problems of the university today. For a response, see Morgan Adamson, "Graduate Education Is the Dubai of Higher Learning," *Academe* 96, no. 1 (2010): 25–27.

54. Washburn, *University, Inc.*

55. Adolph Reed Jr., "A GI Bill for Everyone," *Dissent* 48, no. 4 (2001): 53–58.

56. Jeffrey Williams, "Student Debt and the Spirit of Indenture," *Dissent* 55, no. 4 (2008): 73–78.

57. Aronowitz, *Knowledge Factory.*

58. On union struggles, see Krause et al., *University against Itself,* and Cary Nelson, ed., *Will Teach for Food: Academic Labor in Crisis* (Minneapolis: University of Minnesota Press, 1997), which focus on labor activism at New York University and Yale, respectively. For another recent model of student activism, see http://www.occupystudentdebtcampaign.org/.

59. Edu-Factory Collective, *Toward a Global Autonomous University.*

60. Williams, "Deconstructing Academe."

61. Ibid.

62. John Mowitt, *Text: The Genealogy of an Anti-disciplinary Object* (Durham, N.C.: Duke University Press, 1992); Roland Barthes, "From Work to Text," in *Image, Music, Text*, trans. S. Heath (New York: Hill and Wang, 1977), 155–64.

63. Barthes, "From Work to Text," 155.

64. See, e.g., Fredric Jameson, "The Ideology of the Text," in *The Ideologies of Theory, Essays 1971–1986* (Minneapolis: University of Minnesota Press, 1986), 17–71; David Harvey, *The Conditions of Postmodernity* (Oxford: Blackwell, 1989).

65. Mowitt, *Text*, 33.

66. Ibid., 35.

67. Ibid., 36.

68. Ibid., xvii. See also René Girard, *Violence and the Sacred*, trans. P. Gregory (Baltimore: Johns Hopkins University Press, 1977).

69. Mowitt, *Text*, 40.

70. Ernst Kantorowicz, *The Fundamental Issue: Documents and Marginal Notes*

on the University of California Loyalty Oath, University Archives, The Bancroft Library, University of California at Berkeley, October 8, 1950. An online version of the text is available at http://sunsite.berkeley.edu/~ucalhist/archives_exhibits/loyaltyoath/symposium/kantorowicz.html.

71. Bob Blauner, *Resisting McCarthyism: To Sign or Not Sign California's Loyalty Oath* (Stanford, Calif.: Stanford University Press, 2009), 74–77.

72. This "sign or get out" policy was adopted on a 12–6 vote, with Sproul and Earl Warren opposed. George Stewart, *The Year of the Oath: The Fight for Academic Freedom at the University of California* (New York: Doubleday, 1950), 36.

73. As Kantorowicz put it, "mass decapitations of professors such as have taken place monthly in California's academic abattoir (157 + 6 + 31)." Kantorowicz, *Fundamental Issue,* 19.

74. Stanley Weigel, the lawyer for the faculty who refused to sign, convinced Kantorowicz to withhold publication, fearing that it could negatively impact the nonsigners' legal proceedings. Blauner, *Resisting McCarthyism,* 195.

75. As a German nationalist who was also a Jewish émigré to the United States and who wrote about the foundations of political power, Kantorowicz's personal and intellectual biography has itself become an object of scholarly concern, particularly as recent interest in the political theorists of the Weimar period and their experience with states of exception has grown. On Kantorowicz's history and its relation to his scholarship and politics, see Robert Benson and Johannes Fried, eds., *Ernst Kantorowicz: Erträge der Doppeltagung Institute for Advanced Study, Princeton Johann Wolfgang Goethe-Universität, Frankfurt* (Stuttgart, Germany: Franz Steiner, 1997); Martin A. Ruehl, "'In This Time without Emperors': The Politics of Ernst Kantorowicz's Kaiser Friedrich der Zweite Reconsidered," *Journal of the Warburg and Courtauld Institutes* 63 (2000): 187–242; Alain Boureau, *Kantorowicz: Stories of a Historian,* trans. S. Nichols and G. Spiegel (Baltimore: Johns Hopkins University Press, 2001).

76. Kantorowicz, *Fundamental Issue,* 1.

77. Ibid., 16.

78. Ibid., 16–17.

79. Ibid., 19–20.

80. Ibid., 20.

81. Ibid., 6.

82. Ibid.

83. Ibid., 20.

84. Ibid.

85. Ibid.

86. "A profession, as the word itself would suggest, is based upon conscience, and not upon working hours as in the case of modern trades, or on Time in general. In this respect the scholar resembles the judge whose duties are not disposed of by sitting in court, or the clergyman whose duties are not exhaustively described

by the mention of ritual performances and sermons on Sundays. The conscience is actually the essence of the scholars 'office' *(offcium)* which he is entrusted with and through which he becomes truly a 'public trust.'" Ibid., 21.

87. Ibid.

88. Ibid.

89. Freund, *Legal Nature of Corporations,* 17.

90. Ibid., 18.

91. Ibid., 17.

92. On the cover of *Fundamental Issue,* Kantorowicz added the words "Fiat Lux (The Motto of the University of California)" to the bottom of the page, where one normally encounters publication information. Presumably it was this process of giving light that spurred Kantorowicz's critique.

93. Moishe Postone, *Time, Labor, and Social Domination: A Reinterpretation of Marx's Critical Theory* (Cambridge: Cambridge University Press, 1993), 5–6.

Conclusion

1. Foucault, "Society Must Be Defended," 254.

2. Ibid.

3. Ibid., 256.

4. Ibid., 254.

5. Ibid., 258.

6. Ibid., 260–61.

7. Michel Foucault, *Discipline and Punish: The Birth of the Prison,* trans. Alan Sheridan (New York: Vintage, 1977), 31. See also Elden, *Mapping the Present,* 111–19.

8. E. P. Thompson, *Whigs and Hunters: The Origins of the Black Act* (New York: Pantheon, 1975), 260.

9. Ibid., 262.

10. Ibid., 263.

11. Ibid., 264.

12. Ibid., 265.

13. Ibid., 262.

14. On the nature of this gap, see Derrida, "The Force of Law: The 'Mystical Foundations of Authority,'" in *Deconstruction and the Possibility of Justice,* ed. D. Carlson, D. Cornell, and M. Rosenfeld, 3–67 (New York: Routledge, 1992), and Agamben, *State of Exception,* 37–40.

15. But see William Scheuerman, *Liberal Democracy and the Social Acceleration of Time* (Baltimore: Johns Hopkins University Press, 2004), for an argument to the contrary. Scheuerman, like Thompson, argues that the liberal rule of law's commitment to procedural norms of deliberation and the separation of powers offers a bulwark against capitalist globalization in the sense that law has a different

temporal horizon from capitalist exchange. I suggest that Scheuerman attempts to cordon off a good core of liberalism without fully grappling with the ways those forms are constitutive of capitalist social relations or, for that matter, the ways legal exemptions and emergencies, to which capitalist globalization has frequent recourse, are already internal to the liberal rule of law. Scheuerman has himself demonstrated how deeply the emergency is incorporated into the normal function of liberal capitalist law in his incisive article "The Economic State of Emergency," *Cardozo Law Review* 21, nos. 5–6 (2000): 1869–94.

abandonment, 6–9; Agamben and, 174n24; capitalism and, 12, 111, 115; colonization and, 183n59; corporation-as-police and, 21; globalization and, 38; liberal rights and, 79. *See also* Agamben, Giorgio; ban

academic capitalism, 140, 144

Adidas, 147

administration, federal. *See* federal administration

Agamben, Giorgio, 7, 10; the ban, 6, 174n24, 204n68; *homo sacer,* 137, 174n21; persons 78, 86, 198n79; rights 78; space of law, 108–9, 183n59

Aglietta, Michel, 184n5

Agnew, John, 122, 123

Alabama, 94

aliens, 72. *See also* Constitution, U.S.: Fourteenth Amendment

Allende, Salvador, 123

Alliance for Justice, 66

Althusser, Louis, 14–15, 162, 172, 176n47

American Association of University Professors, 145

American Banana Company, 103

American Banana Company v. United Fruit Company, 102, 105, 107

American Car and Foundry Company, 121

American Journal of International Law, 102

American Locomotive Company, 121

Amnesty International, 129

Andean Pact, 125

Annan, Kofi, 127, 132

anti-Chinese ordinances (California), 71

anticapitalist corporatism, 141

antidisciplinarity, 141, 149–53, 159

antisweatshop movement, 133, 147

antitrust law (U.S.), 59, 99; extraterritorial applications of, 108. *See also* Sherman Antitrust Act

Aquinas, Thomas, 186n30

Arendt, Hannah, 133–35, 137, 159, 183n59

Argentina, support for corporate code of conduct, 125

Aristotle, 10, 174n24

Aronowitz, Stanley, 149

associations: Bodin on, 35; Gierke on 5, 79–81, 82; Hobbes on, 36–37

Australia, 143

Austria, reciprocal recognition of U.S. corporations, 104

autonomy, 16, 20, 35–36, 38, 53, 108, 139, 141, 153–55

Bair, Jennifer, 124, 131

Baldwin Locomotive Works, 121

ban: biopolitics and, 11, 78; capitalism and, 12, 63, 69; corporate personhood and, 75, 76; corporate sovereignty and, 8–9, 20, 54; definition of 6–7, 174n21, 174n24, 196n49, 204n68; geographic dimensions of 108–9; modern liberal state and, 99; public–private distinction and, 187; responsibility and, 114 rights and, 78. *See also* abandonment; Agamben, Giorgio; exception; immunity

Bank of Augusta v. Earle, 52, 92–94, 95, 96, 102

Bank of the United States (2nd), 45–46, 47, 54, 55

Bank of the United States v. Deveaux, 70, 102

Barbados, support for corporate code of conduct, 125

Barnett, Clive, 112–13, 114, 206n8

Barthes, Roland, 150–51

Bayh–Dole Act (U.S.), 144, 149

Beard, Charles, 73, 195n31

Beard, Mary, 73, 195n31

Belgium, reciprocal recognition of British and U.S. corporations, 104

Bellamy, Edward, 4

Bell Laboratories, 216n17

Bender, Thomas, 142

Berle, Adolf, 5; as advocate of shareholder primacy 118–19; 208n22; on corporate property, 117–18, 194n10; corporatist vision of U.S. economy, 119; debate with Dodd, 118–19, 207n20, 208n29; reiterating corporate sovereignty, 120–22, 132, 161; separation of ownership and management, 69, 117

Bermuda, 101, 202n54

Bill of Rights (U.S.), 71

Bingham, John, 195n31

biopolitics: affirmative, 137, 158–59, 165; Agamben on, 7; the ban and, 8; capitalism and, 9–12, 111, 159, 162; corporations and, 81, 96, 120, 122; Foucault on 7, 76, 161–62; liberal, 77, 78–79; totalitarian, 155, 159

biopower, 162. *See also* biopolitics: affirmative

Blackstone, William, 16, 27, 31, 84, 188n49

Blandi, Joseph, 190n54

Bodin, Jean, 35–36, 89

Bok, Derek, 146

Bosse, Abraham, 22

Bousquet, Marc, 145–46

Bourdieu, Pierre, 18, 177n51

Bratton, William, 118, 119, 208n29

Brazil, support for corporate code of conduct, 125

Bretton Woods institutions, 88, 107. *See also* International Monetary Fund; World Bank

Bricks Presbyterian Church v. Mayor of New York, Novak on, 189n49

Bureau of Corporations (U.S.), 43, 59, 98, 191n70

Butler, Henry, 189n54

Cadman, John, 190n54

California: anti-Chinese ordinances, 72–73; tax cases and Fourteenth Amendment, 73, 74, 75

cameralism, 7, 27, 28, 179n24

camp, the, 7–8, 78, 109, 183n59

Campaign GM, 116–17

Canada, 36, 101–2, 143, 147

capital: associations of, 81; corporation as legal embodiment of, 10, 12, 17, 38, 44, 57, 63, 64, 69, 114; limited liability and, 83; living labor and, 11, 113. *See also* capitalism; corporate capitalism

capital accumulation. *See* capitalism

capital flight, 87, 131

capitalism: biopolitics and, 8, 9–12, 121–22; collective power in, 139; comity and 94, 96–97; corporate power and, 3, 14, 15, 45, 85, 164–65; crisis of the 1970s and, 123, 143; critiques of, 11–12, 66, 73, 135–37, 157–58, 160; death and, 161–62; development and, 42, 131, 136–37, 212n91; free market, 14; global, 14, 87, 135, 136, 161, 221n15; government of life by, 10, 12, 88, 114, 130, 137, 161–62; liberal government and, 9, 53, 88, 221n15; liberal international order and, 122; responsibility and, 114–15; sovereignty and, 17, 42, 69, 122, 139, 150, 172n10; spatial expansion of, 74, 88, 91, 92, 96, 97, 98, 100; universities and, 140, 157–58, 160. *See also,* academic capitalism; capital; corporate capitalism; value

Capitalism and Freedom (Friedman), 116, 117

capitalist class, 11, 44, 45, 62, 112, 172, 184n5, 192n77

capitalists. *See* capitalist class

capitalist value. *See* value

Carnegie, Andrew, 62

Carolinas, as colonies, 16

Carr, Cecil, 181n41

Catholic Church, Roman. *See* Roman Catholic Church

CERDS, 124–5, 126, 130, 131

Central Intelligence Agency (U.S.), 123

Chandler, Alfred, 184n5

Charitable Uses Act, 29

Charter on the Economic Rights and Duties of States, 124–25, 126, 130, 131

charters: citizenship of corporations and, 70, 73, 107; colonization and, 34–35, 51, 54, 183n59; comity and, 89, 92; constitutions and, 5; corporation-as-police and, 30–35, 180n27; as gift, 16, 20, 37; liberalization of with general incorporation laws, 56–57, 69, 190n54; as liberty against the state, 20; state territory and, 87, 92, 93, 97; U.S. state legislatures and, 53, 55; as vested right, 46, 48, 52

Chatterjee, S. K., 131

Chile, and Allende overthrow, 123, 124, 209n42

Chinese civil rights cases (California), 72

Chronicle of Higher Education, 149–50

Chrysler Company, 121

Church, Frank, 209n42

Citizens United v. Federal Election Commission, 65

citizenship: African Americans and, 71; Arendt on, 134; biopolitics and, 77, 78; consumers as, 5; corporate (*see* corporate citizenship); Fourteenth Amendment and, 71–72, 77; modern liberal state, 68, 69, 75; universities and, 143

Civil War, U.S., 57, 67, 70–71, 74, 92, 195n21, 201n33

Clarke, Nick, 113

Clausewitz, Carl von, 161

Clayton Act, 59

Clinton Laboratories, 216n17

Cloke, Paul, 113

Coase, Ronald, 184n5

Coates v. Mayor of New York, Novak
   on, 189n49
codes of conduct, for transnational
   corporations, 122, 124–31, 133,
   137, 210n47, 210n50, 211n67
Cohen, Morris, 5, 120
Coke, Edward, 30–31, 84, 182n42
Cold War, 127, 143
Cole, George, 81
Colombia: foreign corporations in,
   104; support for corporate code
   of conduct, 125; United Fruit
   Company and, 102–3
colonization: in Americas, 50, 51, 54;
   comity and, 88, 90; corporations
   and, 13, 16, 20, 34–35, 36,
   38–39, 42, 103, 183n59; New
   International Economic Order and,
   124, 130
Columbia University, 107
comity, 17, 88, 89–99, 108–9, 200n13;
   in international law, 100, 102,
   203n56; as law or custom, 90–94;
   state of nature and, 90, 108–9; in
   U.S. law, 94–99
Commentaries on the Conflict of Laws
   (Story), 92
commerce: foreign corporations and,
   95; insurance as different from,
   98–99, 202n49; manners and,
   182n58; as natural right, 90
Commerce and Labor, U.S.
   Department of, 59
Commissioners on Uniform State Law,
   98
Committee of Experts for the
   Progressive Codification of
   International Law, 107
Committee on Research in Economic
   History, 173n16
common good: commerce and, 50, 93,
   186n30; corporations and, 8, 54,
   57, 99; the fisc and, 24; Foucault

and, 27; police and, 50. *See also*
   public welfare; *salus publica*
common law: antitrust and, 59, 99;
   Maitland on, 82; modern liberal
   state and, 74
Commons, John, 61
commonwealth, 21, 23, 36–37, 77,
   102, 181n29
commonwealth studies, 5, 173n16,
   188n41
Commonwealth v. Alger, 187n36,
   187n37
community, 54, 68; Arendt on, 134;
   Gierke on, 81; as *persona ficta*,
   23; police and, 26–27, 180n25,
   187n36; disciplinary, 153
Community Environment Legal
   Defense Fund, 66
company law. *See* corporate law
concentration, economic, 44, 56, 60,
   115, 119, 121, 184n5, 208n22
conflict of laws, 88–92, 200n13;
   foreign corporations and, 92, 94,
   97, 108
Congress, U.S., 59, 101, 108, 123, 143
Connecticut, as colony, 16
constituted power, 5, 6, 8, 11, 89,
   109; and constituting power, 12,
   174n24, 176n39
Constitution, U.S.: commerce clause,
   95; Fourteenth Amendment, 67,
   70–75, 77, 98; rights for corporate
   persons under, 65, 68, 70, 72–74,
   98; slavery and, 92
consumers: as citizens, 5, 120;
   monopolies and 61; neoliberalism
   and, 112; as political subjects, 133;
   students as, 146, 148
contract: charter as, 42, 48, 52–54;
   corporation as nexus of, 2, 41, 106;
   foreign corporations and, 90, 93,
   96–97, 104; market society and,
   50; natural entity theory and, 68;

social, 21, 23, 75, 108
Cook, Walter W., 97
Corbridge, Stuart, 122–23
corporate body of the state, 20–26,
  35–37, 78, 158, 162–63
corporate capitalism, 41, 42, 43,
  66, 69, 85, 111; consolidated by
  U.S. state, 73–74; corporate social
  responsibility and, 119; law and,
  82, 84, 164; workers and, 209
corporate citizenship, 9, 12, 17, 79;
  corporate social responsibility and,
  111–14; international law and,
  105, 106; Marshall on, 70; *Paul v.
  Virginia* and, 95; personhood and,
  85; *Slaughterhouse Cases* and, 71,
  72–73; Taney on, 95, 102
corporate governance, 1, 2;
  deterritorialization and, 87;
  personhood and, 68, 82; social
  responsibility and, 117, 207n20;
  state and, 119
corporate law: British, 194n11;
  capitalism and, 164, 209n36;
  exported by the U.S. with
  globalization, 42; genealogy and,
  14; international, 88, 95, 98;
  medieval, 16; problematic of, 42,
  164; progressive, 117–20, 209n36;
  shareholder primacy and, 116;
  social sciences and, 2, 171n3; and
  suspension of law, 18. *See also*
  corporate governance; corporate
  personhood; corporate power;
  corporations, theories of
corporate liberalism, 192n77
corporate personhood, 3; in Anglo-
  American legal thought, 82–85,
  200n29; ban and, 86; biopolitics
  and, 79, 120; debates over, 66–68,
  71, 85; as fictional, 70, 80; in
  German legal thought, 79–82, 85,
  200n29; liberal capitalist order and,

  60, 68, 76, 85, 86; liberal theory of
  in international law, 88, 96–97, 99,
  107; reality of, 83, 157; rights and,
  75, 79, 85; will and, 68, 74–75, 82,
  158. *See also* corporations, theories
  of
corporate power: Anglo-American
  legal history and, 5; as articulation
  of capitalism and liberal law, 3;
  as being in common, 141, 153,
  157–60, 165; charters and, 35,
  53, 93; critiques of, 3, 9, 54, 85;
  democracy and, 2, 4, 9–10, 45,
  65–69, 115, 121, 164, 189n53,
  190n54; and economic government,
  43–45, 60–64, 73–74, 112, 119–20,
  181n29; economists and, 2; as gift,
  37; as global problem, 1, 38–39;
  law and, 18, 130, 163–64; as mode
  of political sovereignty, 4, 6, 8–9;
  problematic of, 9, 14–18, 19, 139;
  responsibility and, 113–15; social
  sciences and, 2–3, 15, 61, 75, 143,
  150; spatial dimensions of, 13–14,
  24, 38–39, 87–89; tragedy of, 139.
  See also corporations
corporate property. *See* property,
  corporate
corporate social responsibility (CSR),
  9, 17; Berle–Dodd debate and, 117–
  22, 132, 207n20, 208n22, 208n29;
  Friedman on, 115–19; Hymer on,
  135–36; neoliberalism and, 112–14,
  132; shareholders and, 116–22,
  208n20, 208n29, 209n36; workers
  and, 120, 209n36; I. M. Young
  on, 132–35, 159. *See also* codes of
  conduct; political responsibility
Corporation Act of 1889 (New
  Jersey), 56, 98
corporation-as-police, 16, 20, 28–33,
  35, 42, 158, 163; political rights
  and, 75

corporations: class interest and,
43–44, 130, 164, 172n8, 172n10,
209n36; criticism of, 3, 9, 36–38,
45–48, 49, 62, 63, 65–67, 73–74,
123–24, 130–31, 135–37, 144–49;
as double body of state sovereignty,
4–9, 20, 54, 81, 86, 92, 109, 122,
130, 139, 153; ideology and, 4,
172n10, 189n54, 216n23; as
medieval institutions, 16, 23, 45–
46, 156; as monstrous, 11–12, 37–
38, 45–46, 47, 51, 54, 62, 65–67,
115, 150, 157, 183n67; as private,
2, 16, 17, 41–43, 52–54, 60, 99,
102, 117–120; as quasi-public, 42,
54, 55, 60, 68, 85; resemblance
to states, 5–6, 81–82; as threat
to states, 1, 3, 4, 6, 8, 21, 37–38,
183n66. See also corporate power
corporations, foreign, 87–89, 93–100,
102, 104, 106, 108, 201n33,
201n45, 203n54
corporations, theories of: as grants of
the sovereign, 4, 8, 16–17, 28–38,
41, 180n27, 182n44; as grants
within U.S. law, 46, 51–57, 62, 69–
70, 92, 189n49; as ideological form
for capital, 4, 172n10, 189n54,
216n23; as legal fiction, 4, 11–12,
23, 52, 70, 80, 84–85, 106, 183n66;
as nexus of contracts, 2, 41, 106; as
real or natural entities, 60, 66, 68,
73–74, 79–83, 88, 97, 100
corporatism: anticapitalist, 141; Berle
and, 119; Gierke and, 81; Nazism
and, 155, 158, 162
corpus mysticum, 23, 25
Costa Rica, United Fruit Company
and, 102–3
credit, credulity and, 32
Creighton, Andrew, 56
critical university studies, 141, 150, 153
Cuba: U.S. imperialism and, 103–4;

Commercial Code, 103
custom: comity and, 88, 90–93, 100,
200n13; the university and, 158;
Whigs and Hunters and, 163

Daimler Company v. Continental Tyre
Company, 105, 107
Dartmouth College v. Woodward, 52
Das deutsche Genossenschaftsrecht
(Gierke), 79
Davis, John P., 29, 36
Davos, Switzerland, 127
De Conflictu Legum (Huber), 91
Dean, Mitchell, 28, 64, 180n27
Declaration of Fundamental Principles
and Rights at Work (ILO), 127
Declaration of the Rights of Man and
Citizen, 78
deductive power (sovereignty), 35,
86; Foucault and, 7, 24–26, 76, 79,
179n16; police and 26, 29; salus
publica and, 50
De Jure Civitatis (Huber), 90
De Jure Praedae (Grotius), 89
Delaware, and general incorporation
laws, 56
Deleuze, Gilles, 18
democracy, 2, 4, 9–10, 45, 65–69, 115,
121, 164, 189n53, 190n54
deregulation, 1, 10, 163
Derrida, Jacques, 6, 173n19
deterritorialization, 17, 87, 113
development: corporations in U.S.,
national, 42, 51, 53–54, 57, 63, 85,
173n16, 189n52; critiques of, 131,
135–37, 212n91; economic, 1–3,
115; MNCs in third world state,
122–27, 130–31; as placeholder for
political projects, 131; universities
and, 140, 146, 148, 218n35. See
also improvement
Dewey, John, 68, 84, 97
Dicey, A. V., 95

Dicken, Peter, 1

disciplinary power, 6, 161; academic disciplines and, 15, 141, 143, 147–53, 219n53; antidisciplinarity and, 141, 149–53, 159; capitalist value and, 120, 162; corporations and, 28, 32, 34, 38, 156, 158–59, 162; legal exception and, 20; and the subject, 34, 156

division of labor, 42, 49, 135–36, 185n24

docile bodies, 152

Dodd, Edwin Merrick, 118–19, 132, 189n53, 190n54, 190n59, 207n20

Dred Scott v. Sandford, 71

due process. See Constitution, U.S.: Fourteenth Amendment

Dunlavy, Colleen, 208n20

Dunning, John, 123

DuPont, 125, 216n17

Dutch East India Company (VOC), 19, 89–90

East India Company (English), 13, 19, 34–35, 36

Eastland Company, 32–33

economy: biopolitics and, 120–22, 159, 161–62; dualism with state, 3, 42, 113, 152; global, 95, 100, 108–9, 122–23, 126–27, 135–36; knowledge, 140, 146–47, 216n23; liberal critique of police and, 43, 44, 49–50; as mode of government, 43–45, 57, 64, 158, 184n5; monopoly and, 61–62; national, 41–42, 74–75, 202n54; police and, 27–28, 29, 31, 48. See also corporate capitalism; markets; police; political economy

Ecuador, support for corporate code of conduct, 125

Education, U.S. Department of, 145

Edward VII (King), 101

efficiency, 2, 96, 120, 148

Elizabeth I (Queen), 181n41

El Salvador, reciprocal recognition of U.S. corporations, 104

Emory v. Grenough, 91

England: charters and, 20, 29–30, 45–46; imperial trading companies and, 33–34; international commerce and, 94–95, 100, 104–5; liberal government and, 5, 29, 42, 82; police in, 27, 180n27, 180n28, 181n29; religious conflict in, 21; rule of law in, 163; shareholding in, 208n22; universities in, 142

environmental protections: corporate social responsibility and, 112, 126–27; corporations and, 1, 3, 108, 161

equal protection. See Constitution, U.S.: Fourteenth Amendment

Esposito, Roberto, 78, 86, 137, 196n52

Estonia, reciprocal recognition of U.S. corporations, 104

European Union, corporate social responsibility and, 111

exception: the ban and, 6–8, 12, 99, 174n24, 183n59; charters as, 17, 20, 28, 34, 37, 62, 97; liberal rights and, 44–45, 163, 222n15; needs and, 186n30; personhood and, 78; responsibility and 113, 130; territory and, 90–91, 108–9. See also ban, immunity

exemption, legal. See ban, exception, immunity

extraterritoriality, 17, 18, 203n56; comity and, 89, 92–95; commerce and, 92–94, 96, 102, 108; fisc and, 24; imperial trading companies and, 33

FDI. See foreign direct investment

fault, political responsibility and, 132

federal administration: corporate regulation and, 43, 57, 108; government of life and, 77; modern liberal state and, 74

Federal Trade Commission, U.S., 43, 59, 191n70

Feilchenfeld, Ernst, 105–6

fellowships. *See* associations

Field, Stephen, 58, 71–74, 85–86, 95, 121, 161, 202n49

Figgis, John Neville, 81

Finkelstein, Martin, 145

Finland, reciprocal recognition of U.S. corporations, 104

Firestone Tire and Rubber Company, 121

fisc, 24–25

Fordism, 142

Ford Motor Company, 121

foreign corporations. *See* corporations, foreign

foreign direct investment, 1, 122–23, 127, 135, 140

Foucault, Michel, 6–7, 24, 26, 51, 76–77, 79, 81, 112, 161–62, 179n16; genealogy and, 15, 177n47; *History of Sexuality, The*, 76, 179n16; *Society Must be Defended*, 77, 161. *See also* biopolitics; deductive power; disciplinary power; state racism

Fourteenth Amendment. *See under* Constitution, U.S.

France: police in, 27; reciprocal recognition of British and U.S. corporations, 104; and UNCTC, 210n50; and U.S. Non-Intercourse Act, 101

Frankenstein, 65, 67

Frederick II, 155

Freikorps, 154

Freund, Ernst, 73, 79, 82–83, 141, 157–58, 200n29

Friedman, Milton, 115–19

Fundamental Issue, The (Kantorowicz), 141, 154–59, 221n92

G-77. *See* Group of 77

GI Bill, 142, 149

GM. *See* General Motors

GEP. *See* Group of Eminent Persons

Geiger, Roger, 144

genealogy, 9, 10, 14–18, 44, 45, 78, 81, 86, 113, 122, 130, 139, 153, 159–60, 163–64, 177n47, 207n8

General Agreement on Tariffs and Trade (GATT), 125

General Agreement on Trade in Services (GATS), 147, 218n43

General Electric, 121

general incorporation laws, 43, 55–57, 69, 98, 189n53–54

General Motors (GM), 116–17, 121, 125

Geneva, GEP hearings and, 124

geopolitics, 107, 109

George III (King), 52

George, Stefan, 155

Georgetown University, 105, 117

Georgia, 16, 94

Germany: enemy corporations and, 104–5; Gierke on association law in, 79–82, 200n29; nationalism in 82, 154–55; and police science, 27, 28, 179n24, 180n27; reciprocal recognition of British and U.S. corporations, 104

German Civil Code, 81

Ghali, Boutrous, 211n67

Gierke, Otto von, 5, 73, 79–82, 85, 92

gift, as exemption from law, 16, 20, 37–38, 53, 62, 109

Girard, René, 150–51

Global Compact, UN: 127–32; and neoliberal globalization, 112, 130;

and voluntarism, 128–29, 130–32
globalization: alternatives to, 67, 132; as class project, 130; corporate-led, 2; imperialism and, 19, 38; neoliberalism and, 10, 14, 112, 142; rule of law and, 221n15; spatiality of, 14, 18, 38–39; state sovereignty and, 4; U.S. corporate law and, 42; universities and, 140, 142–43
Global War on Terror, U.S., 7
Goldwater Institute, 145
Goodrich Tire Company, 121
Goodyear Tire Company, 121
Google, 160
governance. *See* corporate governance; government; governmental rationality
government: administration and, 57–59, 61, 190n54; colonial, 16, 51; corporate social responsibility and, 112, 130; corporation-as-police and, 31; economic, 5, 43–45, 57, 112, 119–20, 184n5; efficiency and, 5; ends of, 5, 52–54, 85; liberal, 9, 38–39, 75, 108–9, 122; of life toward value, 7–10, 77–79, 96, 114, 120, 131, 137, 161–62, 209n36; persons and, 68–69; police and, 26–29, 48, 50–51, 60, 179n24, 180n27, 181n29; popular sovereignty and, 45–48; privatized, 1, 112; property and, 41–42; self-organization and, 16, 30, 34, 156–57, 159
governmental rationality (governmentality), 5–6, 26–28, 43–45, 60, 64, 108, 114, 179n20, 181n29, 187n35
Graham, Howard Jay, 73–74, 195n31
granger movement, 58
Greece: ancient corporations and, 23; *polis*, 48, 134, 180n25, 206n92; reciprocal recognition with British

and U.S. corporations, 104
Grotius, Hugo, 89–90, 186n30, 200n13
Group of Eminent Persons (GEP), 124–25, 135, 210n47
Group of 77, 124–25, 130–31, 132, 210n50
group personality, 80. *See* corporate personhood
Guadeloupe, 101
Guidelines for Multinational Enterprise (OECD), 128
guilt, responsibility and, 132–34
Gulf of Mexico, oil spill, 1, 3

habeas corpus, 78
Haiti, 100
Hale, Matthew (Lord), 188n37, 191n64
Hale, Robert, 5
Hale v. Henkel, 74
Hammond, Bray, 189n53, 190n54
Hanson, Peter, 211n67
Hardt, Michael, 108
Harlan, John Marshall, 99
Hartog, Hendrik, 5
Hartz, Louis, 190n54
Harvard Law Review, 118
Harvard University, 66, 154
Harvey, David, 176n40
Havana Charter (International Trade Organization), 123–24
Hegel, G. F. W., 6, 80, 197n57
Henderson, Gerard, 70, 95, 97, 194n13, 200n29, 201n33
Henshaw, David, 46–48, 51, 54, 185n15
Higher Education Act, U.S., 143
Higher Learning in America, The (Veblen), 142
History of Sexuality, The (Foucault), 76, 179n16
Ho Ah Kow v. Nunan, 72

Hobbes, Thomas, 16; fear of corporate
    autonomy, 35–38, 45, 183n67;
    Leviathan, The, 21, 22, 178n6; on
    sovereignty, 21–24, 78, 81, 158,
    183n66
Hohfeld, Wesley, 97
holding companies, 56, 64
Holmes, Oliver Wendell, 99, 103
Holy Roman Empire, 89
homo sacer, 137, 174n21, 198n79
Honduras, reciprocal recognition of
    U.S. corporations, 104
Hont, Istvan, 49, 185n30
Horn, Walter, 154
Horwitz, Morton, 5, 56, 66, 73–74,
    187n35, 194n10
House of Lords (U.K.), 105
Huber, Ulrich, 89–92, 98, 200n13
human rights, 9, 112, 126–29, 133,
    137, 213n93
Human Rights Watch, 129
Hungary, reciprocal recognition of
    U.S. corporations, 104
Hurst, J. Willard, 5
Hymer, Stephen, 135–37

IBM, 125
*ICC v. Alabama Midland Railroad
    Company,* Skowronek on, 191n69
Ignatieff, Michael, 49, 185n30
Illinois, railroad rate setting
    commission, 58
immunity, 4, 8, 9, 20, 38, 54–55,
    60, 63, 130–32, 137, 157; comity
    and 90–91; Esposito and, 78–79;
    Fourteenth Amendment and,
    72; liberal rights and, 78–79,
    108–9; responsibility and, 120–22;
    sovereign, 102. *See also* ban;
    Constitution, U.S.: Fourteenth
    Amendment; exception
*Impact of Multinational Corporations
    on Development and on
    International Relations* (UN), 124
imperium in imperio, 35
Import Rate Case, Skowronek on,
    191n69
improvement, 7, 50, 54, 57, 161–62.
    See also development
incorporation laws, general. *See*
    general incorporation laws
Industrial Commission, U.S., 43,
    59–62, 191n70
In re Ah Fong, 72
In re Parrott, 72
In re Quong Woo, 72
In re Tie Loy, 72
interdisciplinarity, 15, 141, 148–53,
    219n53
International Chamber of Commerce
    (ICC), 125, 128
International Forum on Globalization,
    66
International Labor Organization
    (ILO), 127–28
international law: conflicts with
    state sovereignty, 104–7; foreign
    corporations in, 100; liberal
    theory of corporation in, 88, 100,
    105–7; private, 89, 94; public, 9,
    88; responsibility and, 115, 126,
    128–29, 131; spatiality of, 89. *See
    also* conflict of laws
International Monetary Fund (IMF),
    122–23
International Telegram and Telegraph
    (IT&T), 123
interstate and foreign commerce, 59,
    92–96, 99, 202n54, 203n56
Interstate Commerce Commission
    (ICC), 43, 58–59, 191n69
Interstate Commerce Act (U.S.), 58–59
Iowa, railroad rate setting
    commission, 58

Ireland, Gordon, 104
Ireland, Paddy, 194n11, 208n20
Italy: reciprocal recognition of British and U.S. corporations, 104; and UNCTC, 210n50
ius gentium. See law of nations

Jackson, Andrew, 45–46, 47, 54, 55, 62, 185n14, 190n54
Jamaica, support for corporate code of conduct, 125
Japan: foreign direct investment from, 123; reciprocal recognition of U.S. corporations, 104
Jenks, Jeremiah, 61–62, 192n78
Jhering, Rudolph von, 83
Jones, Dwight, 84
Jones, Gilbert, 125
Joo, Thomas Wuil, 72
jurisdiction, 13, 17, 18, 69–70, 84, 108, 122; charters and, 33–34, 70, 73, 189n54; foreign corporations and, 88–93, 95–103, 105, 203n56, 204n65; spatial expansion of capitalism and, 13, 69, 91, 202n54
juristic persons. *See* legal persons
Justice, U. S. Department of, Antitrust Division, 107

Kansas, 99
Kantorowicz, Ernst, 220n75; *Fundamental Issue, The,* 141, 154–59, 221n92; *King's Two Bodies, The,* 23–25, 174n21, 193n1
Kentucky, foreign corporations in, 201n45
King, Samantha, 146
King's Two Bodies, The (Kantorowicz), 23, 25, 174n21, 193n1
Kloppenberg, James, 181n29
Knemeyer, Franz-Ludwig, 180n25

knowledge economy, 140, 146–47, 216n23
Kolko, Gabriel, 172n8, 192n77
Krueger, Muria, 128, 212n75
Kyd, Stewart, 30

labor: absent in corporate law, 209n36; division of, 42, 49, 135–36, 185n24, 186n30; economy and 28; liberalism and, 79; living 10–13; standards and protections, 108, 127; theory of value, 49; universities and, 145–47, 150, 157, 160
laissez-faire: capitalism, 173n16; constitutionalism, 53, 75, 186n34, 202n52; as critique of state power, 71; liberalism, 28; monopolies and, 189n53
Lamoreaux, Naomi, 208n20
Laski, Harold, 81–82
Latvia, reciprocal recognition of U.S. corporations, 104
law: borders of, 8; capitalism and, 12, 95, 97, 164; and custom, 90–91, 200n13; exceptions from, 4, 6–7, 16, 18, 20, 35, 37, 55, 64, 109, 114, 179n19, 183n59, 187n35; fact and, 103; formation of corporate power and, 2, 4, 5, 18, 39, 52–53, 68, 113–14, 184n5; government of life and, 77–79, 178n7; ideology of, 18; interests and, 83; liberal, 3, 68–69, 74, 79, 86, 114, 120, 164; as limit, 9; necessity and, 25, 179n19, 186n30; as norm, 43–44, 76, 88, 96; police and, 26, 48; pragmatism and, 75, 97, 200n29; property and, 41, 50, 86; public–private distinction and, 5, 41–43, 50, 53, 58, 60, 63, 71, 74, 187n35; and right, 80–81; as socially

constructed, 18, 75, 85, 177n51;
    spatiality of, 18, 78, 88–92, 97,
    106, 109
law, corporate. *See* corporate law
law, international. *See* international
    law
law, natural. *See* natural law
law of nations, 90, 93, 101–2
law, Roman. *See* Roman law
law, rule of, 83, 163–64, 221n15
League of Nations, 88, 105, 107
Lectures on Jurisprudence (Adam
    Smith), 27
legal history, 5, 73–75, 94, 115
Legal Nature of Corporations, The
    (Freund), 82, 141, 157
legal persons, 13, 44, 57, 60, 65–68,
    80, 83, 96, 99, 107, 164. *See also*
    corporate personhood; natural
    persons
legal realism, 5, 85, 97
Leslie, Larry, 143–44, 216n23
Levant Company, 33, 182n44
Leviathan, The (Hobbes), 21–22, 26,
    178n6, 183n67
Lewin, Tamar, 147
liability: limited for corporations, 43,
    56–57, 64, 74, 83, 190n59; Marxist
    critique of, 172n10; and political
    responsibility, 129, 132–33, 159;
    as problem in corporate regulation,
    84, 100
liberal international order, 122, 143
liberalism: corporate property and,
    194n10; government by economy
    and, 44; laissez-faire, 28, 50;
    manners and, 58; persons and, 68,
    78–79; police and, 181n29; popular
    sovereignty and, 38; problematic of
    68, 76–79. *See also* governmental
    rationality; government: liberal;
    law: liberal

liberal law. *See under* law
liberal state. *See* modern liberal state
liberal theory of corporations, 88,
    96–100, 105, 106–7
Liberia, reciprocal recognition of U.S.
    corporations, 104
License Cases, 51
Livermore, Samuel, 91–92
Lloyd, Stuart, 1121–13
Locke, John, 81, 186n30
Lorenzen, Ernst, 97
Louisiana, foreign corporations in,
    201n45
Louisville Railroad Co. v. Letson, 70
Luxembourg, 202n54

MNCs. *See* multinational corporations
Maier, Pauline, 5, 51
Maitland, Frederic, 5, 73, 79, 81, 82
Malpass, Alice, 113
management, 41; as agents of
    shareholders, 116, 118; division
    of labor and, 135; and local
    populations, 3; ownership and,
    9, 74, 118; and planning, 119;
    responsibility and, 115–16, 118,
    122, 137, 208n29; of universities,
    144, 147, 156
managerialism, 145
Manhattan Project, 143
markets: competition and, 57, 59,
    99, 107–8; corporations and, 38,
    54–55, 61; division of labor in,
    42, 49, 186n30; free, 46, 48–50,
    55, 116, 186n30; government
    by economy and, 44; imperfect,
    60; labor, 140, 146, 153, 157;
    multinational corporations and,
    122; neoliberalism and, 10, 14,
    17, 112–13, 130, 143–44; police
    regulations of, 28, 47, 186n30;
    prices in, 49, 57; scarcity and, 64;

as social organization, 10, 61, 116, 127, 130; universities and, 140, 143–44, 146–47

Marshall, John, 52, 70, 101

Marx, Karl, 175n33; on corporations, 64, 193n90; on potentiality, 10–11; transformation of living labor into capital, 12–13. *See also* Marxism

Marxism: on corporate law, 209n36; corporations and, 172, 184n5; critique of law, 163; and text, 151; and uneven development, 135. *See also* Marx, Karl

Mason v. Intercolonial Railway of Canada, 101–2, 105

Mason v. Ship Blaireau, 203n56

Massachusetts: as colony, 16; and *Commonwealth v. Alger*, 187n36, 187n37; general incorporation laws in, 189n53; liability in, 190n59; and Route 128 corridor, 140; Supreme Court of, 101

Massachusetts Institute of Technology, Radiation Lab, 143

Maximum Freight Rate Case, Skowronek on, 191n69

McCain–Faingold Bipartisan Campaign Finance Act (U.S.), 65

McCarthyism, 155

McConnell, Sam, 102–3

McCurdy, Charles, 74–75, 202n52

Means, Gardiner, 69, 117, 119–21, 161, 194n10, 208n22. *See also* Berle, Adolf

mercantilism, 7, 27, 28

Merchant Adventures, 34. *See also* Wheeler, John

Merchants of London Trading to France, 32

Mexico: reciprocal recognition of U.S. corporations, 104; support for corporate code of conduct, 125

Meyers, Marvin, 185n14

Microsoft, 160

Middlesex University, 144

Miller, Arthur S., 5

Mines Royal Company, 32–33

Minnesota, railroad rate setting commission, 58

miserable sectors, 136–37, 158

Modern Corporation and Private Property (Berle and Means), 117, 119–20, 194n10, 207n20, 208n22. *See also* Berle, Adolf

modern liberal state, 73–77, 192n77

monopolies: general incorporation laws and, 57, 69, 189n53, 190n54; as granted rights, 31–34, 45–46, 49, 51, 54, 71, 89, 94, 182n44, 189n53; international commerce and, 89, 94, 102–3; Jenks on, 61–62; markets and, 55, 57, 60–64, 185n53, 193n84; as monsters, 62, 183n67; natural entity theory and, 74; regulation of, 57, 100; Sherman Antitrust Act and, 58–59, 103; over state violence, 20, 87; trust problem and, 60, 193n84; U.S. Industrial Commission and, 59

Monsanto, 216n17

Moon, Hyeyoung, 147

Mortmain, Statute of, 30

Mowitt, John, 150–53

multinational corporations (MNCs): compared to national economies, 5; growth of, 17, 122–23; imperial companies and, 13, 19, 38; UN debates over, 123–28, 133, 135–37

Multinational Corporations in World Development, 124, 135

Multinational Monitor, 66

Munich Republic of Councils, 154

Munn v. Illinois, 58, 118–19, 188n38

Murphy, Thomas, 125
Murray v. The Schooner Charming Betsy, 101

NIEO. *See* New International Economic Order
Nader, Ralph, 66–67, 70
Napoleonic Code, in Cuba, 103
National Center for Educational Statistics, 145
National Industrial Recovery Act, 119
nationalization, 88, 105, 126
National Science Foundation, 144
natural entity theory, 66, 73–74, 82, 84. *See also* corporations, theories of: as real or natural entities
natural law, 182n58, 185n28, 186n30
natural persons, 60, 66, 88. *See also* corporate personhood; legal personhood
nature: human, 21, 34; labor's transformation of, 10–11; transcendence of, 26. *See also* state of nature
Nazism, 78, 155, 158, 162
necessitas legem non habet, 25. *See also* law: necessity and
Negri, Antonio, 108, 174n24, 176n39
Neocleous, Mark, 180n27
neoliberalism, 76; analytical problems with the concept of, 112–13, 163; and depoliticization, 112; as ideology, 14; as market-based government 10, 112–14, 142, 163; responsibility and, 114, 132; universities and, 17, 140
New Code Environment, 127
New Deal, 74. *See also* Berle, Adolf; National Industrial Recovery Act
Newfoundland Company, 33
New Hampshire: *Dartmouth College v. Woodward* and, 52; foreign

corporations in, 201n45
New International Economic Order (NIEO), corporate codes of conduct and, 124–26, 130–31, 210n50
New Jersey: foreign corporations in, 201n33; incorporation laws in, 56–57, 98–99, 100, 188n41
New Orleans (Louisiana): *Slaughterhouse cases* and, 71
New York City: corporate charter of, 188n42; financial markets, 57; GEP hearings, 124
New York State: Court of Appeals, 205n80; foreign corporations in, 100, 201n33; general incorporation laws, 55, 189n53
New York Times, 115, 117, 147
New York University, 147
Neylan, John Francis, 150
Nietzsche, Friedrich, 15, 133–34, 176n47
Nike, 147
Niklasson, Sten, 126
Noble, David F., 144
nomos, 109, 206n92. *See also* law
Non-Intercourse Act (U.S.), 101
norms. *See* law: as norms
Norms on the Responsibilities of Transnational Corporations and Other Business Enterprises with Regard to Human Rights (UN Norms), and legally enforceable corporate codes of conduct, 128–29, 130–32. *See also* Global Compact, UN
Norway, reciprocal recognition of U.S. corporations, 104
Novak, William, 5; on modern liberal state, 74–77; on police, 50, 187n35; 188n49
Noyes, Walter, 60

Oak Ridge National Laboratory, 216n17

Obrecht, Georg, 179n24

Oeconomy. See economy

Olds, Kris, 147

Organization for Economic Co-operation and Development (OECD), 128

On the Genealogy of Morals (Nietzsche), 134, 177n47

Panama, United Fruit Company and, 102–3

Parker, Robert John, 105, 205n79

partnerships, difference from corporations, 83

Pasquino, Pasquale, 179n24

Paul v. Virginia, 95, 98, 202n49

Peck, Jamie, 10

Pennsylvania: Bank of the United States and, 45, 55; corporate regulation in, 188n41; foreign corporations in, 201n45

people, the, 50, 65, 80–81, 86, 198n79. *See also* sovereignty: popular

Perlin, Ross, 146

person, *dispositif* of, 78, 196n52, 198n79. *See also* Esposito, Roberto

personhood. *See* corporate personhood; legal persons; natural persons

Peru, support for corporate code of conduct, 125

Philadelphia (Pennsylvania), 100

Philosophy of Right (Hegel), 80, 197n57

Pincus, Steven, 181n29

planning, 119, 135

Platt Amendment, and U.S. corporations in Cuba, 104

Pocock, J. G. A., 182n58

Poland, reciprocal recognition of U.S. corporations, 104

police *(polezei),* 17, 118; capitalist development and, 17, 42–44, 50, 53, 186n31; colonization and, 16, 35, 50–54, 183n57; corporations and, 16, 20, 21, 28–33, 35, 42, 158, 180n27; defined, 26–28, 179n24, 186n31; in England, 20, 27, 30–33, 42, 180n27, 181n29; Foucault on, 7, 26, 51, 77; in Germany, 27, 81, 179n24, 180n27; as government by economy, 26–28, 29, 43–44, 64, 181n29; Hegel and, 197n57; liberal critique of, 42–44, 48–50; property and, 50–53, 186n34, 187n36, 188n49; in the United States, 42–45, 50–53, 58, 71–75, 118, 186n31, n34, 187n36, 188n49. *See also* corporation-as-police; economy; government; police power

police power, 17, 42–43, 50–53, 58, 77, 92, 99, 186n34, 187n36, 188n49, 201n33; *Slaughterhouse Cases* and, 71–72, 74

polis, 48, 180n25

political arithmetic, 27

political economy, 41, 139; critique of police and, 48–50, 64, 186n30; exception and, 17; Foucault and, 7; free markets and, 46; liberal, 68. *See also* corporate capitalism; economy

political responsibility, 132–34, 137, 159

political theology, 8, 10, 134, 174n21, 179n19

Poovey, Mary, 178n7, 180n27, 185n28

popular sovereignty, 38, 42, 48, 50–51, 54, 62–63

Portugal, East India trade and, 89–90

Post, Gaines, 178n13
Postone, Moishe, 160
potentiality: ban and, 174n24; capitalism and, 10–12, 120; living labor and, 10–12; political possibilities and, 159; space and the actualization of, 13–14
pragmatism, 75, 94–97, 189n54
private property. *See* property, private
privatization, 1, 10, 42, 43, 60, 163
privileges and immunities. *See* Constitution, U.S.: Fourteenth Amendment; immunity
problematic: of corporate sovereignty, 14, 15, 17, 19–21, 42, 44, 114, 120, 137, 190n54; definition of, 14–15, 177n47; and disciplinary knowledge, 150; of law, 164; of liberalism, 68, 75, 79; of governmental reason, 26, 60, 181n29, 187n35; of personhood, 80, 82
profit: corporate social responsibility and, 112, 116–19; of corporations compared to gross national product of states, 5; maximization of 3, 116, 119, 120; public welfare and, 64; short-term, 127; university strategies for, 140–47; and utility, 32
property, corporate: and classical liberalism, 194n10; equal protection and, 72–73; managerial discretion and, 118, 122; nationalization of, 105; as personified, 73, 75; political theology and, 85, 120; public rights over, 48, 53; separation of ownership and management, 69, 74, 117; shareholders and, 115, 118, 122; as vested right, 54, 85.
property, passive, 117

property, private: corporations as, 41–43, 58, 60, 194n10; Fourteenth Amendment and, 71; and freedom of the seas, 89–90; in natural law tradition, 186n30; necessity and, 186n30, 186n34, 187n36; police power as promoting, 42, 186n34, 187n35; and problematic of government, 187n35; regulation of, 58, 118, 187n36
public interest proxy campaigns, 116–17, 207n16
public–private distinction: corporations as blurring, 42–43, 54, 58, 188n42; Fourteenth Amendment and, 71, 74; Hale on, 5; king's two bodies and, 24; liberal capitalism and, 53, 96, 100, 108; monopoly and, 60, 63; police and, 50, 187n35, 187n36; responsibility and, 112–13, 133–34
public–private partnerships, 1, 144
public welfare: corporate body of the state and, 24–25; corporate sovereignty and, 8, 113; corporation-as-police and, 16, 30, 180n27; corporations as threats to, 35, 37–38; legal norms and, 43, 108; market economy and, 42–44, 49–51, 60, 184n5; planning and, 119, 122; police and, 26–27, 49. *See also* common good; *salus publica*
Pufendorf, Samuel, 179n16, 186n30
Pullman Company, 121

Radin, Max, 84–85, 200n29
Raeff, Marc, 28, 179n24
railroads, 53–54, 57–58, 60, 88, 98–99, 118, 189n49
Railroad Tax Cases (California), 72, 85

Radio Corporation of America (RCA), 121

Readings, Bill, 143, 148, 216n23

real entity theory. *See* natural entity theory

Redfield, Isaac, 188n49

Reed, Adolph, Jr., 149

regulated companies, 32

regulatory capture, 3

republicanism, 26–27, 42, 53, 74, 181n29

responsibility. *See* corporate social responsibility; political responsibility

Revolutionary War (U.S.), 16, 50–52

Rhode Island: colony of, 16; foreign corporations in, 201n45

right, law and, 6, 9, 74, 80–81, 84, 85, 87, 162, 179n16, 186n31, 188n49

rights, corporate: biopolitics and, 79; capitalism and, 17, 45; constitutional protection of in United States, 66; limited by police power, 188n49. *See also* charters; corporations, theories of

rights, natural, 90, 109

rights, property: contract and, 54; control and, 83; economic concentration and, 121; interests and, 83; and law, 41, 106, 164, 186n30; as legal norm, 44; liberalism and, 44, 80; police and, 187n36, 187n37; and responsibility, 115, 119, 121, 122; and slavery, 92; shareholders and, 73, 194n11

Rio Declaration on Environment and Development, 127

Ripley, William, 61

Rodenburg, Christian, 89

Rodgers, William, 62–63

Roman Catholic Church, 5, 10, 23

Roman law, 80–81, 89, 91, 92 174n21

Root, Elihu, 103

Rose v. Himley, 203n56

Ross, Andrew, 147

Royal African Company, 19, 34–35

Roy, William, 57, 180n59, 188n41, 190n54

Ruggie, John, 128–30, 132–33

rule of law. *See* law, rule of

Russia: police in, 27; revolution and foreign corporations, 105, 205n81

sacrifice, 24–24, 78–79, 152, 174n21, 187n35

Sadler, David, 112–13

Sáinz, José Campillo, 125

Salimoff and Co. v. Standard Oil Co. of N.Y., 205n80

salus publica: ban and, 8; corporate body of the state and, 24–25; corporation-as-police and, 34; global, 96; police and, 27; problematic of government and, 50, 77, 187n35. *See also* common good; public welfare

San Francisco (California), 72

San Mateo v. Southern Pacific Railroad Company, 73, 121

Santa Clara v. Southern Pacific Railroad Company, 67, 70, 73

Savigny, Friedrich Carl von, 80, 92

Sawyer, Lorenzo, 73

scarcity, 64, 184n5, 186n30

Scheuerman, William, 221n15

Schmitt, Carl, 6, 108–9, 179n19, 205n92

Schooner Exchange v. M'Faddon, 102, 203n56

Schuster, Ernst, 104

Schuster, Jack, 145

Schwartz, Douglas, 117, 207n16

science: capitalism and, 96; corporate will and, 83, 158; economy and,

184n5; legal, 84; physical, 97, 142–43, 147, 149, 216n17; police and (see police); social 2–3, 7, 15, 61, 75, 143, 150
scientific management, 120
security: capital and, 12; economic, 44, 49, 75, 86, 119; police and, 27, 48, 50, 77; sovereignty and, 23, 25, 77, 179n19; of state and population, 7–8, 75
Securities and Exchange Commission, U.S., 123
Sedgwick, Theodore, 45–48, 51, 54, 185n14
Sagafi-nejad, Tagi, 126, 211n67
Santissima Trinidad, The, 203n56
separation of ownership and management. See under property, corporate
September 11 attacks, 132
Servicemen's Readjustment Act (GI Bill), 142, 149
Shapiro, Irving, 125
shareholders: activism of, 116–17; and citizenship of corporations, 70, 104–5, 107; as the corporate body, 70, 122; and corporate social responsibility, 115–22, 137; democracy, 122; diffusion of, 208n22; as independent from corporations, 69, 74, 83; interest of, 2, 3, 118–22, 208n20; liability of, 56, 74; managers and, 9, 41; primacy, 116, 118–22, 208n29; protection of, 62, 72–73; value, 112; and workers, 209n36
Shattuck, Jared, 101
Shaw, Lemuel, 187n36, 187n37
Sherman Antitrust Act (U.S.), 58–59, 103, 191n70
Siam, reciprocal recognition of U.S. corporations, 104

sic utere tuo, 50, 53, 186n34, 188n49
Sieyès, Emmanuel Joseph, 86
Silicon Valley, 140
Sitze, Adam, 187n35
Six Books of the Commonwealth (Bodin), 35
Sklar, Martin, 58, 191n70, 192n78, 202n52
Skowronek, Stephen, 58, 191n69, 192n77
Slaughter, Sheila, 143–44, 216n23
Slaughterhouse Cases, 71–72, 74
slavery, 27, 28, 29, 31, 67, 73, 91–92, 179n16
Small, Albion, 179n24
Smith, Adam: critique of corporate monopolies, 2, 49; on the division of labor, 185n24; Lectures on Jurisprudence, 27; and natural law, 186n30; on police, 27, 48–50; political economy of, 49–50, 64, 116, 185n28; Wealth of Nations, The, 27
Smith, Bryant, 84
sociological jurisprudence, 75, 84, 97
social science, 2–3, 7, 15, 61, 75, 143, 150
Soederberg, Susanne, 130
Social Circle Case, Skowronek on, 191n69
soft law, 129, 133
Sokoloff v. National City Bank, 205n80
Sotomayor, Sonia, 65, 67
sovereignty, 4–9, 114–15, 162–64, 174n24, 176n39, 179n16, 179n19; autonomy and, 156; capitalism and, 12, 122, 139; corporation-as-police and, 28, 31; corporation as threat to, 65, 183n66; disciplines and, 150; divided, 35; modern liberal state, 74–75; national economic,

124–26, 131–32; persons and, 76–79; pluralism and, 81–82; popular, 42, 46, 48, 50–54, 62; of state, 19–25, 155; territory and, 12–13, 87–94, 96, 98–99, 100–9

space, 12–14; colonial, 16, 183n59; development and, 131; economic, 202n54; law and, 88–89, 108–9; and the seas, 90; of sovereignty, 7, 23, 78, 183n59; university as, 156, 158, 160

Spain: Cuban Commercial Code and, 103; reciprocal recognition of British corporations, 104

Spanish American War, 103

spatial division of labor, 135–36

spatiality, implicit, 13–14

Spinoza, Baruch, 15

Sproul, Robert, 154, 220n72

St. Thomas, 101

state, the: corporate body of, 20–26, 35–37, 78, 158, 162–63; corporate rights against, 17, 20, 44, 75; and corporations, 52–54, 84–86; and economy, 42; Gierke on, 80–81; and government, 26–28, 43; and natural law, 186n30; positive power of, 75, 76–79; and regulation of corporations, 60–64; *salus* of, 20, 34, 37–38; sovereignty of, 21–24, 35, 174n24, 179n16; the supplement of, 173n19; and territory, 87; universities and, 142

stateless people, 134; corporation as, 106

state of nature, 6, 90, 108–9. *See also* nature

state racism, 77, 81

State University of New York, Albany, 144

Story, Joseph, 92–93, 96, 98, 200n13

structural injustice, 132

Studebaker Corporation, 121

supplement, the, 6, 173n19

Supreme Court, U.S., 51–52, 58–59; comity and, 91, 95, 98, 101; corporate personhood and, 65–67, 70; and economic regulation, 75; and Fourteenth Amendment, 71–72

Sutton's Hospital, Case of, 30

TNCs. *See* multinational corporations

Taney, Roger, 51–53, 92–96, 98, 102

tenure, 46, 145, 154–56, 158

territoriality, 7, 12, 36, 88

text, 150–51

theory, 14, 76, 163

Thorpe v. Rutland, Novak on, 188n49

Tickell, Adam, 10

Tiedeman, Christopher, 53, 186n34, 188n49

Timberg, Sigmund, 5, 107, 109

Tomlins, Christopher, 50, 186n31

Trading with the Enemy Proclamation (U.K.), 105, 205n79

transnational corporations. *See* multinational corporations

Treasury, U.S. Department of, 103

Treatise of Commerce, A (Wheeler), 34

Treatise on the Limitations of Police Power (Tiedeman), 188n49

Tribe, Keith, 28, 180n25

Trinidad and Tobago, support for corporate code of conduct, 125

Tripartite Declarations of Principles Concerning Multinational Enterprises (ILO), 128

Trust Problem, The (Jenks), 62

trusts, 59–63. *See also* antitrust; Sherman Antitrust Act

Tsuk, Dalia, 209n36

Turkey, reciprocal recognition of U.S. corporations, 104

Turley, Jonathon, 108, 203n56

ultra vires: corporate charters and, 53, 56; foreign corporations and, 92–94, 96
uneven development, 135–36, 163
Union Carbide Company, 216n17
United Fruit Company, 102–3
United Nations: and capitalist development, 130–31; Conference on Trade and Development (UNCTAD), 124; corporate social responsibility and, 110, 122–37; developing states at, 124–25, 130–31, 136–37; Economic and Social Council (ECOSOC), 124–26; Global Compact, 127–32; Group of Eminent Persons, 124, 135–37; and liberal international order, 122; resistance to legally enforceable corporate codes of conduct at, 127–29
United Nations Commission on Transnational Corporations (UNCTC), 124–26; demise of, 126–27
United Nations Global Compact. *See* Global Compact, UN
United State: comity in, 91, 94–100, 200n13; and corporate capitalism, 1, 62, 87, 104; corporate personhood in, 80, 82–85; hegemony of, 122–23; improvement and, 50; interests of, 103–4; international protection of markets, 107; police in, 51, 187n35; universities in, 140, 142–44, 147, 214n7: wars in Iraq and Afghanistan, 132
United States Rubber Company, 121
U.S. v. American Tobacco, 59, 99
U.S. v. E. C. Knight Company, 99, 202n52

U.S. v. Furlong, 203n56
U.S. v. Standard Oil Company, 59, 94
U.S. v. Trans-Missouri Freight Association, 59
Universal Declaration on Human Rights, 127
University of California, 154–55, 221n92
University of Notre Dame, 144

value: capitalist, 10–12, 17, 68–69, 111, 114–15, 120, 130, 137, 141, 153, 157–60, 162, 176n40; corporations and, 17, 68–69, 111, 120–22, 153, 209n36; exchange, 49; Foucault on, 7, 76; government of life by, 10–12, 114–15, 120, 130, 157–60, 162, 165; natural price and, 49; shareholder, 112; socially necessary, 11, 158
Vasse v. Ball, 100
Veblen, Thorstein, 64, 141
Venezuela: reciprocal recognition of U.S. corporations, 104; support for corporate code of conduct, 125
Virginia, 16, 95, 201n33
Virno, Paolo, 10–12
Vitoria, Francisco de, 89
Voet, Johannes, 89–90, 96, 200n13
Voet, Paul, 89–90, 96, 200n13

Wachter, Michael, 119, 208n29
Wainwright, Joel, 131, 212n91
Waite, Morrison, 58, 188n38
Warner Bros., 121
Washburn, Jennifer, 140
Washington, D.C., foreign corporations in, 201n45
Watson, Alan, 92, 200n13
Wealth of Nations, The (Adam Smith), 27, 49, 185n30
Weber, Max, 87, 89
Weil, Simone, Esposito on, 196n52

Weissbrodt, David, 128, 129, 212n75
Westinghouse, 121
West Virginia, 56
Wheeler, John, 34, 182n58
Williams, Jeffrey, 149–50, 214n7
Williamson, Oliver, 184n5
Wisconsin: railroad rate setting
    commission, 58
Wolfman, Nathan, 102, 203n65
World Bank, 111, 123, 146
World Economic Forum, 127
World Trade Organization, 147
World War I, 56, 104, 107, 154

World War II, 88, 107, 122–23, 142m
    216n17
Wotipka, Christine Min, 147
Wuerker, Matt, 65, 67
will: collective, 23, 158, 183n66;
    corporate, 68, 74–75

Yale Law Journal, 68
Yale University, 219n58
Yick Wo v. Hopkins, 72
Yntema, Hessel, 90
Young, E. Hilton, 96–97, 100, 201n29
Young, Iris Marion, 132–35, 159

Joshua Barkan is assistant professor of geography at the University of Georgia.

CPSIA information can be obtained
at www.ICGtesting.com
Printed in the USA
FSHW020852130820
72935FS